Songs of the
Blind Snowbird

by
Robert Michael Jacobs

Jay Street Publishers
New York, NY 10023

Published by Jay Street Publishers
155 West 72nd Street, New York, NY 10023

ISBN 1-889534-83-8

www.robertmichaeljacobs.com

*I dedicate this volume of work to my mother, Thelma,
whose great love and support has always been unwavering.
Mom's devotion to promote and maintain harmony and
mutual respect has always exemplified the most admirable
values which we should adopt and pass along to others.*

Table of Contents

Editor's Note

I met Rob Jacobs on December 18, 1995, just three months after he lost his sight. The first thing we did on that snowy Saturday was to walk his dog, KC. For me it was love at first sight – KC, that is. Rob followed by a few hours, but he was accustomed to playing "second fiddle" to this amazing little guy.

The following March, I threw a surprise party for Rob. OK, it's not hard to surprise a blind man. His mother, Thelma, and her husband, Otto, came up from Long Island for the occasion. The next day, Thelma told me that our meeting was *berschert* (Yiddish for "meant to be"). In the time that has followed I can say that Thelma was quite correct. We have changed each other's lives, in ways that would fill another book. Our closeness, as friends, must manifest itself in a strange physical way as we are often mistaken for brothers or cousins.

Speaking of family, Rob is blessed with a wonderful, loving family, who have supported him steadfastly throughout these last seven years. They have also welcomed me, making me feel that I am *mishpucha* (Yiddish for "family"). His cousins, Norman and Helene Seifert, include me in all Holy Day observations. They have served as models in my journey to Judaism. As both my parents are dead, I cherish my wonderful Jewish mother, Thelma.

There are so many elements of our friendship that have altered my life permanently, but the most important of all is Rocky, my Yorkshire Terrier. Rocky was a birthday gift from Rob and KC – absolutely the best present I have ever received; the gift that keeps on giving, every day.

The Book

I have edited a wide variety of materials: technical manuals, business publications. The most difficult was a Doctoral Thesis for an economics professor; it had a run-on sentence that occupied one and a half pages. Editing for Robert has been a true pleasure. From the first I recognized his unique, lyrical writing voice. Most of the missing punctuatiom errors are the type that a spell-check program would miss. The quality of the copy was always quite high, as Rob had polished each piece for many days before sending it to me.

You should also understand the difficulty Robert faces in the act of writing. All interaction with the computer is through the keyboard and his ear – what he types is converted into sound. Computer actions such as "cut & paste" that we take for granted are intensive memory exercises for him. He must first, aurally, locate the text he wants to "cut," then determine the insertion point, again by ear, remembering where in the text it is. He cannot quickly scan as you or I. After "pasting" the text, he must carefully review the results to ensure that everything was properly selected and inserted. It is not easy. I tried to replicate this task by using his computer and I became mentally fatigued quite rapidly.

The book's foundation Rob's series of columns entitled, **The Blind Snowbird,** published in **Celebrate!,** a local alternative newspaper in Key West, Florida. Recognizing that the columns were a reflection of what was happening in his personal life, he wrote the "backstory" that was concurrent with each column. They have been woven together here in this book.

Note to the Reader

First, all of the columns were writtens as stand-alone pieces; i.e., it was assumed that a reader might not have read previous columns. Based on this premise, Robert had to repeat some information; e.g., that he is blind, the difficulties he faces in everyday life, etc. They are *not* redundancies.

Second, Robert writes "by ear and for the ear;" therefore, many of his pieces are best enjoyed when read aloud. Subtle word plays that the eye might pass by are best heard by the ear. Take the time to read the columns aloud. You will find many hidden treasures.

Mark Hetherington

About the Author

Robert Michael Jacobs was born on Long Island, New York, on March 7, 1958.

Rob earned a Bachelor of Fine Arts degree from the Rochester Institute of Technology in May, 1981. His undergraduate education was primarily in Communication Design, which focused on two-dimensional graphic design. He extended his study into the newly-emerging technologies of computer graphics. Formal education in graphics and fine arts evolved into the application of these skills for Information Technology systems.

Rob designed, created, tested and implemented customized Graphical User Interfaces for Executive Information Systems. Additionally, he wrote the user's manuals and trained the client's staff on these applications. Rob was employed in this capacity for ten years with an international consulting firm, working with both government and commercial clients.

Rob lost his eyesight due to CMV Retinitis in 1995. This resulted in the termination of his professional design career.

Sudden total blindness at the age of 37 was especially devastating as it meant the loss of his greatest passion: the visual arts, as well as a very lucrative career. Rob points out: "My self-esteem suffered at the loss of freedom, privacy and personal control."

Forced to reinvent himself, Robert pursued work in developing specialized social programs for non-profit agencies. Additionally, he continued an on-going volunteer position as a tutor of American English as a Second Language (ESL) to new immigrants. He received an "Outstanding Volunteer" award from JVS

(Jewish Vocational Services) for his commitment to helping new immigrants adapt and integrate into American culture.

Robert studied adaptive computer technology in order to acquire the technical skills necessary to continue writing, teaching and maintaining his independence.

While adapting to blindness, Rob wrote and lectured for the MSPCA (Massachusetts Society for the Prevention of Cruelty to Animals). He also facilitated a support group for others suffering sight loss due to CMV Retinitis.

Currently, he lives in Boston for six months and in Key West for six months each year.

Starting in February 2001, Robert wrote a column for a local alternative Key West weekly publication. The regularly-featured column, titled *The Blind Snowbird,* was very well received, and retained a diverse and devoted readership.

Rob states that his goal for his written work is to engage, entertain, enlighten and educate the general public. He feels that by presenting a unique point-of-view he can recapture his creative ambition for a greater social purpose.

OVERTURE

FORWARD, MARCH!

I've been called brave and courageous. There have been times when I graciously accept such commendation, and want to pat myself on the back. Alas, these self-congratulatory moments usually occur while walking along a busy urban sidewalk. With a cane in one hand, and my attention primarily focused on safe travel, this would be a poor time for such a contorted physical gesture. So I just hold my chin up a little higher, and acknowledge that the mere fact that I am out there among the masses of pedestrians and motor vehicles, really is a major feat in itself.

Aware that at any moment, I could suddenly be run down, knocked over, incur a painful collision, fall into a hole, trip on an obstacle, or lose my orientation, I continue to march forward. My sheer determination is an ostensible declaration to project a calm, confident image. Even if only pure self-delusion, this assertion usually manages to get me safely home.

Is it unfair for me to label this mental practice as a form of deception? My own character naturally tends to rebuff credit or praise, whatever the source. I do not mean to imply feigned modesty, nor deny significant personal successes achieved in adapting to total adventitious blindness. Fluctuating self-perception alters in the context of my immediate emotional status.

As you will read in the following pages, any sense of bravery is fleeting. Admittedly, I do have moments of great pride, but at other times I feel weak and ashamed. I concede that all people occasionally experience sensations of weakness and insecurity, particularly in the face of sudden fear, turbulence, depression and loneliness. Life sure can be a bumpy ride!

What should the reader expect to derive from the contents of this volume? These segments portray personal accounts from a strange journey – one that punctuates stretches of tranquillity with severe turbulence. Viewed in its entirety, by means of several intertwined storylines, I contend that one must seek some applicable wisdom from life's formidable experiences. When perceived as an adventure, complete with curious humor and occasional appropriate acquiescence, acceptance of human limitations may ultimately assist us to defy defeat.

As I choose to regard, with reverence, the whims of fate, I've come to acknowledge that there are certain definite limits to my control regarding situations and events. Assuming otherwise is the major source of anger, frustration and disappointment. This should not suggest that we should stop trying to steer the course of our life's journey, but anticipating unpredictable roadblocks, detours and mechanical failures, can alleviate some anguish and personal suffering.

I recount some very disturbing situations, then I attempt to find a message within. Can unsettling events be reviewed in a humorous light? Should I project sarcasm or cynicism? Well, the choice is not always mine to decide. When I speak directly from my heart, the mood and the tone of my writings openly reveal the emotional impact of circumstances from the perspective of a blind man living in a sighted world.

Through my published columns, I have always endeavored to appear upbeat, and present a viewpoint that would amuse, engage and enlighten readers. But in truth, in the more desperate of times, the resulting segments expressed a bit more raw intensity than I would have preferred to reveal.

My initial aim was to continue publishing a regular column indefinitely. But, when I reviewed the collection contained over the course of one year, I was struck by how many unusual personal experiences occurred concurrent with the production of my regularly-published columns. It became quite apparent that these many on-going events strongly influenced each week's selected theme, perhaps subconsciously. There is a common thread that connects each column, but the stories behind the scene weave a larger mesh in which the contents of the columns should be presented.

I begin with a wearisome account of turbulent airline travel. (Don't become despondent from this initial introduction.) Few people can claim not to have their own personal horror stories. But I ask you to indulge me and try to imagine going through air travel hell with your eyes closed.

Have I chosen to compile these written segments in order to shine light on the comic or the tragic implications of the varied situations? Neither. Life is never fully one nor the other, regardless of extraneous conditional circumstances.

The darkest of times gets averaged in with lighter and brighter occasions. We can only measure the entire picture by the shade of gray. So if the road you travel is a bumpy one, the best you can do is reinforce your shock absorbers and go forward. Don't get caught in the sand trap of despair. It is only temporal.

It is often easy to feel nothing but the pain, lose faith in people and succumb to heartbreak and capitulation. I frequently have done so. But, I would prefer to recognize that there really are some very good souls in this world who care. To the fellow journeyers who have touched my life, provided inspiration, encouragement and cleared away some of the gloom, I want to express my sincere gratitude. I dedicate this book to them. They are my champions.

PRELUDE

The familiar female voice of my talking bedside alarm clock announced the pre-dawn hour of five o'clock a.m. It was a cold morning in mid-November, 2000. Despite little actual sleep, I felt too jittery to be sluggish. I jumped out of bed at the sound of the alarm and went directly to the tasks that had been deferred to the early morning hour. They had been swirling around my restless mind all night. These items included all the business that could not be attended to before retiring for a few hours of sleep, sometime after midnight.

For several weeks prior, I had been composing lists, making notes, scurrying about and eventually crossing things off the written files and voice records. I fastidiously documented everything on my computer, from what needed to be done before I left, while I would be gone, and what to do immediately upon my return. I would be leaving my home for many months, and there were so many things to consider and prepare for in advance of this extended absence.

I had worried constantly, deluged with a myriad of concerns. What would I carry aboard the plane? What would I need to ship? What was my system for handling incoming mail? What medications would I need to carry with me, and which others would need to be ordered and forwarded later? With whom should I leave my spare set of keys? Who would water my plants and keep a vigilant eye on my home? What preparations were essential for traveling with my KC Dog? What about available cash, checks, cards, bills, and the household utilities? Had I thoroughly attended to all appointments and commitments needing resolution?

My 5 a.m. mind was swarming. Months of preparation had tried to consider every conceivable precaution to avoid complications. I had felt unsettled for the last month, and it had finally come to a climax on that morning.

Traveling blind is a terrifying experience for me. I had learned this from previous occasions, times when dozens of unforeseen obstacles and frustrations turned these long journeys into nightmares. The general public has come to accept in recent years that air travel is often a harrowing experience. One main factor is the air carriers' dismal reputation for customer service, along with the lack of reliable information, delays and flight cancellations. Additionally, I must contend with all this crap as a totally-blind man in a crowded public airport, with a computer in my backpack, a dog in a bag over one shoulder, and my carry-on essentials in another bag hanging over the other shoulder. I am stooped over under the weighty burden. Keeping my mind focused on my valuables and tickets, I shield KC and myself from the hordes of oblivious and confused travelers in the airports, on the shuttles and aboard the planes. I navigate through these unfamiliar spaces with only a long white cane, regularly relying on the kindness and accuracy of total strangers.

But on this particular November morning, there was some relief to my anxiety. I would not be traveling the unfriendly skies solo. Mark was accompanying me on this trip to my southern home in Key West. His presence would relieve me of some of the inevitable challenges: directing me through security checkpoints, overseeing my belongings, constantly referencing the changing information on the display monitors overhead, and guiding me through the airport terminal to the proper gate.

A cold and eerie feeling slapped my face as I walked out onto the front stoop of my Boston apartment building to approach the waiting taxicab at the curb. I heard doors creak open, the trunk lid lifted and slammed shut, as I was escorted to a plush back seat. KC poked around inside his Sherpa bag as it was placed on my lap. I tried to comfort him with soothing words, but alas, I was far more anxious than was he. KC fully trusted me to transport him safely, as I had done so many times before. As long as he remained in my presence, even with the mesh of a nylon bag between us, KC felt fully secure. Envying his serenity, I was trying to absorb his calmness by osmosis.

At this early hour, the roads were not yet clogged with rush-hour traffic. The cab bolted through the quiet city streets. I swayed as it swerved along the curvy river roads toward the tunnel under Boston Harbor. Emerging at the far side of the tunnel, the cab abruptly turned toward the entrance to the airport. I fidgeted during the entire ride. As the cab raced along the twisted roadway, my mind raced with all my insecurities: Where was my wallet? My ticket? My passport? Was my bag properly zipped? Had I packed it as efficiently as possible? How easily could I gain access to the contents I would need for the journey? Did I have enough painkillers and tranquilizers available to endure the next eight hours? Plagued by the stress, I neurotically chanted my concerns to Mark. He sat calmly on the seat beside me. He must have known that in all my ranting, I was inconsolable, and there was little he could offer to provide relief.

The cab abruptly pulled up to the curb at the terminal. My mind continued to reel nervously. I relentlessly assaulted Mark with my anxious inquiries.

"What time is it now? Did we arrive here early enough to stay on schedule?"

The door of the cab opened and, once again, I was blasted by the frosty air as I climbed out of the vehicle. Was this second cold slap-in-the-face a harbinger of events to follow?

Mark was already at the curb with the driver; they were pulling baggage from the trunk. I securely adjusted my computer backpack, and gently, but firmly hauled the strap of KC's bag over my left shoulder. I kept speaking to him, trying to keep him calm, as my own guts were quivering; I did not want him to sense my own nervous tension.

My queries rattled on: "Mark, are you sure we have everything? Where is my black bag? Have we paid the driver? Is this the right terminal?"

We enter the airport. With Mark as my sighted guide, I tap-tap my cane as we pass from the chill of the outdoors to a warmer, noisy terminal building. Despite the cold air outside, I have been perspiring under my clothes.

I continue: "What time is it now? Where is our departure gate? How much time do we have? Are they boarding yet? Is the dog OK? Which bags are you carrying? Mark, find the monitor! Is the flight on time? Are we here in time? Which way to the gate? Is the dog still OK?"

Mark does his best to alleviate my anxiety, as he understands my sense of insecurity.

Some time later, we are seated in an overcrowded airplane, the dog quietly in his travel bag at my feet. Can I relax yet? Reflecting, I seek some tranquility. I want to reassure myself that I can take comfort that this journey from Boston to Key West will be smoother than the same voyage one year earlier. Sitting in my assigned seat, in the company of Mark and KC, I recollect that horrendous day one year prior, in November of 1999. Up to this point, I had considered it to be among the most distressing days of my life.

I learned a valuable lesson that day: at all costs, avoid going through Miami International Airport. On that particular trip to Key West, KC and I were traveling on our own. Anticipating my need for assistance in Miami, I had made special arrangements. I was given assurance by the airline that someone would meet us at the gate in Miami to escort us to the proper gate for the connecting flight. Once there, we would board the small plane that would transport KC and me to that remote island 200 miles to the southwest.

Things did not turn out very well. I was ushered off the flight from Boston into a cold, noisy terminal at Miami. Eventually, a small Spanish-speaking woman with a wheelchair approached me. She had been assigned by the airline to see me safely through the maze of hallways, escalators, elevators, shuttles, moving sidewalks, and security points to the connecting flight. Immediately I realized that the language barrier might hamper communication. Additionally, I recognized instantly that having this small woman push me and my belongings through the multi-level maze in a wheelchair would have been rather impractical. Instead, I opted to use the wheelchair as a baggage cart. I insisted on carrying KC's travel bag and bearing the burden of my computer backpack.

The journey through the airport seemed like a marathon. KC was getting uncomfortable in his small compartment, and was letting me know. I opened the zipper slightly and stroked him for reassurance. It was awfully cramped and hot in there. Nearing the end of this fatiguing expedition through the airport, time was running close to the point of departure for my connecting flight. According to my guide, there was only one more hurdle: I would have to pass through airport security again. This meant taking off the baggage that hung from my tired body. I had to put down KC's bag and let him out so that they could inspect it. Then I had to take off my belt pack so they could run it through the scanner. I was told to lay my computer backpack down on the moving belt of the x-ray machine. Afterwards, I would need to reassemble my belongings quickly, and scramble to meet the waiting aircraft. Time was ticking away.

I voiced apprehension about passing my computer through the scanner. Their response to my protestation was that the only alternative was to inspect the computer backpack by hand. While it was still securely on my back, I felt hands starting to unzip the many compartments and reach inside. Then, I heard a different, very authoritative voice insisting it would still be necessary to pass the entire backpack through the scanner. As this delay was jeopardizing my scheduled connection, pragmatism prevailed over my stubbornness. Realizing the serious danger of missing my flight, I relented under the pressure. Someone then started to remove the backpack without warning, and as all the zippers had just been opened, the contents spilled out onto the floor. My agitation increased drastically. KC's whereabouts and well-being heightened my distress, as I heard, from a distance, him once again being crammed into his hot Sherpa bag by a complete stranger. Meanwhile, my computer and its components were scattered all over the floor. Not one person offered to assist me in retrieving my belongings or to console me.

Clearly, I had no allies among the crowd of onlookers. Compassion and gentility was conspicuously absent. I blindly crawled around under their feet, feeling the floor for the dispersed contents of my backpack. Some familiar items that came into my grasp had certainly fallen from the sack, but were pulled away; I was told that they were not mine. I was sure this was untrue. But, I grew more concerned about catching my flight and getting KC to a safer and friendlier environment. I had lost all confidence that a hero would come forth to rescue me from this predicament. Despite feeling betrayed and tormented, KC was always my greatest concern. Any hope of tranquillity lay far in the distance, far out of sight.

My assigned Spanish-speaking escort had been standing silently nearby, observing this debacle. I had just been through the most humiliating experience I could imagine, but she had done nothing to question her superiors' action. Once beyond the security checkpoint, I asked her to identify the security and airline personnel who had been accomplices in this outrageous ordeal. She contended that she did not know any of them. As she was subordinate to these fellow company employees, I am certain that her response was based on her own job security.

Eventually, I made my connecting flight just in time. I will spare the reader the continuous difficult details endured, from boarding the mobbed shuttle bus to blindly climbing a narrow metal staircase to the tiny plane, under the incredible weight of my precious cargo. At last I was on the flight – the final leg of this odd odyssey.

As a postscript to that horrid ordeal, when I got to my home in Key West, I soon learned that many essential computer components from my backpack had, indeed, been lost at that security post. Months of struggle followed in replacing the missing equipment, and I may never get over the anger and humiliation of that unfortunate event.

So, this year, I was not traveling alone and should encounter no such tragic obstacles. I wish I could say that this was true. But a new travel nightmare still lay ahead.

No matter what precautions I take or how stubborn I am, I am still subject to the whims of fate and circumstance. I was determined to hold two things close to my person for the entire length of the trip. Most importantly, KC would never be out of reach. As Mark loves KC as I do, and understands my obsessive concern for his well-being, I had assurance that he would be well protected.

My second obsession was related to the horrendous ordeal I described above, when my computer suffered at the hands of others. For this reason, I refused to let the computer backpack come off my body, no matter how uncomfortable this would be for the next several hours.

But well into the journey, facing our final segment of airline travel, my obstinance was put to the test in Miami. Yes, I said Miami! No matter how hard I tried to avoid that contemptible airport, events out of my control magnetically pulled the course of our southbound journey toward that dreaded airline hub. I had made extra-special efforts and accepted additional expense to be booked on a different airline, in order to make the Key West connection in Tampa. But as we sat in the Tampa airport terminal, me with one hand on KC and the weight of the computer backpack crushing my vertebrae, fate once again callously intervened.

The flight from Tampa to Key West was canceled. We were given few options, other than to take a flight to Miami, and then fly on to Key West with a different air carrier, the same one that had been so offensive to me the previous year. My worst nightmares seemed to be coming true. This experience underscores the lesson that I refer to in a column

I wrote, *Dates, Fates and Interest Rates.* Life was once again providing proof that our decisions and choices are in the hands of a power other than our own.

After reaching Miami, we scurried to the correct terminal for the (unplanned) third leg of this formidable flight. Once again, I found myself in the hot Florida sunshine on a tarmac to board a tiny commuter airplane. I was approached with a dreaded demand. Told that I could not get up the narrow staircase to the plane with my luggage, I would have to relinquish my backpack. I vigorously protested, but to no avail. Under pressure and threats, I reluctantly submitted to this hostile command, and stripped off the weighty burden from a sweaty and aching back. I handed it to Mark with the adamant instruction that he personally carry both the computer and KC aboard the plane. Arms thrusted toward me, coaxing me to board first, up the narrow stairway. At the top, I ducked into the tiny hatchway and was shoved into my seat. Within moments, Mark joined me. I compulsively began to take inventory of all our possessions.

First, I asked Mark, "Where is KC?"

"He's right here at your feet."

I reached down between the cramped seats feeling for his bag, and slid my hand into a small opening in the zippered bag to reassure him with a pat on his furry little head. (This gesture also served to calm me.)

Next, I asked Mark about the storage location of the backpack that contained my computer. He told me nonchalantly that he had to surrender it over to a baggage handler, to be put into the cargo hold. They told him that there was no room aboard the aircraft, so he willingly complied, despite my previous severe objections. Upon learning of this move, I panicked; I had a very clear premonition that this meant something bad was in store.

Anger, frustration, fear and extreme anxiety tightly gripped me, once again.

Three hours later, at my Key West condo, I once again

took inventory of all our possessions. I asked Mark to check out the computer. And, as if scripted, we discovered immediately that the computer was DOA – dead on arrival.

Six weeks of agonizing frustration followed. Mark extended his stay in Key West to help me resolve this latest technical tangle. He was added to the Thanksgiving guest list to join my brother's family, who were spending the holiday in Key West. Meanwhile, Mark worked diligently to help me find a solution to this latest computer catastrophe.

Perhaps Mark is the only person who truly understands how vital my computer is for me to sustain daily life. He knows very well how dependent I have become on the machine for my work, banking and record-keeping. Mark may have felt somewhat responsible for the unfortunate occurrence. And I was so tormented by this event, which I had taken such pains to avoid, that I admittedly persisted in expressing my grief in order to retain his involvement. I disdain this characteristic trait, which tries to dissipate my own suffering by sharing the burden with others. Shamefully, I admit that I wanted him to accept some degree of fault for the problem. I was fully aware, that this tactic might be unfair, but emotional pain does not evoke rational and thoughtful behavior. I had set some very clear objectives to accomplish during my stay in Key West. These goals could not even be asserted until there was first some resolution with the computer.

I had envisioned that my writing would extend beyond the book on which I had been working for the previous three years. My plan was to submit a proposal to author a weekly column in the local Key West newspaper, through which I could present a unique perspective. The book I had been working on was far from complete. It had been more like a continuation of my journal writing, and followed the journey of my life as I grew further and further from my last glimpse of daylight. This winter, I wanted to reach out to an audience in "real-time." (The autobiographical material of my long-term writing project still seemed just a distant glimmer, one that might someday chronicle my personal experience.)

Mark stuck by me through this latest calamity. At first, we attempted to find a local source to repair the machine or recover its data. This endeavor only resulted in some bad technical advice and pages of service invoices.

I grew more desperate in my need for a working computer. Ultimately, it appeared that I would need to replace the old one, try to recover its contents and transfer them to the new machine.

On the recommendation of the local computer service technician, I purchased the latest model of my deceased laptop computer. He assured me that he could JUST take the old hard drive (See "No JUST in Justice) and install it in the new one. The technician was certain that this was feasible and uncomplicated. I would have a working unit again in just days.

Bypassing the harrowing details, this "guaranteed" approach proved unsuccessful and expensive. As a result, I had a new computer, with a baffling new operating system, but still no data from the trashed machine. Desperation engulfed me. On my brother's advice, I sent the old machine to New Jersey, where a technically-proficient gentleman eventually was able to recover the data onto a disc, and subsequently repair the old machine.

Suddenly I found myself with a new machine that had an operating system that was incompatible with my adaptive speech software and voice synthesizer. I will spare readers the other gory details, which involved further expense, time and aggravation. When I finally had a working machine and Internet access, I settled for a less-than-ideal situation, but my motivation to go forward and achieve my primary goal was only further fortified. After all, the substance of these recent problems magnified the underlying intent of my more universal message.

THE HATCHLING

Six weeks had passed since my arrival in Key West for the winter season. The previous account of my recent travel woes reveals how the very technology, on which I am so dependent, can greatly disrupt my life and impede personal goals.

Once my computer nightmare had been sufficiently resolved, with a functional system and access to the Internet, I immediately went to work on a newly-conceived project. I outlined a proposal for submission to the editor of *Celebrate! Key West,* the local GLBT (Gay/Lesbian/Bisexual/Transgender) alternative weekly newspaper. After initial telephone contact with Ginny, the editor, I sent her an email detailing my proposal. This initial written correspondence contained rough drafts for my first three columns and approximately eight other topics for subsequent columns.

My proposal was instantly accepted. Ginny requested that I submit my first column as soon as possible, with the agreement of being published every other week. I was elated with this response. After I submitted the final draft of *The Navigator*, Ginny was clearly impressed, and she encouraged me to submit a column on a weekly basis instead. Hence, *The Blind Snow Bird* was hatched.

In retrospect, I feel that I gave less thought in naming my weekly column, than in refining its mission and content. The column header, *The Blind Snow Bird,* stuck, in spite of my misgivings. I envisioned this column as a series, so I numbered each submission preceding its title. My original intent was to capture a regular readership. Further, I aspired to a noble goal of discreet consciousness-raising, through an engaging and entertaining series of works. I held no illusions of fame or fortune. (And, true to this vision, neither was ultimately realized on a notable scale, although I can now say with modest pride that I accomplished the primary goal of my project.)

I deliberately structured the entire series to build upon a common thread, while presenting individual situations. Each column was designed to stand alone as a unique work, but I would introduce a new theme with each piece.

The editor and staff were very receptive. The only revision I noticed was that the Part Number that I had included preceding each week's column title was omitted in the printed piece. The editor's rationale became clear to me. Ideally, I wanted each column to be read in its serial order, but many of the readers couldn't be expected to follow a weekly series. *Celebrate!* does have a loyal local following, but a large portion of those who pick up the free periodical are tourists and short-stay visitors. Glimpsing a part number on the title line might discourage readers, who may assume they had come upon an ongoing storyline.

Following the first published *Blind Snow Bird* column, I found my voice and my audience. It was paramount to keep the readers involved by producing columns that aroused curiosity, as it would be novel in its approach and different from anything previously featured in such a widespread publication. Timidly, I wondered: how would the general public feel about seeing the world through eyes that cannot see? Would readers be wary or reticent to embrace a perspective which is normally not presented with such matter-of-fact candor? In a generally tolerant society such as exists in Key West, where a drag queen in stiletto heels at the gym would barely receive a second glance, I questioned why should a blind man in leather mufti make people feel uneasy? If this self-proclaimed Independent "Conch Republic" can proudly boast of the diversity of its community, wasn't it worth an attempt to broaden the definition of all-inclusive?

My new endeavor also provided an opportunity for my fellow citizens: to recognize physically-disabled persons as unabashedly visible and creatively expressive as anyone else. I was a member of a minority which seemed under-represented in a social forum. "Disabled" issues that were brought before the public were usually of a political nature and focused on civil rights or equal access. What I felt was missing was a personal angle depicting a range of commonplace experiences.

I employed my warped witticism and simple, unpretentious anecdotes, with particular effort to have each column location relevant. The "Key West" angle was important. And, although the embedded messages were of a global nature, I was attempting to introduce myself as a member of this small island city, which boasts far more than its share of "characters". The newcomer, a blind guy seen around town, had something special to express. I knew that the substance of my message needed to be contained in an attractive verbal package.

The writing flowed easily, as I had so much subject matter to impart. My first realized challenge came as I struggled to edit each week's column to fit within the imposed word count limit. This was a good discipline in that it forced me to refine each piece into a succinct and polished product.

Fully recognizing that my subject matter would be of an unconventional nature to a general readership, I endeavored to crack the shell of social barriers. My words presented a perspective with which most individuals had never been confronted. Since the total loss of my eyesight in 1995, I found that the subject of blind individuals, living within mainstream society, was unfamiliar to the average American. Frequently, a person's only encounter with a visually-impaired individual was typically through an elderly family member, such as a grandparent. (This is quite understandable, inasmuch as the vast majority of blind and visually-impaired Americans are senior citizens, whose diminished sight has occurred slowly with age, from illness or degeneration.) Rarely did the general public interact with visually-impaired young or middle-aged adults. Seldom had such an encounter been in a public social setting. Therefore, I knew that I would often be the first blind and/or disabled person with whom they may develop a casual relationship.

Through the distribution of my writings, I deliberately wanted to expand beyond the box of familiar news, opinions, gossip, entertainment listings and reviews. People would be exposed to written words that reflected the view of a blind man, perhaps for the first time in their lives. I hoped to allay prejudicial fears of casual interaction with disabled citizens living amidst the community, a fear and awkwardness commonly shared by many individuals. Inspired by my love of language, creativity and socially-motivated ideals, I was eager to tread into this unventured frontier. It was an informal attempt to illuminate an often-hushed topic to others, delivered in an unthreatening guise. The sublime messages contained within might all be new, yet comfortable, as they should tap the common human conscience of all readers.

Daily experiences continuously provided me with anecdotes that I could easily integrate into my weekly themes. In a very short time, my writing attracted a devoted readership. I received positive feedback and commendations all around. It was a pleasant surprise to have total strangers and neighbors approach me to express sincere appreciation. They appeared to represent a more diverse spectrum of society than I had originally assumed comprised the readership of this alternative paper's circulation. I felt that my own expectations were being exceeded.

The book, which I had been writing for the previous three years, needed to be shelved for a time. I knew I would want to revisit it in the future; it maintained its own special value. But I was eager to utilize this new publishing opportunity as a platform to present my message within the community I have come to feel is my second adopted home.

I refused to allow all the technical obstacles that had littered my path over the previous two months to dampen my resolve. In fact, these adversities may have even provided a greater incentive for me to proceed through a creative outlet to express personally an important, socially-relevant set of ideas. Many times during the course of the year that followed, I had been challenged repeatedly with problems that could have impeded my drive, but I doggedly pursued my goal.

For the first thirteen weeks, I submitted my work by email to the newspaper office, located only six blocks from my home. I personally visited this office just a few times over the course of the season, because it was very difficult for me to locate the specific door among the many other storefronts in the plaza.

The only means I had to read the publication was on-line. As the paper was distributed around town by early Friday morning, I would have to wait until Saturday in order to read my words on the newspaper's weekly updated web site. Eagerly accessing the most current edition on-line, I would listen to my computer speak my words, carefully reviewing the material for any errors or edits by the staff. Only once in that first thirteen weeks, did I find one word censored. As an artist, I felt that the editor's extreme caution might have dampened the power of my tag line. (All columns contained within this printing are in their entirety.) On just a few other occasions did I notice altered punctuation or words. These were either due to a translation error in the file conversion, or the copy editor misunderstood a pun or word play I had intentionally, but subtly, embedded in the text.

When I left Key West in May, I asked Ginny if I should continue to submit my column. She enthusiastically responded that she would be happy to publish as much work as I was able to submit from Boston. This was not unprecedented; there was at least one other contributing writer who sent in his column from his summer residence. I set the objective of meeting a bi-weekly deadline until I returned in the fall.

ESL tutoring, on-going projects and other commitments in Boston compete for my available time each week. In order to maintain the quality standard I demanded of my writing, I needed to re-assess my rate of output. What I could not foresee was that several unanticipated events would further diminish my productivity. Despite much personal turmoil, I did not allow these difficulties to prevent me from "getting it right." It is against my nature to miss deadlines. However, due to highly unusual circumstances, I felt it was excusable. Unconsciously, many of these tribulations influenced the themes of my published works.

The year 2001 provided no shortage of distractions, repeatedly making it more difficult to achieve my preset goals. On the other hand, each adversity I encountered provided me additional subject matter. I was concerned that the bleakness of my state of mind would negatively affect the quality of my writing. But my compulsion to write was fortified in that life provided an unexpected source which forced me to explore a wider range of human experiences. Concerned that my humorous demeanor, which had characterized earlier columns, was being overshadowed in darker tones, I understood the importance of being true to life.

Many times I would review a completed piece, and judge it ill-suited to be a *Blind Snow Bird* column. I submitted them with misgivings. Although they did touch upon more intensely serious themes, many were highly acclaimed. My commitment to keep expanding my message necessitated that I employ more raw and somber emotions. Some very personal compositions developed over the summer were not intended for publication, but all my writing, whether to be published or remain private, was colored by the turbulence in my life. Yet, I still needed to keep my column engaging and enlightening, despite its altered tone. This demanded a special fortified effort.

Severely concerned that my mood would reflect my dire situations, I had to undertake particular precautions from appearing too morose, defeated or whiny in my Snow Bird columns. I strove with earnest determination to incorporate humor and irony within the context of the work. Once again I was challenged to keep my standards high and hone my craft to accommodate ever-changing situations.

The Snow Bird was in flight, and I felt that I had to keep flapping my wings, even when flying into the face of a storm.

SECTION ONE

CALL ME ROB

In January of 2001, I submitted my proposal to write for *Celebrate!* Self-acclaimed as "the most colorful newspaper in Key West," this tabloid regularly featured talented columnists and writers that fairly represented the diverse spectrum of the community. Their love of Key West, with its unique social and cultural climate, shined through in their words. Content ranged from drag queen folly to religious commentary to political news and social events.

Celebrate! covered local and national news, conspicuously presenting items of special interest to Gay and Lesbian residents and tourists, but also had wide appeal to the city at large. The editorial content was intelligent and focused. Under Ginny's editorial direction, the publication had become highly respected throughout the entire city. With my initial debut, my voice represented a new perspective. It took a bold and innovative newspaper editor to provide this previously unknown author with a forum. I had come out of nowhere, with a proposal far from mainstream, even for an alternative publication. It was imperative that I prove myself from the start, through my first column, to garner acceptance and retain the readers' interest.

Celebrate's circulation was more extensive than I had originally realized. Within the first month, personal recognition indicated that my readers were ubiquitous. I was reaching a larger audience than I had first anticipated. After three years in Key West, I had suddenly attained a positive, distinctive identity through my writing.

Ginny requested that I preface my first column with a short introduction. My personal background was kept very short. Further biographical details would emerge in subsequent columns; readers would come to know me more intimately. I held no pretense that my foray into this world of publication would be self-serving. Rather, I desired to present an example that could break social barriers by toppling inhibitions, both my own and those of the readers. Aware of the awkwardness felt by others about interacting with disabled persons, I held onto the ideal that if people became familiar with someone such as myself, they would become more at ease in general. I am out there in the world everyday, mingling with the crowds on the street, in the stores, at the theaters and other public places.

Often, people do not even realize that I cannot see them. When this realization finally does occurs, they may be as startled as I am from this sudden confrontation. For instance, when a pedestrian inadvertently bumps into me or trips over my cane, we share an awkward moment. Sighted people may be at a loss of how to react. Should they apologize or offer assistance? They may be embarrassed or feel uneasy, so their first instinct may be to flee. Of course, I do not want others to experience such confusion, whether in an unexpected confrontation or in a social setting. This provides incentive for me to be tactful in order to spare others any discomfort or embarrassment.

Ideally, people need to be more alert to their immediate surroundings, paying better attention to others in their environment. But realistically, we all get distracted along our way. I don't want to walk the streets with tension or suppressed anger, nor do I want to be fearful out in public. Perhaps *The Navigator* and its subsequent columns will cause my fellow citizens to be more vigilant and to feel comfortable asking a disabled person not only if they need help, but also how they can provide such assistance.

For those readers who never would get to meet me directly, they would have the opportunity to realize that all people, regardless of circumstances, share common experiences in life. Each column is designed with the aim of touching upon a universal theme with which every individual can relate in some way. Suddenly, my blindness becomes only one factor, not the prime focus, for our common concerns. And the particular perspective that I present of going through life with this major impediment becomes just another human condition. Blindness is revealed as a challenge to be scaled, rather than as an impenetrable roadblock.

I have always encouraged the inquisitive. When others stop to consider things they take for granted in their everyday lives, they are rewarded with a new sense of appreciation. The courage, for which I have been so frequently credited, should be viewed as a personal willfulness, and can represent a strong potential that may lie dormant in each individual. If my resolve to overcome hardships becomes an inspiration for others to inventory their own personal barricades, they will come to know themselves better.

I have used my columns to illustrate some instances in which the small daily details of life, for most, do become monumental challenges for me. But I use these situations not for an opportunity to whine or generate sympathy. Instead, I am trying to use my personal experience and KC's teachings to propagate mutual respect and appreciation, which all people should have for one another.

Allow me to address one major point of curiosity: How do I write or work on a computer if I am totally blind? Technology! But technology alone makes nothing happen. A systematic integration of technology, albeit flawed, into a larger scheme provides the means to empower. I use "adaptive technology" to interact with my laptop computer. My only input is via the keyboard. A synthesized voice provides me with the audible feedback I need to visualize the appearance of the screen, and to navigate its contents. Frequently, some of the operations can be very intensive and frustrating. Fortunately, I had a prior professional technical background in computer systems. I designed interactive graphical interfaces for fifteen years, before losing my eyesight.

(It would be fitting at this point to make one relevant note: I am an avid reader. My access to published material is primarily through *Recordings for the Blind and Visually-Impaired.* Hence, the process of reading a book is purely an auditory experience. This has greatly influenced my linguistic style. My method of writing is unconventional inasmuch as I never see the printed words. I compose and edit all my work by audible feedback. The selected words, phonetics, cadence and rhythmical patterns which characterize many of my pieces are a thoughtfully designed integral element. Many word plays and puns are purely effective only when consumed aurally. The publisher of my columns inserted a special note to the readers to alert them of these nuances. The message is this: The maximum effect is realized when the portions are read aloud. To expand upon this may I suggest that, if possible, two readers alternate reading sections aloud to each other.]

Additionally, I own several electronic gadgets and small devices for recording lists, notes, numbers, etc. I even have a speaking thermometer. I always carry "Digi" (my portable digital recording device) and "Pocket Lady" (my talking clock). Inspiration can strike me anywhere, as it often does at the gym or just while walking down the street. With Digi at hand, I am always prepared to "jot down" a thought, a rhyme, a significant word or number. Often, I can be seen stopping in the middle of a gym workout or on the sidewalk, speaking into this tiny digital device. The germs of many columns can trace their origin to such moments.

In response to Ginny's request to present a brief introduction to her readers, I composed the paragraph below, which preceded my first column, *The Navigator:*

Call me Rob. You are more likely to have seen me than I am to have seen you. I claim no celebrity, it's just that I am totally blind. I am a seasonal resident of Key West. I dislike the title "Snowbird." I prefer to see myself as a winter-weather refugee. I spend my time in Key West pursuing some personal goals in this tropical climate. In Boston, I am a writer, public speaker and an ESL tutor.

1. The Navigator

"More to your right! More to your right!"
BANG!!
(Embarrassed) "Sorry, I meant to *your* left.
I must be dyslexic!"

This is a typical confrontation I have with
fellow pedestrians. Call them the "Well-Intentioned". Although I would prefer the "Well-Intentioned" to have a better sense of direction,
I'd still rather walk away bruised from these encounters than from those with some other types
I (sometimes literally) run into on the streets of
Key West.

I share the sunshine and balmy breezes with
you when the ice coats my front stoop back in
Boston. I also share with you the sidewalks and
the crosswalks of this city. I do a lot of walking.
It's my most reliable form of transportation, and
gives me back some of the freedom I had before I lost my sight five years ago. Although not
the same as a set of keys to an automobile, then
again, I don't have to pay insurance on my
shoes. I may be more likely to be hit by a car
than someone who is driving, but no amount of
insurance money can repair a broken body, as
a car fender can be unwrinkled or replaced. I
learned long ago that metal is stronger than flesh.
But that's another story.

As everywhere, I encounter many types of
people who have little or no experience with
meeting a blind person. It has become a fascinating study to observe the type of reactions I
receive when mingling with the masses. The
"Well-Intentioned" may be no better skilled in
their approach to me than others, but I cherish
their desire to assist one with impaired naviga-

tional tools.

I recognize that, as a blind person, it is my duty to instruct the sighted on how to best guide me. Though impractical for me, in a momentary encounter, to give lessons in geography, street layouts, or orientation and mobility techniques, I do try to explain pleasantly that the use of certain words or gestures are meaningless to me. Examples: *"Over there." "That way."* Or the pointing of fingers to indicate direction. I suppose that before blindness, I would have been equally challenged.

The streets are also populated with pedestrians whom I will refer to as the "Fearful and Self-Conscious." These are tourists and locals who do not want to appear foolish or ignorant, so they will scurry past, thinking I cannot detect their presence. I hear their conversations fall to a hush, moments before they get near, the increased pace of their footsteps and many other clues that I am sworn not to reveal. They are no less skilled at assisting me than the "Well-Intentioned;" it's just that they fear the confrontation because they may embarrass themselves.

Perhaps they are less self-assured. Maybe they are timid, or just give me more credit than I am due in perceiving my immediate environment. Some do not have as highly-developed sense of direction that they feel they need, or more likely, they do not know how to explain directions without gestures and reference to visual landmarks. Undeniably, most do not know the street names as well as I need to learn them.

Few people ever seem to know on which street corner they are standing. When I inquire, I can almost feel the breeze as they swivel their heads around searching for a street sign. (I cannot determine whether signage does not exist, or if the city chose to make them too subtle.)

In other instances, I have heard of people being rebuked when offering assistance to the blind, and this experience has left them unwilling to take the chance of this happening again.

To be kind, I will refer to the last major type of pedestrian that I encounter as the "Oblivious." A friend of mine watches these individuals in amazement and proclaims them to be the "Sighted-Blind." They wander around the sidewalks as if in a fog, or they are lost in the occupation of window-shopping. If they are too busy people-watching, I must register as invisible. How else can I explain the people who park themselves in the middle of the sidewalk and expect everyone should walk around them and their parcels? Or if they are moving toward me, how is it that they so frequently trip over my cane? Perhaps it is not obvious that the man approaching with the dark glasses and tapping the white-and-red cane is blind. What shocks me is how many stumble over my cane and nearly knock me over, and then either accuse or excuse me for almost tripping them.

I do not want to come across as whiny or arrogant, I only present this perspective because I live this existence.

If you see me out there on Duval Street, please do not hesitate to say "hello," or ask if I need guidance. I will be happy to help you to help me.

(2/1/01)

2. More Than Meets the Eye

It is said that beauty is only skin deep. For that reason, as an admirer of beauty, I try to touch as much bare skin as possible. And I make no excuses for being so forward – of course I only take this approach in the appropriate places.

Whether or not we admit it, even to ourselves, we all make some sort of pre-judgment based on the first impression, i.e., the visual scan. Shallow as that may seem to those of us who believe we are most open-minded and liberal, it is commonly accepted social behavior.

As a blind man, without being too offensive, I need a tactile means for getting my first impression...perhaps: *"May I Braille you?"*

This method of introduction may be rather bold, but I explain it this way: my hands must be a replacement for my eyes. And as "checking someone out" is acceptable in many social environments, I am employing my only means for doing the same. Besides, my sense of touch is sharper than my eyesight ever was.

It may be superficial that we judge each other first on impressions we receive regarding age, clothes, bodies, etc., yet we are all somewhat guilty of this means of choosing people to whom we introduce ourselves. I have been deprived of the ability to select others from afar, in a subtle and discreet manner, as a sighted person would. Interestingly enough, I have found this to be an enlightening experience. I have less hesitation to start conversations with those in my immediate vicinity, whereas before, I may have felt self-conscious or intimidated. My circumstances preclude approaching others based on appearances. I am forced to be less judgmental. I feel I can be more open and relaxed, and therefore, it often puts the other person at ease as well. I find that I end up talking to people whom I otherwise may never have met.

On the other hand, I am aware that I may not be up-to-date in style. Recently, a friend derided me for wearing workout clothes to the gym that were no longer fashionable. Although I had always just considered such clothes as merely functional and comfortable to work out in, I began to feel it necessary to update this part of my wardrobe. But then, what of the rest of my appearance? Is my haircut out of style? Do my street clothes appear dated? And most of all, how much should I really care about all this?

Truly getting to know people and developing friendships and relationships should transcend such superficialities. Yet, our society places great emphasis on style and appearance, and it can be said to be a cornerstone of our commercial capitalism. As a blind man, am I not fulfilling my duty to consumerism? Bold ads do not entice me as they slip by unnoticed. Attention-grabbing displays at the ends of the store aisles and the allure of the shopkeeper's window display have no impact on me. This situation may keep me from impulse buying, saving me dollars and calories in the end, but my contribution to the local economy is inhibited. I find it difficult enough obtaining what I truly need, let alone things that may enrich my life: things of beauty and luxury, such as art or culinary delicacies.

But who am I to pretend to be so down-to-earth that my appearance does not concern me? I want to look my best. I am embarrassed when friends point out that my shirt is on inside out or that I am wearing two different-colored socks. But I am grateful for their blunt observations and get the chance to make the appropriate correction.

Basically, I have always assumed (even before blindness) that glamour is over-valued. I never tried to be fashionably trendy or a slave to the designer label. At the same time, however, I prefer not to be noticed as a fashion anachronism. Will someone please tell me when I can no longer get away with wearing tie-dyed tee shirts or army fatigues?

Although I contend that we should consider that there often exists more to everything than meets the eye, it just may be those other superficial discretions that people sometimes crave. So if you find me in a dark place of ill-repute, it should be considered that I either made a bold, determined effort to find my way there, or else it was a complete accident that I stumbled into such a lascivious environment. I will allow you to decide which one it is.

(2/08/01)

3. Ironies and Iron Knees

"Expect a letter from our agency. You will need to fill out the enclosed form in order to receive our services."

This statement came from the Division of Blind Services when I requested assistance with reading my mail. I found this rather disturbing.

More upsetting is when I am challenged about my blindness. This often occurs when I first meet someone, and after a conversation, it is revealed that I am totally blind.

"Prove to me that you are really blind!"

"How should I do this?" I respond. Should I bump into a wall for them?

Actual recent street encounter: I was walking past the Green Parrot in the mid-afternoon, heading toward Duval Street. As I was weaving my way through the usual obstacles on the sidewalk (bicycles and other clutter), I heard obnoxious shouts aimed in my direction. Suddenly, standing right in front of me was a man who kicked my cane and blared: "Shit! That's all this town needs; some guy pretending to be blind!"

I replied, "Well it sure has enough stupid, drunken assholes like YOU! Why would I want to pretend to be blind?"

His only smug response was: "Oh, I can tell that you are not really blind!" as he stumbled past me. If anyone ever deserved to be smacked with my cane, it was this jerk. Alas, as a blind man, I have a hard time trying to hit a moving target. So all I could do was hurl a few verbal assaults in his general direction to unleash my immediate rage, and continue my journey.

That hadn't been the first time I have heard such a question. How do I possibly respond to an accusation that I am faking blindness in order to get attention? Should I even respond at all?

"I don't believe you are blind! Who dresses you!?"

Should I take this to mean that I can get away with my selected attire by claiming that I am always forced to dress in the dark? By the way, on that particular occasion, the inquirer was actually complimenting me on my outfit, and wanted to know who it was that had the good taste. It surely could not have been me.

Life is full of absurd experiences for us all. I seem to face an extra measure.

Fellow pedestrians may warn me of an open manhole up ahead, but I may not find it until it is too late, and I could be standing in deep shit by then.

Warnings are given to me with good intentions. But, when advice lacks enough information for me to deal with the situation properly, I must rely on my intuition alone.

"Do you have a pencil?" I am often asked.

I truly wonder how many blind people carry around pencils. I often carry with me a small digital recording device to make notes. Sighted people (the "light-dependent") almost never have anything with them to do the same, so they always ask me for something to write with. I cannot usually meet this request.

I do, however, always have with me my cane and wear dark sunglasses for protection. When out at night, I have often been ridiculed for wearing sunglasses by those who think that I am trying to make a cool fashion statement. To avoid embarrassing anyone, I may need to point to the cane to give a further clue. That does not always work, especially in a leather bar, where it might be seen as some sort of novel sex toy. Then, a more detailed explanation must follow.

The cane's purpose is more apparent when fully extended and seen in full light. I have been complimented on my adept use of this device, even to the point of being told by good-natured passers-by that I am "doing a good job." Assuming they are referring to my navigational skills, I smile. But they have not seen me in my less-stellar moments.

I sometimes feel like a cockroach using its antennae to explore its immediate environment. In a way, the cane does act in this very manner; the cane should be moved side-to-side, preceding each footstep, working sort of like a radar system. I move forward into "safe" territory. Yet, some things do slip under or over the radar screen. Fire hydrants at knee-level can cause an unexpected shock (ouch!). Side-view mirrors on large vehicles are at face level and pose a harmful threat, as do impacts with bicycle handlebars (in the ribs), tree limbs, awnings and table umbrellas.

Danger lurks all around, so if I appear somewhat tense or remote, it should be understood that I am always anticipating the next frightful collision.

Expressing rage at unwarranted comments made at me is one thing, but when I start chastising fire hydrants and bicycles, it may be time that I re-evaluate my mental well-being.

(2/15/01)

4. KC At The Gate

KC cocks his head slightly and peers back at me over his narrow shoulders. One furry little ear stands straight up while the other flops forward.

I feel his forlorn gaze and am well familiar with his inquiry. I let out a pair of sighs; KC lets out a pair of pants. Once again, I am forced into the role of protective parent and have to tell him to go left on the path. He wants to go right and exit the gate of our insular community.

I repeat the same sad warning: "It's a dangerous world out there; someone has to shield you from the world." He cannot understand how his world has shrunk from several square miles back in Boston to the smaller acreage of our present gated community.

It was a deliberate choice to live in a part of town that has more walkways than roads. Two years ago, when I lived on a straight, narrow suburban street near the White Street Pier, we ran into trouble. Or I should say trouble almost ran into us. Upon leaving the house, KC would walk down the front path to locate the sidewalk. But there was no sidewalk. So he saw the street as one very wide walkway. One day a car came barreling down the street and almost hit us both.

Afterward, he was very reticent to take walks, and declared the backyard as his only safe zone.

KC is well known in Boston as the mascot for an MSPCA (Massachusetts Society for the Prevention of Cruelty to Animals) program that assists people with illness by enabling them to keep their precious pets. When I lost my sight five years ago, KC was my primary concern. Fortunately, this program came along just in time, and allowed me to keep our small family together while I went through the necessary rehabilitation to adjust to a life of blindness. His companionship and devotion has gotten me through this last turbulent decade.

People often ask me if he is my guide dog. As KC is a ten-pound Yorkshire Terrier, I jokingly respond that he does a good job in that regard, but he did not pass the height requirements to be certified. Many times, the inquirer does not realize that I am joking.

One can always know when a pet is communicating with us. Even without seeing him, I feel KC's thoughts. I know when he is watching me and what he wants me to know. Three years ago, he observed me writing at the computer. He sent me a message telepathically. (He sends messages in his East Coast Terrier dialect of Dawglish.)

I interpreted his comment: "I can do that."

"Do what?" I asked.

"Write," he answered. "If it were not for me lacking opposable thumbs, I could share my wisdom with the world."

I acquiesced and volunteered to let him channel his thoughts through me. So I put his words into my computer. The next thing I knew, he had an advice column in a local newsletter for the MSPCA. His advice column covered subjects ranging from teaching tolerance and diversity among four-legged creatures to advising pets on how to look after their two-legged friends.

Animals are gifted with means of non-verbal communication that far exceed human methods. They are also fortunate, in my view, in that they arrive in this world knowing their true purpose in life. Think of how many of us never find that calling.

Not unlike me, KC was forced to change careers in mid-life when I lost my sight. At the age of seven years, he was forced to take on new roles and responsibilities. He adjusted better than I did, and rose to the occasion with honors.

My pride of KC shines through, although I do feel a bit jealous when people pass us by and say hello to him and not to me. He thrives on the attention. I indulge his ego, somewhat relieving my guilt for being over-protective. I hope he can forgive me and understand my anxiety.

KC has traveled extensively, and has logged more air miles than have most Americans. He has accompanied me hiking the Southwest deserts and throughout the Rocky mountains. (One of my favorite photos of him is called "KC on the Rocks.")

Although his fame has put him in magazines, documentaries, live televised broadcasts and even on the pages of annual reports and calendars, his most important role is just being my friend.

Who else but our pets give us such warm welcomes when we come home, whether we are gone for five minutes or for five days. And how is it that they know how to make us smile, when nothing else in the world can bring us joy and comfort. I have often stated, in terms of our friends, "dogs, they never make other plans."

I advise you to give thanks for your furry companion everyday. I certainly do.

(2/16/01)

KC SPEAKS

THE KC DOG SONG.
Sung to the tune of the "Brady Bunch" theme

This is the story
Of a dog named KC, who has the middle name of Theodore.
He was adopted by a dad named Robert,
Who even loved him more.
He lives in Boston, on a street named Beacon,
And he loves to play endless fetch and ball.
KC stands for Killer Canine,
Though he's just eight inches tall.
He has a column
That's called "Dear KC."
In the pet world, he gives the best advice.
To those who know him and those who love him,
There is no better dog at any price.
The KC Dog, the KC Dog!
That's the way he became the KC Dog.
Arf! Arf! Arf!

Not many dogs have their own theme song. But I have never really thought of KC as a dog. He has been a member of my immediate household family since 1989. Although he appears to the casual observer to be a dog, I know better. KC came into my life in a canine form. But over the years, KC has revealed to me, and to the many others who have had the honor of getting to know him, that this ten-pound package contains a unique soul. The extent of his character and power is nearly impossible to measure. KC has always been a catalyst that set things in motion. He is the spark that ignites action and inspiration in the world around him.

Several years ago, I took a weekly Torah study class with a beloved and revered Rabbi. My friend, Mark, who was raised and educated severely Catholic, joined me in attending this class. Mark adored this Rabbi, as did most of her colleagues and congregants. He was enamored by her special demeanor from the first time he heard her speak. As a teacher, she inspired the attendees of this study group to a high level of sophisticated analysis and intellectual curiosity. We all looked up to her, but she made us realize that, we students, all had so much to learn from each other as well.

At one session, we were discussing the presence of angels as they appeared in the ancient scriptures, and how angels still are involved in our present lives. The following week, Mark brought to class a beautiful framed photograph of KC. I was unaware that he had stashed this in his bookbag, nor was I alerted of his plan. He held up the photograph before the class and identified KC as an angel in a dog disguise.

Then he told some of the story of KC: the miracles he worked as he touched my life, as well as in those others with whom he had contact. I knew all this to be true, yet I was a little nervous about the reaction of the Rabbi and our fellow students. Although I knew this to be an open-minded group, I was fearful that Mark's bold assertions might be pushing the envelope of sensibilities among these witnesses. Would they think this "Goy in their midst" was precariously walking the tightrope of sacrilege? Instead, Mark's demonstration only reinforced the class's mutual conclusion that angels really do enter our contemporary lives in many forms. As you will come to read, this notion of KC is very understandable, even to the most cynical.

In March 1996, exactly six months after losing my sight, I stood at a lectern before a gathering at a volunteer orientation session. On that cold winter day, I was the featured speaker. This occasion was the first time that, as a blind man, I would publicly address a group. I had diligently prepared a detailed outline for my presentation, as I had so much to impart to this group, and did not want to omit carelessly any vital points. My primary function at this session was to present a client's perspective, which, at that time, only I was qualified to provide. Several dozen prospective volunteers had braved the cold wintry weather on this Saturday afternoon to learn about a new program being launched by the MSPCA (Massachusetts Society for the Prevention of Cruelty to Animals). The mission of this program, from its inception, was to enable pet owners to maintain their loving relationships in the face of disabling personal health issues. Directed by a professional staff, the program's structure relied entirely on volunteers and contributors. The original concept for this local program was being incubated just as I was confronting the total loss of my eyesight. At that time, with the new initiative still in its developmental phase, KC and I were its first and only prototype clients.

Although I had taken great effort to be well prepared for my presentation, I had never spoken to an invisible live audience. Despite thorough planning, I would not be able to refer to written notes. So I attempted to memorize the basic outline of my talk.

Upon being called to the podium, I soon realized that I did not need to depend on prepared notes, as the words I spoke about my experiences flowed directly from my heart. Meanwhile, unbeknownst to me, KC was working the room. He methodically approached each attendee individually – personally introducing himself, not missing a single person present, and bewitching each one with his warm charismatic greeting.

As I spoke from the podium, I heard inexplicable sounds of reaction from the audience. I had no clue that my best friend was upstaging me. Or was he? To the observer, we were working in tandem. As if scripted, KC served to magnify my verbal message. I discarded any attempt to keep to my formal speech, as it proved unnecessary. My aim to herald the benevolence of this emerging program was made clear by KC's presence in the room. His own style of conveyance only served to illustrate the message further than any person could verbally communicate.

Within the context of my talk, I was relating how KC had saved my life by just being there for me in the darkest of times. Upon losing my sight the previous fall, my health was poor, and I struggled to find any meaning for which to live with the advent of my new circumstances. But KC's love and devotion was enough to remind me of my original vow to be there for him for the entirety of his natural life. He made it clear that I could not even think of deserting him, and even more incredibly, he brought me a new sense of peace and loving comfort in my hours of desperation. I spoke candidly of this to the listeners before me.

From the lectern, I heard both sniffling and giggling. Somewhat mystified by this mixed reaction, apparently my words moved them to tears, while KC's conviviality evoked mirth. I concluded my talk by expressing gratitude and admiration for the staff and volunteers – declaring my pleasure that this organization, known for its devoted humanity toward animals, was as equally concerned with the human lives which they invariably touched.

This occasion would be the first of many times in which KC and I worked as a team to solicit support for this incredible MSPCA program.

In March 1999 KC wrote the following piece for an invitation to a fund raising event to benefit "Phinney's Friends," the program to which I refer.

My name is KC. I was the first dog in the Phinney's Friends Program. Three-and-one-half years ago, my Dad, Rob, lost his vision from CMV. Since we have been clients of the Program, we have had the opportunity to make public appearances. (Dad always complains that I manage to upstage him. It's not my fault that I am cuter and more playful.)

I write a column for the Program's newsletter in which I share my wisdom with troubled pets. But the most exciting thing for me has been all the wonderful people that we have come to know through Phinney's Friends. I love walking with my volunteers. I am a great tour guide and love to share with them the fine features along my routes. (I have several favorites, although I enjoy varying them slightly each time.) Both Dad and I treasure the long-standing friends that have come into our lives to help us stay happy and healthy together.

We are both so grateful for this wonderful program.

After the publication of my fourth column, "KC at the Gate," my editor at *Celebrate!* asked me to send her some of KC's advice columns to which he referred. To my delight and surprise, Ginny requested a "Dear KC" advice column to be published every other week in *Celebrate!* (Amusingly, I received a smaller financial compensation for the "Dear KC" columns, proving that we still live in an inequitable society, where pay scales are not based exclusively on production and quality.)

KC was an instant hit. This was no surprise to me. The editor sent a photographer to my home so that KC's photo would appear next to his column. I had never been given the same offer. But I relish him the honor he deserves, as the source of the responses actually do emanate from him. I am merely the conduit that composes the text files. He has always channeled his original thoughts directly into my head and my fingers enter his words into the keyboard, to submit for his bi-weekly column.

KC's wisdom is apparent to anyone with whom he has contact. I frequently quote him and turn to him for guidance. As you will read in his words, his mastery of universal realities is exemplified by his in-depth understanding of situations, far greater than the limits of human consciousness. His scope broadly embraces the physical and metaphysical realms. I have always envied his ability to exude peace and disseminate it to others in need. KC frequently has awed the staff at hospices and nursing homes by demonstrating this natural inclination and skill. His reach is immeasurable by human comprehension.

As a source of wit and wisdom, KC continues to mystify me more each day. But a gift such as KC's should never be questioned, only cherished and revered.

DEAR KC [1]

Dear KC,
I am a house cat who lives with my brother and dad out in the quiet suburbs. I have an issue with you members of the dog species. The more of your type that I meet, the more I am convinced that dogs are from Mars and cats are from Venus. My littermate brother and I have discussed this and we are both quite puzzled about your canine appetite for toys and attention. Why must your emotions be expressed with such irrational exuberance?

Your loudness is often overbearing and your constant need to be busy is quite alarming. How is it that you overlook the art of being coy and subtle or cannot appreciate the joy in mellow activities such as a peaceful rest? I cannot recall how many times I have been rudely awakened from a peaceful afternoon nap by the loud barking from a neighborhood hound.

Dogs' passion for playing and running about wildly makes me think that some of you fellas never grew up. It occurs to me that each of you tries too hard to retain that silly title as "man's best friend". Is it some macho thing? I do not mean to offend in any way. I just thought that your wisdom and fairness could enlighten some of us curious felines.
Furrily Yours,
Alexis

•

Dear Alexis,
Your observations are well noted. However, I believe it is just a matter of difference in style. But it would also be inaccurate to paint all dogs

or cats with the same brush. Differences between felines and canines and even differences among ourselves is the true beauty of diversity. We should all learn to appreciate our different styles of behavior and be united and proud of our essential role in assisting our human friends get through their crazy lives (Talk about irrational behavior...) It's a blessing to know how much they really need us.
KC

•

Dear KC,

I am a four-year old Yorkshire Terrier, and much like you, I am very active. This is a two-part question:

First, whenever I lick my 'private parts', my human dad says, "I would if I could!" – I don't understand. And second, I REALLY like to hump – dad's arm, leg, whatever. Sometimes my dad will say, "You're limited to once-a-day, mister. I don't want you to be like the former President!" Who is this "President"? Is it a big dog? Does he hump a lot? I am confused – I don't think that I have done anything wrong.
Respectfully yours,
Rocky

•

Dear Rocky,

You've done nothing wrong! As to the first question, humans are not designed as well as dogs. While they do have that neat "thumb" thing on their paws that allow them to open doors and cans, they cannot lick themselves. Humans might be just a bit jealous of us animals who

CAN lick ourselves. They must get another human to lick them and, I guess, not all humans like to lick each other, especially their private parts. But many do – I've seen it and you may have also. Those humans who have learned the joy of licking private parts are usually just as eager as we are.

For the second question, the former "President" that your dad is referring to is a human politician. From what I have heard from the talking box or TV, this human does a lot of humping, licking, and other things that we do. But for some reason, some other humans thought he was bad for doing it and he got in a lot of trouble. I heard some people say that the former President is a sex addict. But your love of humping is absolutely natural.

It is no different from licking yourself. Some humans do not like to see us do these things – it makes them feel bad that they can't do it themselves. Those humans are known as "Republicans."

Rocky, keep sexual yearnings and politics separate. Feel free to express yourself by licking and humping!
KC

5. Sounding Off

Welcome to the Information Age. Information is a strange thing. Either we are awash in too much information, or, sometimes, information is in an inaccessible format. Try to understand how this is a reality for me as a blind man. Imagine if everything you read was in Swahili or spoken in legalese jargon. You would find yourself surrounded by information that was useless to you. But what if everyone else around you did not notice this problem and carried on normally?

As a teacher of the English language, perhaps my experience has made me more empathetic to my students who come to this country and struggle to understand our culture and our language.

Maybe I have developed an extra sensitivity to the barrage of audio media that targets us wherever we go. Waiting rooms, coffee shops, bars and restaurants all seem to have television monitors aimed at their captive audience. We are interrupted from having private thoughts because Martha Stewart is telling us how to live a more elegant lifestyle, or financial reporters must keep us up-to-the-minute on the stock market's gyrations. When did Dunkin' Donuts conspire with CNN to keep us both awake *and* well-informed?

It is a myth that when one loses one's vision his/her sense of hearing improves. In actuality, having lost my primary sensory input, all other senses move up on the hierarchical scale. As a result, the sense of hearing captures more attention in the brain. The effect on me has not been clearer hearing, but instead, an increased audio range. In other words, sounds, regardless of their point-of-origin, compete equally for attention. I must consciously distinguish which sounds to focus on and which ones to ignore.

When the conversation at the next table is more intriguing than the one I am part of, my mind tends to drift in that direction. When a song that I particularly like comes on over a public speaker system, I get lost in what should only be background sound.

The unsettling part of this situation is when I am overwhelmed by an audible background that most sighted people don't even consciously hear. I have trouble concentrating on the more important sounds intentionally directed at me. When a friend takes me shopping at Winn-Dixie, I feel swamped in a sea of music, announcements *and* advertisements. It becomes a tedious process for me to get my shopping cart filled and complete this task.

If you think that you have heard every gripe there is about the proliferation of cell phones, here's one more:

On more than one occasion, when receiving verbal guidance from people on the street, suddenly, I notice that their statements are punctuated with non-sequiturs. One sentence will be appropriate and sensible, and the next will be disconnected and contain totally irrelevant flotsam from another continuum. My bewilderment grows until I am made aware that they are speaking on a cell phone at the same time they are speaking to me. While on the subject of cell phones, when people use them in public places, the volume of these one-sided conversations is at least twice as loud as that of normal conversation.

In a completely unscientific study, I have observed that children are louder when playing in

water than when on dry land. I think that children should come with a warning label:

*"CAUTION: When wet, volume will auto-
matically increase drastically."*

Similarly, dogs bark louder at night.

In my world traffic sounds can be quite useful. The flow of traffic provides me with a sense
of direction. Likewise, the buzz of an approaching motor scooter or the rumble of a large truck,
lets me know that crossing the street would best
be delayed. Sadly, the City of Key West is not
only missing street signs, but also lacks audible
crossing signals for pedestrians. When asked
how I know when it is safe to cross, I reply that
it *never* truly is. Without knowing who has the
green light, I just perk up my ears, step off the
curb bravely, cross my fingers, pray and move
swiftly in search of the opposite curb.

Sounds can provide many clues when
sorted out properly. Water fountains, air conditioners, wind chimes, roosters, leaf-blowers and
bar music – all can clue me in on my location.
Even hard-soled shoes give me information. If
I walk closely in the wake of these well-heeled
pedestrians, I will likely be safe from surprise
impacts.

(I do miss the woman who stood out in front
of Crabby Dick's last year and announced in a
loud, booming voice that it was a great place
for lunch. She served as a great audible land-
mark.)

In enumerating the many sounds above that
are part of the character of Key West, consider
this: I had a most pleasant surprise early one
morning last week. I was walking my dog, KC,
and was suddenly struck by nothing but the
sweet sounds of nature. A gentle breeze rustled
the palm trees overhead and I heard twittering

songbirds nearby. Just then, a warm ray of sunshine splashed on my right shoulder and whispered to me the reminder that I was still living in Paradise.

(3/01/01)

6. Gooey Phooey!

The Gooey Phooey is a dance. It is done in the presence of a mechanical rodent in the dim light of a phosphorescent monitor. Physical movements express frustration. They incorporate obscene gestures, hair-pulling and nail-biting, accompanied by pleading and shouted invectives. The dancer pounds out the beat with fists on any hard surface to the sound of whirring disc drives and electronic computer tones. For us computer geeks, the Gooey I refer to is spelled GUI. This is one of those computer-age acronyms that stands for "Graphical User Interface."

I was present at their inception.

Once upon a time when keyboards were the domain of musicians and typists, a mouse was an unwelcome visitor that paid its rent in little turds, and windows were for letting in fresh air. We dreamed of a future of robots, automation and the paperless office environment. But something went wrong. A lot of people want to place all the blame on Bill Gates (co-founder of Microsoft), but there were many others involved in this plan to change our lives. I, for one, feel partially responsible.

Years ago, I was an artist-turned-engineer who conceived of a world that enabled the dumbest CEO (Chief Executive Officer) to have the status symbol of a PC (Personal Computer) on his desk. As typing was not in the curriculum at CEO school in his day, we needed to give him the means to interact with this desktop device. He needed to appear to consult it for important decision-making company information. The large ego of a top executive would not allow him to admit that his grandchildren were more adept at using a PC than he was. So his company spent fortunes on consultants to build him a system to facilitate this new technology. This is where I came in.

I was caught up in the lure of big MIC (Military Industrial Complex) spending by the Reagan-era administration in the 80s. As a consultant for an international firm that fed off a huge DoD (Department of Defense) budget, I was selected for my graphic design skills to create graphic computer screens that allowed the user to bypass technical computer idiosyncrasies. An executive could interact with this machine via the same single finger he would use to pick his nose when no one was looking. He would not have to learn how to type; typing was a skill beneath his dignity and was a task for his personal secretary, earning a small fraction of an executive's salary.

Our consulting firm pioneered touch-screen technology, graphical representation of data and drill-down menu systems. Now my former career has come back to bite me on the ass.

As a blind man, I stand helplessly in front of an ATM (Automatic Teller Machine) while it prints a message on the screen asking me which language I want to use for our electronic conversation. Even if synthetic speech were included as an option, I would not know where to place my finger on the screen to make the selection. It follows that living in a point-and-click world, as we now do, some commonplace interactions have become inaccessible to me. If one cannot point, how can one click?

I sit at home in front of my laptop computer, and using only a keyboard as input, I try to navigate a GUI to interact with each computer screen. Although my computer is equipped with special software that reads the printed text on the screen to me in a robotic voice, as so much is non-text (depicted as graphic icons, or image frames), I struggle with each unfamiliar screen. Unfortunately, I am more dependent on computers than are most people. The PC is my only method for keeping records, paying bills, writing, accessing information, reading newsletters, doing research, creating instructional material and sending text correspondence. Hence, you may often find me standing in front of this machine with which I have a love/hate relationship, doing the dance of the Gooey Phooey.

Today, many use the PC mainly for on-line pornography and chat rooms. For obvious reasons, this has no value to me. Call me old-fashioned, but I prefer my sex partner to be in the same room with me, and prefer real space to cyberspace in which to hold my conversations. Although the World Wide Web (WWW) has made the world a smaller place, I still prefer to be within touching distance when being intimate with others.

There have been standards published and guidelines offered to creators of web sites and computer application software that would make a more user-friendly environment for the visually impaired. But unless mandated by law, private companies need not adhere to such a framework. In a strange twist, all government agencies are legally required to do so. But who trusts the government, anyway?

My only comment here: GOOEY PHOOEY!!!

(3/8/01)

DEAR KC [2]

Dear KC,

I am a two-year old poodle who is spending the winter months here in Key West with my family. The rest of the year we live in the suburbs of Chicago.

Excuse my ignorance, but I am perplexed about something peculiar in my new neighborhood. There is an abundance of flightless birds that wander freely through the streets and yards. They squawk endlessly and throw mulch all over the sidewalks. In the last several weeks, I have noticed they are followed around by little versions of their kind, who "peep-peep" all day and raise quite a ruckus when I go out for a walk. I have heard these birds referred to as "chickens."

This is where I am confused. I had always thought that chicken was a kind of food, and was for roasting, frying or barbecuing. The younger members of my human family have even fed me this food secretly, under the table. If these feral birds running around are the same species as the much beloved food, why do they pass a barbecue without cringing, and have permission to run around freely without constraint, when we, man's best friend, enjoy no such freedom.

Curiously yours,
Gracie

Dear Gracie,

This island community is an unusual place indeed. Freedom to act with little constraint is a valuable hallmark of Key West. Yet, I agree that sometimes these freedoms are not equally applied to all. Regarding the chickens, they do seem to take advantage of their safeguarded status. We all wish they would be cleaner and make less noise (especially the males, referred to as "roosters," who stupidly announce the sunrise all throughout the night). We must accept living among all the species, even those with far less intelligence and character than ourselves. Besides, I wouldn't want to eat these wild birds, seeing how unfit they are for our consumption. I would bet they are not very tender, and would probably taste like mulch. I recommend you walk past them with your head held high, as I do, proudly knowing that our human families choose to love, feed and shelter us! Besides, chickens can be vicious if aroused and chased. They give a whole new meaning to the term "pecker."

As for the lack of open space for us canines to run freely, I have been informed that there is an initiative under way that would allow us to exercise freely our canine vitality in certain public spaces.

We hope to ultimately repeal the pet ordinance that bans domestic animals from all county parks.

Our human allies should also discuss plans to set aside an enclosed space for a "dog run," which would allow us to mingle amongst ourselves, unleashed.

If afforded this opportunity to expand our freedom, let's agree to leave the streets to the chickens and form our own alliances among ourselves.

KC

7. Alone in the Crowd

As a blind man, I often feel very alone in my immediate surroundings, whether in a mob, or just walking along a street.

Frequently, clueless about who is in close proximity, I get an odd feeling of isolation.

The other day, I was peacefully relaxing at the pool. The wind was fresh, the sun was warm,and the environment was tranquil. Voices around me were soft. I had my earphones on and was listening to a mellow radio station. The pungent aroma of a cigar suddenly overwhelmed me. A gentle breeze brought the fumes directly to my nose. Because the wind direction was fickle, I could not tell where the offensive aroma originated. I faced a dilemma: I could possibly move, but it would not be easy for me to find an empty lounge without stumbling over neighboring sun worshippers. I wanted to ask politely for the smoker to relocate or put out the cigar, but I did not know where to direct this request. I felt a bit trapped, but did not want to leave the pool area. Instead, I opted to go in the water for a swim.

I swim lengthwise along the edge of the pool to keep my orientation. I swim using only my legs to propel me with arms stretched out before me. This gives me ample warming of the end of the pool and avoids unexpected head impacts. It took only one concussion to learn this. Meanwhile, I pray that others see me under the water, as bodily impacts could be rather embarrassing.

I had hoped that during my exercise, the smoker would complete the consumption of hiscigar. Unfortunately, cigars burn slower than

I swim.

Similarly, I was sitting at the bar at the Green Parrot listening to some good live music. A drunken man with both offensive mannerisms and breath sidled up next to me. He attempted to make small talk in his slurred speech. I maintained a polite disposition. His talk was nonsense and I wanted to listen to the band on stage. He commented on some women sitting across the bar from us. I encouraged him to go over and speak to these objects of his lust. He told me that he had once tried to start a conversation with them but that they had dissed him. I told him, in all honesty, that perhaps conversation was not his strongest point, and he should try another approach.

He preferred to ramble on next to me and barrage me with his foul breath and mindless chatter. Once again, I was trapped.

It's not easy for me to slip away discreetly, or say that I need to go to the restroom. In most instances, I need someone to direct me there, particularly in an unfamiliar environment.

At the gym, I hear people all around me. Lively conversations ensue. Rarely do I get approached for conversation. I listen quietly while vigorously pursuing my fitness goals. Meanwhile, I hear chat about dinner parties and weekend adventures of which I was not a part. I feel lonely. But at least the vision of athletic bodies all around me does not distract me from my true purpose for being there.

It has been implied that I use my blindness as an excuse to do a lot of shameless body contact in a crowded bar or club. If surrounded by a lot of hot bodies, I do admit that the hands-on approach is a simple, and possibly pleasing way, to travel through the masses.

When I find myself in a waiting room, such as in a health clinic, I may be surrounded by patients. But the kind that I need is spelled P-A-T-I-E-N-C-E. I get quite bored there very quickly. Most people can find refuge from this boredom by picking up one of the outdated magazines or newspapers lying around. People-watching can provide enough entertainment to let the time pass more quickly. Neither of these are options for me. I usually curse myself for not having brought along my portable radio/headset. I find video monitors blaring at me to be annoying, and never showing anything I would choose to watch. So the time passes slowly. I am left to do a lot of thinking. It's OK; I like to think. But then I usually crave my recording device to store my more profound thoughts.

When visitors come to Key West to spend time with me in this beautiful climate, it is usually perfunctory to attend the sunset activities down by the waterfront. Live entertainment abounds. The crowds scream "OOOH!" and "AHHH!" I nudge my companions, "What am I missing?"

When the crowd laughs at the performer's visual gags, once again I feel left out. "What just happened now?"

I recognize that I am most often the only blind person in any particular setting. And although I often miss what is going on right before my eyes, I know, with some comfort, that there is still a lot going on inside my head that may be just for me. It's sad that some people would never think to look within for life's true value.

(3/15/01)

DEAR KC [3]

Dear KC,

Thank you for sharing your wisdom. In a world ruled by humans, we four-legged species cannot always understand the logic of these irrational beings. I understand from your words that we are here to give them the love and emotional support they so badly need. But when they make decisions that directly affect how we live our lives, I wonder about their ability to see reality, as we know it to be.

I have been designated as a house cat. My freedom to wander ends at the thresholds of our comfortable home.

I see other cats outside through the windows, and realize they have no such constraints.

I often long to hobnob and fraternize with my fellow felines as they climb trees and chase birds in the warm sunshine. Yet, I am confined to this human dwelling. The call of the wild is drowned out by radios and televisions.

I know my parents love me and shower me with all the luxuries and necessities of life. But why do they feel the need to confine me within their habitat?

Your loving admirer,

Duncan

Dear Duncan,

You said it: Your parents love you. In this instance, you must understand that they are doing what they feel is best for you. The outside world is not all as pretty as it may appear from your window. The grass is always greener on the other side of the sill. In reality, it is often a cruel and dangerous world out there. There are dangerous predators that can maim and kill; there is hunger and disease from which you have been protected. Your worries are few, you are guaranteed love and regular meals, and serve your most important role in life – bringing animal wisdom into the home of our often stressed and confused human hosts. Those who go looking elsewhere for their hearts desire are often surprised to learn that it is right there in their own backyard. (In your case your human home.)

KC

•

Dear KC,

I am a Harlequin Macaw with a relatively large vocabulary and I live in a golden cage. The other day I read an article in the newspaper on the bottom of my cage, that valuable exotic birds were being stolen from their homes! I read that there is a Black Market for our finely plumed kind. Once bird-napped, there is difficulty in identifying and returning us to our rightful owners. This report has ruffled my feathers and frightened me greatly. What steps can I take to ensure my safety and, if bird-napped, aid in my return to my beloved owners? I wait from the edge of my perch for your wise advice.

Your fine-feathered friend,

Larry Bird

Dear Larry Bird,

This is nothing to squawk about! Your extensive vocabulary can be your best ally. Make it a goal to memorize your owner's name, home address and telephone number. In the event you are victimized by such a crime, keep repeating your true identity and home address. Words are powerful. They can assist in your return to your loving home.

KC

8. House Guests and House Pests

Undeniably, come the winter months, we live in an enviable part of the country. Friends up north remind us of this often when we speak to them on the telephone. This is not news to us; perhaps that is why we are here. But, considering most of those long-distance telephone conversations start with weather as the topic, we get a little chance to gloat while they complain. Oddly, it is they who broach the subject, so we do what is expected of us, and tell them of our glowing suntans, or how we enjoy our meals al fresco.

Sometimes friends have called me from Boston to tell me what the weather is like here in Key West, after they see on the news that we are the warmest place in the lower 48. Most local residents can get the weather update by looking out of the window. As I cannot see out the window to observe that the sun is shining, when told this news, I feel obliged to go to the pool for a swim and to soak up the rays.

Key West's southern latitude makes it an enticing destination for our family and friends up north. Who among us has not enjoyed the privilege of playing host to a string of houseguests? I do not use the word "enjoy" sarcastically, as I really appreciate the company. I miss my friends in Boston during my winter exile from there. Yet, I sometimes feel that friends make a greater effort to travel the long distance down here to see me, but while I am up north, I may rarely get such a visit over the course of the summer months.

Once they arrive, visitors always turn immediately to the weather channel to see how lousy the weather is back home.

I appreciate the opportunity to enjoy the highlights of Key West that I would not likely do, when I do not have out-of-town guests staying with me. (It is the same situation that occurs where most native New Yorkers have never visited the Statue of Liberty or the Empire State Building, yet nary a tourist does not include these destinations on their agenda.)

As a blind man who lives alone with his small dog as a companion, things are different for me when playing host. I do my best to ensure that my home is clean and comfortable for all. I make special efforts in this regard. As I cannot always know when the ants come marching in, or the floor needs mopping, I engage in a series of preparations. Sadly, in this town it is easier for a blind man to find a dead insect on the rug than it is to locate a reliable and affordable housekeeper to help me. But I do all that I can. Guests are requested upon arrival to please excuse me if the tablecloth is on upside-down, or if the bed sheets are inside-out or do not make a matching set.

I need to state a special set of rules to accommodate my blindness.

Robert's Rules of Order:

1. Guests must do their own housekeeping. When they "check out," I request they help launder and make up the bed in the guest room. (Making up a bed is a formidable task for me.)

2. Don't forget to turn off lights. I never turn on lights when living here alone, so when sighted people leave the house, I appreciate it when they accommodate this request.

3. Do not leave breakables in my way. If a visitor leaves a glass on a table or a counter, I will invariably knock it over. (Usually after they leave, so I am forced to locate shards of broken glass scattered about. This is not only difficult, it is scary and dangerous for me.)

4. All visitors' belongings should be neatly stowed in the guest bedroom. I hate finding unfamiliar objects by sitting on them or tripping over them.

5. Please don't ask me if the clocks around the house are set to the correct time. As I never see them or use them I am likely to answer sarcastically, "They are not necessarily set to Key West time."

6. Don't rearrange the furniture. This even includes leaving chairs pulled out away from the table or leaving drawers and cabinet doors open. I am easily injured.

7. Don't try to be my sighted guide if you are inebriated.

I am more capable of safe mobility when drinking because I am *always* forced to pay extra-close attention. I never fall off curbs as sighted people do.

I know that the above rules may seem anal and restrictive. I want to be a happy and relaxed host, not a bruised and confused host. My compulsion to live this way is not merely a choice, it has become a necessity. Please understand.

Now, dear guest, let's have some fun and perhaps break some of the more conventional rules while together in this beautiful town!

(3/22/01)

DEAR KC [4]

Dear KC,

I am a blue Abyssinian cat, directly descended from the Egyptian cat goddess, Bast. My purpose in this life is to instruct my humans to be more Bast-like, so they can attain cat-serenity. Mama Ana is coming along fine with staring into space and napping, and she abundantly demonstrates her adoration of the Bast in me.

But I'm having trouble with an elemental appreciation lesson. When I demonstrate how to savor the cool, deep water contained in the perfect porcelain decanter, Mama Ana does not follow suit. In fact, she laughs and calls out things like "bowl diver!" and "toilet tongue!"

May I assume you, a dog, are a fellow partaker of the best water in the house? Why do humans find this amusing? Do you think perhaps their peculiar custom of standing on two legs, puts their heads too far away from this wonderful fountain to appreciate it?
Fondly,
Rafiki

•

Dear Rafiki,

Perhaps your theory on their upright posture has some merit, however it might be more likely that with their heads way up there in the clouds, they miss much of the world we so well know and appreciate, closer to ground level. *(The following letter addresses a similar concern.)* Do not be discouraged when our human friends are slow to comprehend so many of the overlooked perspectives to which we attempt to enlighten them.

I personally have not partaken in the libation ritual you refer to. I am a bit too short to get my face at that level. However, I can understand your annoyance at the condescending name-calling. Let's just accept that humans can act rather immature, regardless of their age.

Instead of focusing on your failures with Mama Ana, you should feel proud of your successes.

We share the wisdom of knowing our purpose in life, as you have so stated. Sadly, our human friends spend most of their time searching for purpose in their own lives, and are blind to the peace and serenity that we, their furry companions, naturally incorporate into our own existence. I suspect that your humans have learned more from you than you are even aware, and the admiration they express is proof of this. Be patient with humans. We have a lot of work to do in order to help them learn.

KC

•

Dear KC,

I am a four-year-old beagle. I love to take long walks with my house-humans. There is so much I want to show them, but it is obvious that they consider our expeditions as little more than bathroom breaks. There is so much to sniff, but my folks do not seem to be aware of the abundance of aromas. They may stop to smell a flower on a bush, but are too lazy to put their noses down to the ground and take in all the information that is right there at their feet. Why do they seem so short on common scents?

Barney

Dear Barney,

Good pun! Unfortunately, it is even more accurate than you may realize. Their lack of common sense/scents is another example of their inferior body design. Their noses are too far from the ground to know what we know, and when we try to direct them, they look down their noses at us. It is also a fact that they are smell-challenged. You hounds are the most gifted in this area, but all dogs have a far more acute sense of smell than do humans. Even if we could convince them that the grass and earth hold volumes of information about who has scurried there before us, I do not believe that they would be able to appreciate it as well as we can.

Perhaps we must accept that some of life's pleasures and secrets will forever be beyond their reach. As for convincing them that you would appreciate longer walks, why don't you find trails where both you and your house-humans can both find treats to enjoy.

KC

9. Even A Blind Man Knows When The Sun Is Shining

"Hi, Rob! It's me!"

Who is this "me?" I wonder. With so little information as a single line and a voice, what is the proper etiquette to ask politely, "Who are you?"

Without visual information for identification, unless the voice is very familiar or distinctive, I am bewildered as to how I should respond. Usually, I just return the hello. As I walk away, I worry that they think I am unfriendly.

Sometimes an additional remark will give me the clue that I need. Others spare me the conundrum by giving me their name instead of the "me."

While walking down Duval Street yesterday, an unfamiliar voice greeted me: "Hey, Hot Shot!" At first I took this as a derogatory remark, but realized suddenly, that he called me by the words that are printed on the front of my cap.

I frequently wonder how aware people expect a blind man to be. It is not uncommon to be given credit for having some kind of clairvoyance, or else I may be assumed to be totally "in the dark." If perceived as clairvoyant, it is because I pay more attention to details than most people do, out of habit and necessity. I do absorb more information than people realize.

It is a peculiar position to be in; either being overly attended by well-intentioned people, or to be overlooked because they think I know more than I actually do.

In another instance of communication problems, I often wonder how to return a compliment with sincerity. If admired for my appearance, I know that it is common courtesy to reply, "thank you," and follow with a similar kind remark. But it would be silly for me to say something such as, "I cannot know for sure, but I assume you are looking well also."

If I appear always to be upbeat and optimistic, it is only because I hide my dark and brooding side from the public. (When I want to play the blues, I remember that I only play the violin, not often found in a blues band.) The appearance we project may only be a facade. But if we pretend to be something often enough, we are liable to infuse that manner into our character. When we portray confidence in order to make others feel comfortable, it does more than just cover our fears and insecurities; it restores our wholeness and self-esteem.

I do get lost and disoriented more often than I usually let on. There are entire neighborhoods and pathways that are total black-out zones for me. If I did not have my trusty dog, KC, to get me home, I might wander unsuccessfully for hours. This has happened. But it should also be noted that I would not likely find myself on those unfamiliar pathways, in the first place, if it weren't for my adventurous and nosy dog. It is when I am alone and nobody seems to be around, that I may panic. Last week, I had the strange feeling that I was being followed. I became nervous. When I arrived home, I discovered that I was only hearing the "glug-glug" of the water bottle in my backpack.

I prefer pathways and streets to be straight and to cross at perpendicular angles. From my memorized street map of downtown, I can usually determine my location. Alas, all roads and paths are not straight, nor do they intersect at right angles.

Winding paths or streets present a real challenge. The unexpected crook in the road up ahead can rob us of our confidence and self-assurance, not unlike in life itself. (I never could have foreseen losing my vision at age thirty-seven.)

Our paths cannot always be plotted with certainty. The road that lies before us is constantly changing and may be as unpredictable to us as our future. We all lose our direction at some point. The best that any one of us can do on our journey is to accept our immediate circumstance and try to find the place that we call home.

There are times I long to run away from this life and get lost on purpose. But as Stephen Sondheim so aptly put it: "When running away, know how to get there...And how to get back... And eat first."

In the older parts of Boston, where the streets have no apparent logical design, I dare not even try to keep a sense of direction. It is said that the streets follow the original pathways of wandering cows and drunken sailors. When we find ourselves in such an environment, we must improvise, until we figure out the right course.

I recently explained to someone that I do better finding my way home on sunny days. The reason is simple: LIGHT is INFORMATION.

As I leave the gym in the late afternoon, the warmth of the sun caresses my face, thereby guiding me westward into the setting sun, toward my home. Even without the slightest visual perception, I hear the comforting voice in my head saying, "Walk toward the light!!" And soon, I am safely at home again.

(3/29/01)

10. Art Ache

"It's PINK!" says one.

"No, it's PUMPKIN!" responds the other.

"It's dull and mundane!" demands the first.

"Its loud and brassy, like you!" argues his ex-lover.

Sitting quietly nearby, I listened with amusement. This squabble seemed more like a transfer of deep personal feelings between them.

"I only wanted to select the color coral," I interject at this point.

I had been redoing my bathroom, and it was time to select a wall color from sample paint strips that I had picked up at the local hardware store. The color I had envisioned was clear in my mind, but I needed a sighted person to help me choose the correct hue and tint to match my description. I thought that by surveying my friends, this exercise would be very uncomplicated. It should have been the easiest part of the entire project. Yet, this exchange proves the axiom: No two people see things the same way.

Acknowledging that aesthetic values vary widely, I have always observed with interest the debate over good art and bad art, over what is beautiful and what is repulsive. My extensive background in art has taught me that the objective is not merely for the sake of creating beauty. It should be a means of personal expression to evoke emotional responses from both creator and observer.

The dialogue above proves that a simple response to a color can unearth subconscious feelings. Take this a few steps further and it becomes apparent that each one of us has a unique perspective of our world.

My connection with art and design started at a very early age. My parents encouraged what they saw as talent. Every plaything I received related to art. Far beyond pastels and paint sets, I collected such forgotten items as "Spin-Art," and "Etch-a-Sketch."

Naturally, this was not only my avocation, it developed into my career. My professional work involved designing graphic interfaces for computers.

Pursuit of the fine arts was my favorite leisure time activity. I viewed nature as the ultimate inspiration and expression of art. I was driven to define my life by such passions.

On September 15, 1995, the day I woke up totally blind, the headline in the Rob Chronicles read: ART IS DEAD TO FORMER DESIGNER.

It has taken years, therapy, and much introspection to learn that this obituary was premature. If art were my main form of recreation, I would have to redefine my understanding of what art could be for me personally.

Shortly after the black veil descended before my eyes, I realized that my creative soul cried for expression. I walked over to the dusty violin case that had been sitting undisturbed for years in the corner of my room. I pulled out the delicate wooden instrument, placed it under my chin, and played. A need I had buried inside for too long was given a voice.

Following this action, I realized that I needed to resurrect other neglected forms of artistic expression, as well as to accept that I must see visual art again through other peoples' eyes. (This would prove to be a greater challenge than relearning how to write, sculpt or play music.) It pains me greatly that I can no longer view much of the world directly and must rely on the perceptions of others.

I still go to galleries and museums. I also foray out into nature. But I cannot do these things alone. A sense of loss mixes with elation as I request my companion to interpret visually the scene before and around me. Aware that I might see it very differently than they do, I request they start with an objective description before sliding into subjectivity. I re-create in my head what I hear from their words. When previously familiar with the piece, their words can conjure up the image from remote corners of my mind. Even if I only know some of the artist's work, I can begin to feel his genius once again. And this is why you might see this blind man standing before a painted canvas appearing totally involved.

I crave tactile art. I always ask the curator if I can touch the sculptures, and have never been denied this request.

Without claiming to be extremely gifted as an artist myself, the admiration of great art has always enriched my life. It still can, to a certain degree.

The true test of friendship is the one who will sit next to me in a theater and accepts my constant badgering, "What is happening on stage now?" A well-written play can often ignite my imagination and fills in most of the stage action. Musical theater can frequently express the story line through the music and lyrics, although, I do miss some of the sets, costumes and special effects. Alas, any choreography is lost on me.

Live musical performance invokes feelings directly in my mind, bypassing the need for visual interpretation. In the appropriate setting, I am drawn to dance with little inhibition as to how I may appear to others. I'm just a boy who wants to have some fun!

Lastly, there is my attraction to the greatest art of all: the natural world. No longer able to venture into the wilds of nature alone, I miss the solitary communion with the universal Divine Masterpiece. Take me hiking and leave me on a rock in the deep woods. I listen attentively, and the purity of nature speaks to me. I relive the passions I experienced from my previous sighted life.

Regarding my bathroom, the ultimate true color will forever remain a personal mystery.

(4/5/01)

The Humble Thimble

(Author's Note: for maximum effect,
it is suggested that the following section be read aloud.)

Take one humble thimble –
Seems simple.
How can one humble simple thimble
Seem a symbol for a rumble?
When one humble simple thimble
Creates an ample cause to consequently crumble.
My story is a sample
Of how a simple humble thimble
Leads to tsuris from a tumble.
Pardon if I ramble
Of a simple humble thimble wreaking trouble,
But recall – a single simple needle
Can burst a bouncing baby's bubble.
Trouble from a thimble?
If the simple humble thimble
Is the basis of a legal wrangle tangle
And is said to leave a tiny little dimple
In the middle of the sheriff's shiny Chevy.
The consequence was heavy
Since the dimple in the Chevy
Caused the constable to scurry
To seek vengeance in a hurry.
Simply see it from my angle –

I could not foresee this tangle
As they slyly sneaked behind me, blindly,
To double-trouble me unkindly!
A couple callous cops commenced
To mingle and to wrestle
So I subsequently struggled
To avoid a muscle tussle strangle,
Thinking this hustle bustle hassle,
A rumble tumble tangle,
Was some danger from some strangers off the street,
Whom I'd never seek to meet.
These surly civil servants snatched me like a silent secret missile –
I wished I'd had a warning whistle
To avoid a shuffle scuffle.
Accused of hitting cars –
Brought the blind boy behind bars.
My brain was badly boggled.
Reality had toppled.
Sacred Civil Rights were trampled
By the unruly rowdy rabble.
So, see this simple humble thimble
Caused a rather rancid wrinkle,
And I called my cousin Finkel,
For logistic legal counsel.
Justice is not simple.
Mangled physical and mental,
It is not a gentle jungle to fumble blindly from the middle
Of the rubble of this fangled tangle riddle
Stemming from a simple single humble metal thimble.

The lesson from this Fable?
Do not underestimate
The perilous capacity
Of a simple single humble thimble
To start a sidewalk scuffle scandal.

The sad story truly did all begin with a thimble. Despite fastidious preparation for my seasonal departure from Boston, I had overlooked one important item. I had neglected to pack a spare cane. As this accouterment is an essential element of my everyday ensemble, I maintain no shortage of backups back up in Boston, stashed in my closet. Most are refurbished hybrid versions of previous working models that I had re-assembled from the bastardized parts of previously damaged and broken canes. It was unfortunate that this very season I had but one cane to spare for my quandary.

Never before was it necessary to employ one of my reserve accessories, but this winter my cane suffered a minor mishap. Somewhere out there on Duval Street, probably stuck in a storm drain, lay the detached plastic tip of my cane.

It came to my attention one afternoon as I returned home. The feel of the cane against the pavement seemed uncharacteristically rough. Once safely inside, upon closer inspection, I found that the silicon tip that resembles a mushroom cap had deserted me. Surely, it had already been worn down enough to warrant replacement. But I had assumed that it would survive until I returned to Boston, where I'd have access to a store supplying such specialized merchandise.

Had I continued to use the cane in its damaged form, the tip-less narrow end that remained would constantly get caught in the cracks and irregularities beneath my feet. I was stuck with a walking stick that would get stuck in the sticky walkways. Without the proper protective tip, the tense elastic cord, which tightly held together the detachable segments of my collapsible cane, was exposed. As the vulnerable cord wore against the concrete surfaces, it would soon snap, quickly rendering the cane's point moot. Without a cane, I am totally immobilized. An immediate mend was highly recommended.

I sat at home in search of a quick, creative, clever solution for a rapid recovery. What could I affix to fix the tip-less tip to temporarily fit this function? I rummaged through all my odds and ends for a hardware tidbit to fit on the tip bit. I found no fitting fixture.

I enlisted the mechanical minds of others to envision an end to my arcane cane calamity. We searched for a substitute for the lost mushroom cap. One friend spontaneously conceived of a plan, and on the way to an afternoon concert, he ducked into a store that peddled pet supplies. He emerged moments later with a small collection of cat toys. His simple notion was to append a feline notion to the end of the cane. In theory, his was a clever innovation. However, as often happens, reality proved the inadequacy of this makeshift remedy. We glued a simple plastic ball, with a jingle bell inside, to the end of the cane. But, alas, the strongest polymer available was insufficient to attach the tiny toy to the tip, to hold it firmly in place. Besides, the jingle ball did not have the durability to withstand the rugged pavement against which it would repeatedly rub. So, once pasted in place, the cat ball failed on its first short test run.

The following day, I received a phone call from this friend. He had conceived an alternative proposal. Introducing The Thimble. It fit well over the narrow tip of the cane, and even attached well with ample fixative. So, the long white walking cane and the humble metal thimble were united. Not a perfect marriage, but a good temporary relationship. Trouble was that it was still very narrow and had the propensity to get snagged in the crevices of the sidewalks. And, ultimately, the metal did not have the mettle to contend with the course concrete. It shortly showed signs of wear.

And, as you will read, this thimble's eventual contact with a vehicle set in motion a much larger problem than a tipless cane.

11. The Bare FAQs

Note: FAQs, pronounced "fax", stands for "Frequently Asked Questions"

"May I ask you another question?"

I am asked this often. Perhaps not often enough, as some people are timid about being too inquisitive. Frankly, I am happy when people want to learn what the life of a blind person is like. I feel I do a service for all people with disabilities when I respond with first-hand experience. I welcome inquiring minds, as such curiosity benefits us both with this exchange of information.

The items below are not necessarily in order of importance, frequency, or popularity.

"If you see nothing, not even light, what color is nothingness?"

It is not blackness, as most believe. I usually can only describe it as the absence of any color. Perhaps it is a fashionable shade of gray. When I first lost all my sight, the grayness had a slight suggestion of a hue that seemed to reflect my mood. I selected a therapist who was also blind, believing that only such a person could help me navigate my way back to a semblance of normalcy. She was a Jungian psychologist. From her perspective, dreams and visual illusions held important subconscious meanings. As I arrived at my weekly appointment, she would ask what color I was seeing that day. My answers ranged from purple to mustard to deep black.

I often get asked about dreams. Usually, I dream visually with very vivid detail. I am aware that I am blind, but seeing does not surprise me. It is scarier when I awake and find myself once again totally deprived of visual senses. I have often said, "I go blind every day (when I awake)."

Five years ago, when I first went blind, I would wake up at night, and my mind would trick me. I clearly saw my surroundings in the darkness. These hallucinations were exciting. They seemed so real, I thought I had regained my sight. Presently, I wake up with the last image of the dream clearly stuck in my brain. Without anything to overwrite the imprint, the image sometimes lingers throughout the day. Hopefully, that image is a pretty one.

When I have non-visual dreams, I often wake up with an emotional reaction, but cannot recall the situation from the dream.

"What is it like being blind?"

Please be more specific. Overall, as you might expect, life is very challenging. Some of the most basic daily tasks become very complicated, or totally impossible. For me personally, it was very humbling. For the first time ever, I realized that life was not all in my control. Previously, I never thought that I might need assistance from others. To paraphrase Blanche Dubois, "I have learned to rely on the kindness of strangers." I am deeply grateful for the volunteers, who often become friends, for their assistance with food shopping, reading and responding to my mail, and a variety of other tasks.

Five years ago, in Boston, Social workers from many agencies immediately came to my home. I learned mobility using only a long white cane. They taught techniques for daily living. Organization is essential to survive, and memory becomes a primary device. I learned to make Braille labels, marked folders and boxes.

Everything had its place.

Few modern appliances are designed to be used by visually impaired persons. But have you ever noticed that on most telephones, the number 5 on the keypad is tactually marked, as is the home row on your computer keyboard? Remote controls are nightmares! I must mark switches, buttons and knobs on microwave ovens, washers and dryers, stoves, etc. Next time you reach for that instruction manual to re-program your speed dial or VCR, think of me.

I also learned many tricks to identify the contents of cans, boxes and paperwork. I memorize things such as which cans are marked with two rubber bands or which documents I distinguished with three paper clips. In codifying my CDs, I invented a means of identification, which would be rather esoteric to the casual observer. I often buy food products for the unique shape of their packaging. Paper money must be folded in a distinct manner so that I can determine the denomination.

I also must be less conscious of making embarrassing blunders in public. I get nervous when eating out. I make so much effort to stay clean that I am probably the neatest eater in the place.

"How do you shop for clothes?"

If you have seen me out and about, it should be obvious that I do not put clothes shopping or fashion at a very high priority. In the rare cases that I do need to add to or replace items in my wardrobe, I trust the advice of good friends or sales clerks.

"Have you considered getting a guide dog?"

I could never do that to my canine companion, KC. He has acquired many guide dog skills, but I would never upset him by introducing a second dog into his turf. I couldn't imagine how he would feel if I left the house with another dog, leaving him home alone.

"Is it better to be born blind, or to lose sight later in life?"

"If you had to choose between blindness or deafness, which one would it be?"

Neither of these questions can have a good answer. I am glad humans do not get given such choices. We must just accept whatever fate befalls us.

"How do you. . .?"

Many questions that start off like this can only be responded to with:

"Very carefully,"

"Very poorly"

or simply

"I don't anymore."

(4/12/01)

DATELINE: KEY WEST
FRIDAY, MARCH 30, 2001:
"SNOW BIRD TURNS JAIL BIRD"

"I READ THE NEWS TODAY...OH BOY!"

Note: Personally, the details of this incident are all too easy for me to recall, and, inversely, extremely difficult for me to recount. Having to retell this story repeatedly and composing the documentation contained in this volume have been a formidable, heart-rending task. Additionally, in the telling, I must do my best to relate the incident from two perspectives while maintaining a cohesive, comprehensive presentation. My first-hand account as a blind man, alone, would be restricted by the limited information that was accessible to me during the incident.

Sightlessness rendered me oblivious to many details and activities in my immediate surroundings, which would otherwise be apparent to a sighted person. Therefore, the accurate retelling of the incident had to be presented in an unconventional structure. In order for the reader to follow the course of the action, I needed to insert information that came to me afterwards. Mark's visual perceptions of the events fill in some very relevant aspects and elements, of which I was "in the dark." I have inserted his personal observations and experiences in the appropriate places in this narrative.

1. Another Day in Paradise

Since arriving in Key West on the last Wednesday in March, Mark was to be my house-guest for one week. On the following sunny, Friday morning, we had gone to the pool for a few hours. It looked to be just another typical, beautiful spring day in Paradise.

Our schedule for the rest of the day was set. First, we were to run some errands. I needed to go to the bank. We were then to do some minor shopping. Mark had a massage appointment for later that afternoon. When Mark was to go to his appointment, I planned to return home to complete my next weekly column. We had tickets for a show, early that evening.

We left my house at about 1 p.m. I was feeling very proud, about to cash my first paycheck for my "Blind Snow Bird" series, which had been running weekly, for two months. As we left the bank, I mentioned that I felt an odd premonition. Mark helped me to inventory my belongings, as I thought that I might have left something behind. Everything checked out okay, so we continued on our way. We turned right at the corner of Simonton Street and walked east on the south sidewalk between Southard Street and Angela Street. Mark was acting as my "Sighted-Guide." He walked alongside me on my left, between me and the curb. My left hand held his right elbow for guidance, as my white cane, in my right hand, alternately tapped the pavement directly before my feet and the storefronts to my immediate right.

It was approximately 1:15 p.m., when we started across the driveway that runs beside the Fire Station. Mark noticed a white Chevrolet Lumina sedan speeding down the ramp toward the street. (I was unaware that we were crossing a driveway at the time, as their was no noticeable slope of the pavement, nor was there any detectable curb or change in sidewalk level.)

I heard Mark's cry of warning and then felt him push me backward. His sudden physical gesture startled and confused me.

(Mark told me later: "I thought at first that it [the sedan] would stop at the end of the building, before crossing the sidewalk – as required by law. But at the last moment, I realized that it wasn't slowing down. I yelled, "WHOAA!" and shoved you backwards out of its path.")

Mark had extended his right arm across my chest to push me backward out of the car's path. The vehicle did not stop until it was blocking the sidewalk, its front bumper aligned with the curb. Mark's loud cry alerted the driver. The vehicle screeched to a halt only two feet from us. I nervously asked Mark what had just happened, and he answered that we were almost hit.

The driver called out from his window and I heard his apologies, "It was my fault. I wasn't looking where I should have been. I was looking to the right. I didn't see you."

Mark angrily answered, "You should be more careful! You could have killed us!"

When Mark started to lead me around the car, I bumped against the fender, and for the first time, realized how close the vehicle had come to hitting us.

In order to circumnavigate the sedan, Mark led me off the curb, and into the eastbound traffic lane of the street. I continued to use my cane as before – tapping the pavement in front of my feet and making contact with the front of the vehicle to my right, as it protruded well beyond the building line (which had been serving as my right-hand guide). Mark directed me as I walked between him and the vehicle. I used my cane by tapping the pavement on the left, then raising the cane higher to make contact with the vehicle to stay clear of its front bumper. (I need to raise the tip of the cane when passing closely to a vehicle, or else it will slide beneath the chassis, and give me no clear information about its distance.) We continued to pass in front of the car.

When we had crossed completely to the other side of the vehicle, Mark led me back onto the sidewalk. The driver then got out and called to us, "I am sorry. I was wrong. I was looking to the right and didn't see you on the sidewalk."

Mark then witnessed the driver speak into his radio. I was unaware of this. The driver then walked over to us and said that he had not actually hit us and that it was no excuse to hit the vehicle with my cane. I heard him scold me: "You just hit a county vehicle!"

I was annoyed with his attitude as he gave the impression that a county vehicle was sacrosanct, so I responded, "I don't care what kind of vehicle it is, the real important fact is that you came dangerously close to killing us – and you are not concerned about that?"

I was very disturbed at his callousness, and saw no further reason to confront this hostile man. Mark was still angry, but I suggested that we just move on, since we were already running behind schedule in completing our errands. Despite my prodding, it seemed that Mark did not want to let us continue on our way. I did not understand this delay, so I again urged him to let it be, since neither one of us had been hurt, nor was it worth angering this man with further argument. I had no idea of who this man was, nor what kind of "county vehicle" he had been driving. For some reason, I had envisioned it to be a van or a truck. (Unfortunately, I am rather accustomed to such dangerous incidents while walking in public, and this seemed like just one more.)

As we had turned to face the man during this verbal confrontation, I had let go of Mark's arm. I stood alone, unsure of his exact whereabouts. Mark told me afterward that he watched as several men quietly sneaked up behind me. Of course being totally blind, I could not detect their approach toward me. They kept silent, and did not identify themselves. Suddenly, someone grabbed my left hand and swiftly pulled it behind my back. As I felt something sharp against my wrist, I was severely alarmed. This sudden contact surprised and frightened me, so I instinctively tried to pull my hand away. I did not know what this sharp item was, or who these assailants were. Terrified, I assumed that I was being mugged.

I loudly called out for Mark, but could not determine where he was. (Mark told me afterward that he watched as they were starting to put on one handcuff.)

Without knowing who was grabbing at me, I had no clue that the sharp metal against my wrist was a handcuff.

Again I desperately called out to Mark, "Who are these people? What are they doing?"

I received no reply, and became very irritated with Mark for not coming forward to assist me, nor even providing me any information. Mark later told me, "When I tried to speak to you, to explain what was happening around you, another officer pushed me back and said, 'Move away or I'll arrest you too!'"

The next thing I felt was having my legs and cane kicked out from under me and being slammed face down on the pavement. My face and my right hip hit the cement hard, my front teeth split my lower lip. I was rolled onto my right side. Then I was pinned to the ground by a sharp jab of a knee on my upper back.Another person grabbed both my wrists behind my back and put me in restraints. The knee pressed the full weight of a man into my rib cage. My lip swelled and became instantly numb and bloody – I thought that my front teeth had been broken.

The unidentified assailants then pulled me up off the pavement and pushed me toward a parked vehicle. I was suddenly aware of the intense pain in my right leg and back, which disabled me from standing upright. They shoved me against the vehicle so that my groin rammed up against metal. Completely bewildered, I kept calling out to Mark, "What is happening? Why are they doing this? Who are these men?"

I could not figure out where he was. As he did not respond, I assumed that he was being similarly roughed up and restrained.

A nearby voice responded sarcastically to my panic,

"Don't you get it? When you are put in handcuffs, you're being arrested."

This statement was my very first clue that they might be police officers. But I was still perplexed and dubious, considering the brutal force I was subjected to during this unprovoked assault. Perhaps I was naïve, but I refused to believe that police officers would act this way. Such violence was a display of cruelty and utter contempt.

I asked this stranger the reason for this arrest, as I couldn't conceive of what I might be charged with having done. Nobody would answer me. I told them that I was in great pain in my ribs, and that the cuff on my left wrist was too tight. The restraint was cutting into my skin and I felt it obstructing blood circulation to my hand. A male voice responded that he would loosen it. Then I felt him tighten it even further. My level of fear rose even further.

Next, they pushed me head first into a vehicle onto a hard, plastic surface. They kept demanding that I sit upright, but I told them that I was unable to move my torso without sharp pain. I remained lying on my left side. I could barely breathe and started to hyperventilate, while coughing up phlegm from my throat and lungs. My swollen lower lip was bleeding.

I began to have a panic attack, a chronic condition I have had for many years since losing my sight. These attacks occur under extreme stress.

(Panic attacks are characterized by fast, shallow breathing and muscle convulsions throughout my entire body.)

As I lay on this hard surface, in addition to the jolts of pain in my back, I felt soreness around my right eye socket and on the bridge of my nose, where my sunglasses had pushed into my face when I hit the ground. I also was aware of bruises on my chin, my left hand, and the area on my outer thigh, beneath my right hipbone.

The car was parked in full sun, so the inside was extremely hot. I was drenched in sweat. My mouth was dry except for the mucus I was spitting up from my throat. My sinuses became completely blocked and my nose was totally congested. I struggled to breathe.

As Mark would later relate to me, the man, who was driving the car that had almost hit us, identified himself as a County Detective. He searched through my backpack and wallet, then began filling out a report on the trunk of the cruiser. Again, Mark asked permission to speak with me.

They finally allowed him to do so.

(Mark later quoted to my newspaper editor, "I opened the car door and tried to get Rob into a sitting position but he was in too much pain and couldn't breathe. I asked permission to provide him with his inhaler from his backpack and they agreed. But Rob couldn't exhale enough to use it.")

When Mark opened the door of the car, he offered me the inhaler. It was very difficult to speak, but I kept asking who these men were. He told me that they were police officers. Still doubtful, I asked him if he was certain of this. He assured me that they were – that some of them were in uniform. So I requested that he immediately get their names and badge numbers. I then related to him the extensive nature of my pain and physical injuries. He tried to help me readjust my position in the back of the cruiser, to take my body weight off the injured ribs.

(Mark turned to the officer standing beside the vehicle. He said, "It's roasting back there. The air conditioning isn't getting through the partition. There's only a three-inch hole – that's not enough!" The officer opened the front door of the cruiser, and replied sarcastically, "The A/C is on full. It's cool in here," pointing to the front seat.)

Mark turned back to inform me that they were going to take me to the County Jail, but would not allow him to accompany me. I asked him to take my wallet and backpack home. Mark promised to get a cab and come down to the jail as soon as possible. I requested that he go immediately to the newspaper office *(Celebrate!)* and alert them as to what was happening.

(Mark later told me that when he had asked to accompany me to the jail, they said only if he wanted to be arrested as well.)

Before Mark left, the plainclothes officer asked him why I was upset. Mark responded that almost being killed was a frequent occurrence for me, that I had been hit before, my cane had been run over and had been broken several times, and that most drivers do not stop. The officer lectured that I shouldn't get angry when drivers almost hit me.

Mark told this officer of my many near-fatal experiences. He replied, "Oh, they probably aren't looking for a blind man. I haven't seen one down here in four years. I don't believe drivers would just deliberately do that, they're just busy."

(Sadly, Mark's statements were accurate; in every instance but one, when a moving vehicle had struck my cane, or me, the driver had continued on his way.)

Mark then left the scene to return to my home to make phone calls and notify others as to what just had occurred.

Snow Bird Turns Jailbird
(CONTINUED)

2. Adding Insult to Injury

Mark had departed the scene. I lay in the hot vehicle, drenched in sweat and aching profoundly for at least another half hour. Eventually, I heard the driver's door open and someone get in the front seat. He identified himself as "Jay," and told me that he was taking me to the County Jail. When I queried him further, this driver would only answer that I had just been arrested. I told him that I was in terrible pain from the battering I had just received. He assured me that there would be a doctor to examine me at the jail. This statement seemed mildly comforting, so I thought he might be somewhat civil and understanding. I tried to relax somewhat. But, as I inquired once more as to the reason for my arrest, the driver turned up the car radio's volume, making additional communication impossible. Unable to hear anything else the driver might have said, I was again overcome with despair and tension.

It seemed like a very long time that the car remained stationary, while the driver sat at the wheel. I was confused and irritated by the blasting radio music. Then, I became aware that the car was on the road. Every turn and jolt of the vehicle caused extreme pain in my ribs, left wrist and right hip.

The driver eventually lowered the volume on the radio, and kept harshly demanding that I sit upright. I repeated that my injuries prevented me from changing my body position.

Once arriving at the county jail, as I couldn't maneuver my torso, I requested assistance to exit the vehicle. I was pulled out by my legs until my feet could feel for the curb. One man insisted that I would have to walk. I told him that I could not stand upright, and I would need to lean on someone while being led. I used my left arm to distribute most of my weight onto the man's right shoulder. While we walked ahead, I was hunched forward.

I was brought inside a building and told to sit on a hard chair in front of me. In order to sit, I attempted to straighten my back, but the pain was overwhelming. So, I bent at the knees and sank to the floor, leaning my elbow on the chair. I asked for medical attention. Many voices were directed at me. They kept telling me that I was not really hurt and they demanded to know what I had been drinking that day. I told them I had not been drinking. They continued badgering me about what drugs I was on – marijuana, cocaine, heroine? As my mouth was so dry, I became even more agitated, and was unable to articulate clearly. I requested to see a doctor as had been promised; I was told that a nurse would soon attend to me.

They barraged me with continuous interrogation. My mouth was too dry and painful to speak – I kept requesting a drink of water. No one would comply with this plea. After a while, a female voice approached and identified herself as a nurse. Once again, I was ordered to sit upright. I explained to her that I was badly injured in my ribs and right hip and was not able to straighten my back. I pleaded with her for pain medication. She asked me what medications I was on. I told her that I take Ibuprofen regularly for chronic pain and use various inhalers for asthma. She asked me if I was on antivirals for HIV (an illegal question). I answered all her questions to the best of my ability.

She asked me my birth date. She asked me how old I was. She asked me if I was on any special diets. I kept trying my best to answer, but I needed to have a drink of water. A male voice repeated again that I should tell them what I had been drinking that day. I grew even more distressed from this harassment when I realized I would be receiving no more compassion here than I had back on Simonton Street.

I appealed to the nurse for relief for my immediate pain. She answered that she couldn't give me anything unless I told her what medications I was on, implying that I had been evasive or untruthful up to this point. Her rapid-fire questions continued. She asked me if I had passed along or contracted any sexually transmitted diseases in the last several months. I answered that I had not.

She asked if I had. . .(she rattled off a list of diseases and medical conditions). The only one in the list that I said yes to was "seizures," which I meant in reference to my panic attack disorder. She asked me if I was suicidal. All throughout, I kept pleading for a glass of water, but was repeatedly ignored. It was getting even more difficult to speak.

Again, upon demand, I attempted to sit on the chair. I remained bent forward, to try to mitigate the pain in my back and ribs. She put a cuff on my arm to take my blood pressure. Then she took my pulse. I asked again for pain relievers, and she promised I would get them soon. Then she took my body temperature with a device that she put in my left ear.

I told her of my injuries from being knocked down on the pavement, and requested that she examine the painful area around my ribs. Finally, after my constant urging, she lifted up my shirt and I pointed to the specific location on my back. She touched the area lightly with her fingertips and I flinched. She said she saw nothing wrong and curtly dismissed my complaint. She rose to leave, still promising that I would receive pain medication. I heard her brisk departure.

A man identified himself as a sergeant. He pulled me off the chair and started to lead me away from the area. I again asked for a drink of water, and he accommodated my request. He brought me through a doorway into another room, and insisted that I sit on a metal bench against the wall. I explained to him that I was physically incapacitated and unable to sit upright. When my knees felt the bench, I crouched down on the floor beside it. I asked him for my cane, but he said he could not give it back to me. When he observed that I could not sit on the bench, he told me to wait one minute, and then threw a thin plastic-covered foam-rubber pad on the floor in front of me. Still maintaining some hope that someone would treat me with kindness and respect, I asked him how long I would be in this room, and when I would see a doctor. He said he did not have any answers for me.

The door slammed shut with a loud bang. Alone and miserable, I fell onto the plastic pad, gasping, as another wave of panic advanced on me. My chest tightened and I was still coughing and spitting up phlegm. I was too disoriented to have a sense of my surroundings – only the general direction from which I heard the door slam and its relative location to the metal bench.

I felt filthy and was still sweating profusely. The renewed panic attack brought on muscle convulsions. Trembling and nauseated, my torment erupted in cries of anguish; I screamed uncontrollably. By this time, I felt that I was losing grasp on reality, and called out for someone with whom I could speak. My voice echoed loudly, and gave me the impression that my confinement was a small, bare space.

The passing of time was barely perceptible. Unable to distinguish minutes from hours, only the abject agony endured. Although fully conscious of each torturous, indefinite moment, succumbing to total inactivity would remove any device to measure this dire existence. And, without a means to escape this impalpable moment, I would lose any vision of an end to this lamentable situation. When I eventually regained a clearer perception of passing time, it felt as if I might have been in there for many hours.

As I became aware of this desolation, I started to crawl around the space near the door, away from the filthy mattress and cold metal bench. My hands reached out to feel cement block walls and located the door. I banged on the door with the palm of my hand to gain the attention of anyone outside this room, desperately seeking some answers as to why I had been arrested, and why I was not being given any medical attention. No one responded to my calls or knocking, even though I clearly heard continuous footsteps passing just on the other side. I needed to urinate by this time, so I crawled over to a corner to the left of the door and pulled myself up with my hands against the cement block wall. Leaning into the corner, I relieved myself.

I crawled back to the space in front of the door and continued to knock. A long while later, a man came to the door and before he opened it, he insisted that I move back. I cooperated. Through the opened door, he threatened that if I kept banging on the door, he would put me in restraints. I told him that I only needed to speak with someone – I wanted to know how long I would be detained, when I would be seen by a doctor or get the pain reliever I had been promised, and why had I been arrested. I also asked if my friend had come down to the jail for me. He said that he would go out front and check my paperwork.

Someone (the same man?) came back some while later and said that the report indicated that I had been arrested for assaulting a police officer. I tried to point out how absurd this was, as I was totally blind. When I repeated my other questions, a female voice from behind him scornfully interjected that I would not be released until the next morning at the very earliest. She said that no friend of mine had come down to the jail to inquire of me, and when I asked again about pain relievers, she derisively scoffed that it is not their business to provide such.

While the door was still open, someone put down a tray on the edge of the bench. The woman said that I better eat because I was not going to be released for a very long time. I asked how I would be able to eat whatever was on the tray, and she smugly replied something like, "I'm sure you have eaten before without sight." She did not understand that I had no idea what was on the tray, how it was arranged, or that I could not discern how to feel over the tray for its contents. I said that I only wanted something to drink, and she said that there was some kind of juice on the tray. The door was then slammed closed. I reached for the tray to find the juice, but because it had been placed precariously at the end of the bench, I inadvertently tipped over the tray as soon as my hand felt for it. Everything splattered to the floor. I knocked on the door again to alert them of this. Surprisingly, someone responded shortly, and offered to bring me another tray of food. I told the man that I only wanted a drink of water. He came back within moments to hand me a tall cup of water.

At the prospect of staying in this agony overnight, I became totally despondent. I took the cup of water and crawled to a space farthest from the door and lay down on the cold floor, since the mattress was filthy with my sweat and phlegm. Eventually, a chill enveloped me in my wet clothes as I sat on the floor leaning into the corner. A series of emotions deluged me – ranging from despair, to disbelief, to anger at Mark for not getting me out of this horrible situation. I was sobbing uncontrollably, in total dismay as to the brutal police tactics and their contemptible disregard for civil rights. But eventually, I was able to calm myself, somewhat.

More indefinite time slipped away, then I heard someone approach from outside the door. The door opened and a man's voice identified himself as a nurse. He claimed that he had been observing me from outside my cell, and that he was concerned. As if to comfort me, he mentioned that he had recognized me from the pool at the Orleans House (a gay guesthouse). This man said that he might be able to help me, but that I better be straight and honest with him, as he warned me that he was, "very astute at recognizing false answers or deceptive behavior."

This statement seemed to insinuate that I previously had not been honest or cooperative, which strongly offended me. What reason had he to doubt my veracity? But I suppressed any visible emotional reaction, as I felt that this man was my first hope for some compassion, and a subsequent termination from this terrifying ordeal. Grateful to have someone willing to listen, I gladly provided him all the answers that he sought. I was uncertain, but felt that there was another presence in the room with us, as he interrogated me. (I heard no sounds from a second person, but instinct told me that he was being overseen during his visit. This feeling was based on his gruff approach, which seemed artificially stern and severe, and a stiff, detached attitude, which he projected in his use of language.)

After a lengthy interrogation, he seemed satisfied with my responses, as he eventually said that he would try to expedite the processing of my release. I expressed my sincere appreciation and gratitude. He concluded his visit by finally informing me that my friend (Mark) had been waiting outside for me.

Not long afterward, I was led out of this cell. Someone physically helped to support me, as it was apparent that I could not walk upright. They presented me to two persons – one male and one female, who treated me kindly. They assisted me in all the procedures required for release.

A clerk behind a counter then informed me for the first time, contrary to what I had been told, that Mark had paid my bail many hours earlier, and had been waiting patiently at the jail for my release. After all the necessary processing was complete, I was put in a wheelchair and escorted outside the building to where Mark was waiting for me. One attendant helped Mark lift me out of the wheelchair. Mark tried to get me to sit down on the bench beside him. I still couldn't sit up straight and immediately crumpled to the ground. Overcome with physical and mental exhaustion and pain, I could barely speak. After eight hours of torment, I felt infuriated, fearful and disillusioned from this incredulous experience.

Mark wanted to take me to the Emergency Room at the hospital right away. Despite my severe pain and trauma, I pleaded with him just to get me home. There was nothing I craved more than to return to the safe, familiar comfort of the home that I had left nearly nine hours earlier. There, in private, I could take strong pain and anxiety medication, unabashedly release my emotions, and hold onto my dearest friend, KC.

Although it was difficult to articulate at the time, I knew from previous experience that on a Friday night at the ER, I would be made to wait for many torturous hours before being seen by a doctor, if at all. I could not withstand the pain for that long, and promised Mark that I would get to a doctor as soon as I was able.

Mark called for a cab and we returned to my home.

Note: In the days following this incident, there was a great deal of publicity in all the local newspapers. Less than one week following the events I recounted above, the Chief of Police announced a change in department policy regarding arrests. Generally viewed as a direct response to my experience, an arrest could only be made in the presence of an officer of superior authority.

12. An Uncommon Town

I often mention Boston, my other adopted town. Not unlike Key West, it is unique, yet they share many things in common that have attracted me to both of these places. Boston is no longer the bastion of blue-blood Brahmins, as was once its reputation. Today, it is a composition of various cultures and communities. Boston owes its diversity and cultural richness partly to its large numbers of colleges and universities. Many folks originally came for higher education and ended up staying.

Boston, like Key West, boasts a long and fascinating history. It has been nicknamed the "Hub," or the "Athens of America." This may be a leftover from the days of the arrogant Brahmins who first settled on a small hilly island in the middle of Massachusetts Bay. Back in 1630, Boston was only connected to the mainland during low tide. But even before they chopped down the hills for landfill to expand its geographical area, the citizens set aside a large portion of open space on the south side of Beacon Hill to be accessible to all residents freely. Hence the creation of the green oasis in the center of this growing city, known as the Boston Common. Nearly 400 years ago, cows grazed on this green space, and citizens assembled to express their ideas freely. (Of course, they had to be careful about where they stood.)

I haven't run into a cow there recently, fortunately, as that would be quite a shock! Yet, it remains a public space.

Perhaps the concept of the "Town Common" first began in America in New England, as settlers first arrived from its namesake. I have never known of a town anywhere in the six New England states that did not have a Town Common.

The Common is a place for people to gather, to get to know each other, to exchange everything from ideas to recipes. People get to see their neighbors and visitors alike. Unlike bars, clubs or restaurants, it is not segmented into different societies. The Common reveals the reflection of the entire spectrum of the surrounding community at large. I wish that the founders of Key West shared this notion to set aside a centrally-located open space for its citizens. Key West needs more public green-space with few paved boundaries, walls, fences, curbs or iron gates.

I noted that KC promoted a similar concept in his advice column, by advocating a designated place for dogs to run freely. He has expressed his grievance: Let the dogs run freely! The chickens do! He feels that chickens have more rights than man's best friend. But I will leave canine politics to him.

Key West is also similar to Boston in that it is rare to find a native-born citizen. Key West residents have come here from all over the country and the world. Some originally just came to visit, and then decided never to leave.

Apparently, many are attracted to this remote island city for the natural beauty, or possibly because Key West nurtures progressive and artistic ideals. The result is a society with a highly-visible component of artists and writers. Creativity flourishes, as does the tropical vegetation.

When I lost my sight, I faced even harder challenges with the onset of winter weather. I selected a place where the climate would suit my clothes. My closets in Boston are stuffed with woolen scarves, sweaters, gloves and coats, which I prefer to remain there unworn. Living in Key West, I have more free closet space. In Key West, there is less need to be in the closet. Winter ice and snow is hazardous for a blind person. But equally important, I need to be more connected with the outdoors. Cold winter weather becomes a forced state of detention within the confines of my home. Weather-wise, Winter in Key West is warmer and sunnier than is summer in Boston. I thrive on warm sunshine. As I seek open outdoor space without encumbrance, I also seek open-mindedness. We call Key West "Paradise." but this ideal demands continued generosity, compassion and mutual understanding among its communities.

Key West is unique in its contrasts: One finds everything from honky-tonk to high brow, from casual and quiet to colorful and creative, from serene to sensuous, from sophisticated to sophomoric (especially during Spring Break). Tourists are Bewitched, Beguiled and Bewildered, but beseeched to "be yourself."

Lest you think my intention is to illustrate the many parallels between my two adopted hometowns, their disparities are equally distinguishable.

I love each place for some things they have in common, as well as for their distinct differences.

When in Boston, before going out for the evening, I always step outside first, to determine how MUCH clothing I need to wear. In Key West, I step outside to determine how LITTLE clothing to wear. I love living in a town that has no need for coat checks; nor must I worry about catching the last subway home at night.

Until Key West, I never before went to a Passover Seder riding on the back of a motorcycle. And only here in Key West could I have the following experience. I was standing at the bar listening to the live band. Someone tugged me away. I thought I was being asked to dance. I heard something that sounded like a reference to an astrological sign. I thought he was using some rather dated pick-up line. As we moved onto the dance floor area, I was aghast to learn that he was pulling me away from a six-inch scorpion that was crawling up to me. In Boston, I have been approached by a lot of creeps in bars, but never have I been crept up on by a fucking scorpion!!!

(4/19/01)

Consolidation, Consultations and Counsellors

The horrific incident of my confrontation with the Police on March 30th, left me restless, rattled, battled and bruised.

Mark returned to Boston from Key West in early April. In order to assist me in dealing with my recent crisis, he had delayed his originally scheduled departure by several days. One month remained of my seasonal stay in Key West. Legal Charges by the Police Department were still outstanding against me. My body continued to ache from the physical assault. My muddled mind was traumatized. To whom could I turn? My trust in people had been shattered. As many times before in the face of stress and despair, I clung to my loyal friend, KC, for comfort and solace.

Seemingly, out of the clear blue, early-spring sky, a quagmire of new problems had suddenly sprung up around me, like mushrooms after a spring rainstorm. Predictably, I would be in great trouble without legal and emotional counsel. Even through my personal haze of confusion, I recognized that I could not untangle myself from this intricate web of woe without professional support and intervention. Uncertain where to turn, I first looked to Ginny, my newspaper editor, for direction in terms of seeking legal assistance. Ginny was acquainted with the established network within the community. This enabled her to provide me with multiple legal contacts. On the other front, a friend, a year-round resident of this remote island city, referred me to his therapist. Apparently, my final month in the sunny subtropics would have this dark ominous cloud hanging over me. I would need to move hastily to manage my legal predicament, and consult with a mental health professional to soothe the consequential emotional distress.

About this time, I accepted an invitation from a friend to attend a Passover Seder at his local synagogue. Perhaps I felt that I needed a respite from my turmoil. I reasoned that this occasion might serve as a diversion. Hopefully, it would help me to reestablish a sense of fortitude by engaging with others in an environment of camaraderie. Additionally, the comfort of a familiar springtime ritual might help me to restore a sense of normalcy in my life.

At the Seder everyone around me was happy; they jubilantly socialized amongst their community of friends. I felt like an outsider, self-conscious and conspicuously isolated from this unfamiliar crowd. My presence amidst this revelry only served to contrast my own troubled mood. Before my place setting, there passed the traditional symbols associated with the commemoration of freedom from slavery: the unleavened bread (ceremoniously referred to as the "Bread of Affliction") and the bitter herbs (symbolic of the sting of oppression). I felt nothing but my own misery, as I sat at the holiday table, crumbling inside like a piece of last year's matzoh. Throughout the meal, I wished that I had declined the invitation and had chosen to stay quietly at home instead.

Every influential local member of my tribe was in attendance. It struck my friend and host to introduce me to some of the other guests in the room. Projecting my best impression of an eager participant in this traditional Passover ritual, "the Festival of Freedom," I smiled and cordially shook many hands, suppressing any trace of internal strife. Concealed were my true inner thoughts: preoccupation with getting home to KC as soon as possible, and away from this merry mob. But since this was not an easy option without risking embarrassment, I accepted my host's invitation to meet some of his friends, and acquaintances from the congregation, many of whom were members of the legal profession. Repeatedly, I was prompted to speak of my recent, widely-publicized confrontation with the Police. Many of the guests with whom I met were somewhat familiar with the incident from the media coverage.

Among my host's many introductions, there was one outstanding woman who took a particular interest in my case. Diane had been affiliated previously with the City government. She had many insights to share with me. In addition, she was eager to connect me with one of her associates, a partner with the best legal firm, in her opinion, in South Florida. Diane conveyed an optimistic attitude congruent with a sincere intent to act in my best interest. She inspired confidence. This personal introduction lifted my spirits and renewed my faltering hopes. My attendance at this gathering, in spite of my earlier regrets, seemed to have been rewarded.

I phoned Diane the next morning, as per her offer. We set up a meeting to be held at her office. By the time I had arrived at our appointed meeting, Diane had contacted her associate at the Miami law firm, to which she had previously made reference. Diane and I began by discussing in greater detail, the facts of the incident; she then initiated a telephone conference with the Miami lawyer. This gentleman listened to my story and made further inquiries. By the end of our conversation, he expressed interest in assuming the role of being my legal representative. He was confident that the Police Department would drop the charges against me (which they subsequently did). Before terminating our conference, he outlined a legal strategy to seek justice. But first, he would need to confer with his law partners to review the case before committing their definite participation in his proposed course of action.

Through this period, I still had been methodically contacting other local lawyers and was yet to retain any representation. After consulting by telephone with a distant relative who was a prominent lawyer in South Carolina, it became clear that if

Diane's associates would agree to work with me, this would be my best option. About one week later, Diane gave me the good news: the Miami law firm had agreed to take the case on my behalf. I met again with Diane and shared with her additional details, medical information, photographic evidence, my written statement and the witness deposition that Mark had given to a paralegal. The lawyer's plan was to keep hushed my intent for litigation, using the next six-month period to gather additional evidence. By that time, which would coincide with my next seasonal return to Key West, the law firm would inform the town of their intent to pursue litigation.

Meanwhile, as a response to all the publicity resulting from my arrest, many citizens publicly voiced their alarm. Apparently, my incident was not the first police action to prompt angry community outcry. But unique to my run-in with the local law enforcement officers, was that I was blind. It had subsequently resulted in an action, from within the Police Department, that would change their policy and tactics in regard to all future arrests. This gave the appearance of an admission of wrongdoing on their part for the brutality with which they treated me. And the fact that the charges were dropped so readily was an indication that they conceded that my arrest was groundless from the start.

Under the advice of my lawyers, I had to remain silent about the incident. This was a formidable challenge, as I was so tempted to share with the public, and my readers in particular, the deplorable details of my shocking story. Here, I had the perfect forum to reply to the barrage of inquiries, yet I was forced to withhold an adequate response. I had to tell others that they would need to be patient until I could provide the ultimate outcome, assuming it was within sight. Again, my hands were tied.

My one consolation was that I felt reassured by the stated support of the Miami law firm. I was free to return to Boston with a renewed sense of security. Relieved that I could put the legal ramifications of the issue behind me temporarily,

I began in earnest to work on mending the emotional damage it had caused. It was not the first time in my life that I sought therapy, but never before had it been such a case of urgency. My spirit had plunged, all faith and reason kicked out from under me from that terrifying episode. It was paramount that I become grounded and rational in order to cope with this latest blow.

My meeting with Diane at the Passover Seder, the celebration of freedom, had indeed sparked a renewed personal quest for freedom worthy of reflection. Summer was around the bend, and life was poised to rejuvenate.

13. Migrations

This season has been my longest stay in Key West yet. In no rush to head north and endure a cool and wet New England Spring, I chose to delay my departure. I recall the disappointment I felt due to my early northward migration last year, when I faced another two months of damp and chilly weather. I cursed myself for not having remained longer in the more favorable Key West climate. Now, according to the calendar, it is halfway through Spring, but as the daffodils are just blooming in Boston, Key West is well on its way toward Summer. Noticeable changes have occurred in the last few weeks. On my morning walks with my KC dog, I am serenaded by a symphony of songbirds singing a springtime sonata.

Quickly-moving cumulous clouds scurry across the sky. They can barely contain themselves; they cast a five-minute shadow and spit down a few droplets of moisture, and then continue on their way.

The tropical sun takes on a new ferocity. It loiters high in the afternoon sky like a street-corner vagrant, and appears to be in no rush to sink toward the western horizon, to extinguish its light in the Gulf.

The earth shifts its bias to the northern hemisphere, and naturally, life gravitates toward the northern latitudes.

In Key West, songbirds replace snowbirds. Heat and humidity resume their summer romance. Plum-colored clouds set the stage for impromptu matinee performances featuring the ensemble of thunder, lightning and torrential rain.

Up north, the sun reigns once again, and

rains shower the blooming New England landscape. In the city, the winter's potholes are filled in as the college dorms are emptied. Students leave for their summer exiles. Suburbanites flood into the city neighborhoods in their minivans, to bemoan another season of Red Sox heartache.

In a few days, I will call KC over to his Sherpa bag, and he will reluctantly climb in. As a veteran flyer, KC has complete confidence in me. He knows that the next time he crawls out of the bag, he will be back home in Boston. I envy his sense of security. Air travel is much more stressful for me. All my fears and anxieties are heightened. I wish I could just climb into a snug bag with a few toys, as does KC, and be woken up hours later in the back of a cab speeding through the tunnel under the Boston Harbor.

We all have air travel horror stories. I certainly have mine. If there were support groups for distressed air travelers, we could fill stadiums.

As a blind person, I find traveling on my own to be a harrowing experience. Getting around an airport, making flight connections and minding my belongings, make ordinary hassles and frustrations seem so minor. What is losing a bottle cap on the floor or getting tripped on the sidewalks of Key West in comparison to subjecting myself to the rigors of air travel? There is always plenty to bitch about while in transit for any sighted traveler, but I cannot even locate the person toward whom I should direct my bitching. As I grow weary during my travel, I worry about my most precious cargo: KC, who gets jostled and bumped around in his Sherpa bag. But he barely complains. If I am lucky, I may get an opportunity to place his bag on an empty seat beside me. I give him a mild tranquilizer one hour before the flight and I calm myself with a cocktail or two, once safely aboard. From there on, everything is up to The Fates. The Fates haven't been too kind to me lately, so they sort of owe me one.

In a few weeks from now, my northern life will begin to take shape. I will reconnect with my friends, and with the agencies for which I work. Last year's projects will be resumed. KC will rejoin the canine tennis ball-fetching league at the local park. (This brings out his incredible competitive spirit, where he strives to maintain his number-one ranking over the dozens of younger recruits. I cannot understand how I raised such a jock.)

The first few days back in Boston will be a period of adjustment. I will wake up in a different bed, and must apply conscious memory to determine where I am. A nighttime trip to the bathroom can be a little hazardous, as I try to recollect the layout of my apartment.

What has changed during my absence? Do I have new neighbors? What businesses have come or gone? What is the schedule for all the outdoor concert series?

I salivate at the prospect of the twin Maine Lobster Specials at the local Irish pub; I eagerly crave indulging at my favorite Chinese restaurant just a few doors further down Beacon Street.

The brief summer season will eventually work its warmth into New England. Sea-water temperatures may approach 70 degrees by late in July, and I may take a visit to Provincetown or Ogunquit, Maine, once or twice. I already have a head start on my suntan. Having visited these places so often as a sighted person, I can recall their facades easier than I can visualize Key West, which I have never seen through my own eyes.

As hurricane season approaches, I will use all my telekinetic* powers to steer the storms away from Key West.

It would be a worthy endeavor to hone such telekinetic skills as I may eventually enable myself to bypass the commercial airline industry altogether. If successful (at telekinesis) before my return to Key West in November, perhaps I can spare myself one more frightful air travel experience.

*Telekinesis: The movement of objects by scientifically inexplicable means, as by the power of the mind alone.

(4/26/01)

Rob and KC as puppy.

Walking up Beacon Street, Boston

Mark, Rob and Rocky.
Key West, Florida

KC on the rocks.
(See *KC at the Gate*, P. 49

Sergeant Rocky on duty.

Ella Karabel en pointe.
(See *People Who Need People,* P. 137)

SECTION 2

14. Accentuate The Positive

When we last left Rob, the Blind Snow Bird, and his faithful canine companion, KC, they were preparing to migrate to their northern domicile in Boston. In Rob's last column as the Blind Snow Bird, ("Migrations", which appeared in Celebrate on May 4), he related his anxieties regarding the transition from Key West to Boston. Rob's main concerns about the move between these two distant locales were the trip and the subsequent adjustment to the different environment. As predicted, the travel day did present the unavoidable complications. Always looking for solutions, Rob planned on developing telekinetic skills to avoid future airline woes. But we are happy to report that the pair has made it back to Boston safely.

"Hello, are you Unit 3?"

"Yes, that's me," I answer.

"I am the new letter carrier. My name is Common," a female voice answers.

I am standing in the vestibule of my building with KC on his leash. He is anxiously anticipating his first sniff of the sunny New England morning in six months. He has a lot of catching up to do: re-marking his territory and nosing around the old neighborhood.

What a bizarre name: "Common," I think to myself, or is it just an expression of low self-esteem or modesty.

"What happened to Richard?" I ask politely.

"Rich-ahhd has retired and moved to V'ginyahh. "

Oh! I bemuse silently, If "Rich-ahhd" = "Richard" then "Common" must = "Carmen."

This algebraic equation reminded me that I

was back in Boston. I turned to the dog and said, "KC, I have the feeling we're not in Key West anymore!"

Weather-wise, I was greeted on my return with a warm welcome. A record-breaking heat wave was gripping the region. I wouldn't have taken notice of this if it weren't such a hot topic around town; for me the transition from the Key West climate to this was seamless. I walked outdoors to the same warm sunshine that I had left the day before. No more clothes were required than the gym shorts and footwear that I had become so accustomed to wearing for our morning walk. Aware that this is springtime in Boston, I realized that these temperatures could be just a tease. It could be 45 degrees the next day. But as it turned out, the three-day heat wave brought Lilac Sunday to the Arboretum a week earlier than scheduled.

As expected, my pre-planned air travel itinerary was a mere script to be discarded. Flight cancellations and airline changes threw as many curves at me as possible. After enduring a six-hour layover in Ft. Lauderdale for my three-hour flight, I realized that I was fortunate to be traveling with a VIP (Very Important Pet). As soon as I boarded the final flight for Boston, two dog-loving flight attendants greeted me enthusiastically. It is true that we are judged by the company we keep. I was given the royal treatment. Traveling with KC can sure have its privileges: I was lavished with free drinks and special attention. I finally realized that I had the right connections after all; he was sitting peacefully on the seat beside me. The flight attendants frequently checked in on my comfort (or was it KC's?). The airline's sparse attention to cuisine is something that even the flight attendants joked about when they handed out their "gourmet" snack pack – a few cookies and other unidentifiable treats. But they kept bringing me extra cookies "for KC."

I have often stated my envy of dogs; they know their purpose in life and can truly experience peace in the most trying of situations.

Now, back in Boston, KC reminds me of the urban pastime of pedestrian watching that we call stoop sitting. However, he was a bit rattled on our first Sunday morning back. When we walked down the front stoop, we encountered 20,000 people streaming by on the sidewalk for the annual "Walk for Hunger." I tried to encourage him to direct me to the Dunkin' Donuts for my morning coffee, but even though it is just a few storefronts away from my front door, he chose to turn the corner and seek a more peaceful side street. I couldn't blame him. He hadn't seen such a forest of legs in months.

We had both grown accustomed to our small piece of personal outdoor space in Key West. The closest thing we have here is a splintery wooden deck four floors up on the roof (which is shared with fifty other units). But there is always the nearby park, dozens of local dogs and tennis balls for all.

The seasonal transition from one residence to the other presents its expected problems and challenges, especially for a blind person. Adjusting to my new spatial (not spacious) home environment brings pain and anxieties. Bumping into walls in one's own home is a very humbling experience.

So is forgetting which drawer in the kitchen is the one for the silverware. And as I am missing the Florida Keys, I am also missing the keys to the trunk in which I locked my valuables.

After receiving a new 20-pound bag of food for KC (twice his weight in kibble), I accidentally let the bag fall over and, hence, experienced a kibble spill reminiscent of my Great Spaghetti Spill of '94. But I was sighted back then and it was an easier clean-up. Kibble crunched beneath my feet for days afterward, as the tiny morsels found their way into corners of my kitchen that I didn't even know existed.

In days that followed, I found myself stuck in that indefinable hole in the time continuum known as "waiting for the cable guy."

The old-fashioned city neighborhood supermarket, known for their reasonable prices and great selection of coffee beans, is going upscale. This typifies the real estate value boom occurring around me. As new two-million dollar condos are being built down the street, the longtime residents fear being priced out of their own neighborhoods. (Reminds me of Key West.)

But as Common (Carmen) reminded me on my first day back, this is still the Boston I left. And as I once recounted the similarities and disparities of these two cities, I have enough around me to remind me where I am.

In Key West, assorted sex and seafood specials are served up daily around town, whereas in Boston, it is a Friday night tradition to get scrod.

(5/11/01)

TAX ATTACKS

I surely didn't foresee this incoming tax missile!

Two months ago, most Americans had already completed their income tax obligations. By now, many taxpayers have since received their refunds, and have probably spent it on themselves for discretionary luxuries, as this money is often viewed as a year-end bonus with which to be frivolous.

I, on the other hand, due to my absence from my home in Massachusetts past the dreaded April deadline, still return each spring to face this taxing issue.

Added to my obligatory burden to accomplish this task, which I was fully able to handle by myself before blindness, I must now rely on the accuracy and integrity of others. It still remains my responsibility to compile all pertinent forms methodically, unearth relevant records and ultimately enlist the assistance of trustworthy friends to review all my financial documents. There goes that privacy issue again! My life becomes an open book, or should I say several open ring binders, in which I orderly store each month's bank and brokerage statements.

Last fall, before I left for Key West, my tax accountant had estimated my year's tax liability. I paid my quarterly tax estimates as per his instructions. But things went very wrong. He underestimated my quarterly payments, the faltering economy altered my financial landscape, and unforeseen events muddled the mix. The unfortunate result was that my accountant had to recalculate my personal income for last year, which drastically revised my tax liability. In short, I came up short. I found myself owing the government more money than I had available. Uncle Sam had me by the proverbial balls.

Somehow, dividends and capital gains from existing investments had appeared to boost my yearly income. But by the time the tax on this income was due, the investment portfolio had severely slid in monetary value. So, in taking stock, I had to take stock in order to pay for this stock's income. Is this clear?

These tax impacts became my latest financial foe. I paid the government what I could, and my accountant filed for extensions on the remainder. It was not a pleasant way to start the summer. Frugality kept a constant vigil on my wallet.

In previous times, I had a knack for stock market savvy. My investment skills were widely admired. One particular stockbroker from a major Wall Street investment firm had recognized this, and had developed the habit of calling me regularly to tap my intuition and insight. In the end, I gave this professional financial adviser much more valuable advice than he had ever imparted to me. Without being a mercenary mogul, I did manage to build a portentous portly portfolio over the years. But that previous profitable period in my life was a much different time.

Then, I had the leisure time and capacity to read my investment firm's newsletters regularly and thoroughly. This data helped me to predict, prognosticate and prevail. I could plot P/E ratios, dissect market sectors, formulate figures, review reports and manage mutual funds. But, shortly after losing my sight, I needed to turn my attention to adapting to more mundane daily concerns. Just paying my bills, keeping house and maintaining health and home demanded excessive time and effort.

I could no longer normally navigate the newsletters, periodically peruse proxy materials, systematically speculate securities strategies, scrutinize stock statements, accurately analyze annual reports or okay my 401K. I floated financially on my former success. But, like an untended garden, brokerage accounts will not grow without oversight. My Wall Street wizardry withered on the vine. My fiscal fitness suffered and assets drooped. Meanwhile, my living costs constantly increased. I now need to pay for practical services, which I could formerly do as a sighted person. Additionally, new expenses are incurred in procuring specialized devices and adaptive technology to retain my independence.

Ever-changing tax codes are as incomprehensible to me as the changing dress codes. Each year the politicians promise to simplify life with tax reforms, but only create more complex tax forms.

Wall Street has become just another dark alley in which I wander blindly. And now, due to current circumstances beyond my control, I would have to pay the piper (and the accountant, and the IRS and the Commonwealth. . .)

HELP WANTED, INQUIRE WITHIN

Aftershocks...

I put out an S.O.S. (Save Our Sanity). The events of March 30th, the brutal police confrontation that resulted in my arrest and the subsequent incarceration, left me emotionally scarred. The nightmares still plague me constantly day and night, as I relive the horror of that incident. Any faith and trust I may have formerly had in law enforcement authority has been severely damaged. Bottled-up rage mixes internally with fear. Contrary to my previous nature, I host feelings of insecurity, violation and confusion. Depression constantly courts me as I despair about the larger issues of social justice, personal safety and my ability to regain a degree of control.

Immediately following the incident in Key West, I sought professional guidance to steer through these turbulent emotions. Now back in Boston, I acknowledge that I need to continue some form of therapy to help me deal with the trauma. An appointment with a mental health counselor at my HMO could not be scheduled until several months hence. One other alternative presented itself for the interim period. There is a free clinical program at a local community health center that counsels victims of violence. My experience with the Key West Police seems to fit this definition.

I have scheduled an upcoming appointment.

15. People Who Need People

"I have never been blind," says the voice over my left shoulder. This is stated as if it is a very profound confidential revelation. The man trails closely behind me for three blocks, enthusiastically coaching my every move. He warns me of every street lamp and parking meter along the route. Constantly calculating my distance to the next corner, he calls out his estimate on how many steps I have before the next curb. (I had not solicited his assistance. I happen to be very familiar with every step along this route, as I travel it several times each week.) Yet, I did not want to rebuff him. He displayed a sense of self-importance, and this gave him a purpose for being out on the sidewalk that afternoon. He felt needed. Regardless of his current circumstances, he is by nature a do-gooder.

Curiously, I seemed to have developed this new relationship with the people of the street. I refer to those urban dwellers known as the homeless or vagrants. Society calls them drunks or bums. They are the discarded remnants of a social order in which they seem to have no place. Some are antagonistic, belligerent and contentious; others are amiable, benign and considerate. Many are panhandlers. This population includes many mentally or physically disabled. Most are invisible to passersby. Yet, since I have become blind, they are perhaps more visible to me than are the masses that swell the downtown sidewalks.

It appears as if I confront them more now than I ever did as a sighted man. Some interactions have been good; other times were very negative experiences. In previous columns, I spoke of some confrontations. There were those who insisted I was faking my blindness for attention. Some have tried to trip me or pull my cane out of my hand after being inadvertently tapped as I strode down the sidewalk. I have stumbled over people who sat blocking my path on the stairs to the subway station.

One man sits in a wheelchair in Boston's fashionable Back Bay asking for spare change. When he sees me coming in his direction, he yells for me to alter my course to warn me of his location. The first time that I followed his direction, I subsequently collided with his chair. I explained his misdirection, and he has never confused [my] left from right since that time.

In Key West, an exceptionally friendly man, who badly needed a bath, insisted on bringing me into a sculpture gallery. He wanted me to feel the works of an artist whom he greatly admired. I was grateful for his cheerful desire to share with me this experience. When I revealed that I was a columnist for a gay publication, his whole demeanor changed from affable to repulsed. Looking back on this event, I wonder: is it likely that some people who are looked down upon by others, perhaps need for themselves to look down upon someone else?

I never understood before why Barbra Streisand sang, "People who need people are the luckiest people in the world." Maybe because society feels little need for these people of the streets, they appeared to me to be far from the luckiest people. My stubborn independent attitude always had me believe that all people who need people are needy people. I was dense and arrogant. It has taken my loss of sight to learn some obvious lessons.

I now know that people who need people, touch other people's lives. In doing so both sides can benefit. The one in need teaches the helper during their exchanges. Doors and windows are opened, and the interactions breathe fresh air into the lives of each one. Thresholds are no longer barriers, but instead, become passageways.

My personal experience is testimony to this enlightenment. Since losing my sight five years ago, I have needed to rely on others on a regular basis for some basic needs, such as food shopping and opening my mail. For many years I resisted being on the receiving end of others' assistance. I thought that I could go through life entirely as the giver. This is an unrealistic assumption for anyone.

The giver in me (the ESL tutor, the friendly nursing home visitor, the dependable volunteer) has always known that I actually get more out of giving in most exchanges, than I could ever receive through others' assistance in a hundred lifetimes.

For over ten years, KC and I have visited with a former neighbor who presently lives in a nursing home not far from my apartment. Ella is now 94 years old. She was once a highly-regarded talent in dance and musical theatre. A cherished photo of Ella hangs on my wall. It captures her standing on point as a young ballet dancer from 70 years ago. I can no longer see this photo, but it is imprinted in my heart. She never had children, nor did any of her four other sisters, who also worked and performed in the theatrical arts. Now she is alone, nearly anonymous in this world. I may be the only one left who knows of her illustrious past. I have retained the posters and promotional glossies from her stage career. Ella is humble and quiet, therefore nobody around her knows that she once was a famous, talented beauty. When KC and I walk into her room at the nursing home, even this blind man can feel the radiance of her smile upon seeing us. She lets out a squeal of joy, and for the first time in months, she is once again someone very special.

(5/25/01)

16. Fates, Dates and Interest Rates

Is it Fate? Destiny? Karma? Or when the planets align? Or perhaps, just being in the right place at the right time?

The Wisdom of KC

"Robert, why don't you have a boyfriend?" my mother asked while visiting me in Key West last winter.

"I guess I'm just too picky," I quickly replied.

My therapist asked me the same question a few months later. Again, I had to think of a good response. After a few minutes of some soul-searching, I conjectured, "Perhaps most guys are hesitant to get involved with a blind man."

"Rubbish!"

Feeling that my excuse was flimsy, he proceeded to rattle off my best attributes.

Thus, I added a new goal to my list of summer endeavors: Dating for keeps.

It has been a few years since I have had a steady partner. Yet, I have been out and available. The times on which I have employed Lady Luck as my agent, I have ultimately concluded that the Lady is a Tramp. I have lured men, with the hope that I might wake up the next morning beside someone to whom I would want to serve coffee and exchange meaningful conversation. Such encounters have not developed into the enduring relationship that I seek. It often ends with a hangover and making sure that this new acquaintance has subway or cab fare home.

I decided on an alternate method for securing prospects: the personal ads.

It was essential to select the words carefully. My ad must be sincere, succinct and efficient. I wanted to include the words: honest, open-minded and intelligent. As I highly value integrity, I needed to mention that I was blind. But I was concerned that if I was too blunt, I may find that men might instinctively pass over my ad. So I came up with a subtle way of implanting this information; I opened with the title: "BLIND DATE AND MORE."

I spoke candidly by phone with respondents to my print ad and felt confident that they would feel relaxed and interested in meeting me. The results were mixed. After initial telephone contact, some men immediately dismissed making a date with a blind man, despite expressing interest in me. That's okay with me. I wouldn't want to date someone who felt uncomfortable about this issue.

But a strange thing happened. My therapist had theorized as to why I had been unsuccessful in developing relationships: I had been sending subtle signals unknowingly. But once I determined that I wanted more than just sexual encounters, new things started to happen.

Despite the ad, I began to meet interesting prospects. Men at the (predominantly straight) gym started flirting with me admiringly. I was approached on the sidewalk and asked for a date by a complete stranger. I had a good laugh when a very close friend answered my ad without realizing it was mine.

I am learning that, in life, things occur where and when you least expect them. One should always be open to opportunity. Unfortunately, we also must accept that when opportunity knocks, we may be in the shower or out walking the dog.

We delude ourselves that we have more control over our destiny than we really do. Accept the notion that we each have limited power to tinker with the odds. We may not be the captain of our fate, but merely an oarsman in a turbulent river. By my estimate, over fifty percent of life's journey is determined by chance and coincidence, affected by choices made by others. The lesson: use wisely whatever powers you may have.

Nearly six years ago, I lost my sight as a result of several maladies occurring concurrently. In late summer of 1995, I assumed that I wouldn't be blind for long, that I would not live to see 1996. I was half right. The universe threw an "O. Henry" twist into my story. I lived into the new century, but not to SEE it.

Fourteen years earlier, unforeseen circumstances totally altered my planned career path. My first boyfriend mentioned my talents to a man sitting next to him on a business flight. That event ultimately resulted in this man becoming my new employer in a different profession.

Embrace the unexpected. My therapist assured me that I had a guardian angel. That's not always easy to believe when things look bleak.

Nobody ever expects good telephone customer service anymore. Imagine my SHOCK when I called the IRS last week for an answer to a tax question. I was eventually connected to a man who not only knew the answer, but also displayed a genuine interest in my personal situation. He gave me praise and encouragement. He closed our conversation with a remark that caught me by surprise: "There are angels everywhere."

Life holds no guarantees. A past lover of mine often said, "If you want a guarantee, go to Sears and buy a battery."

It is unwise to depend entirely on experience, intuition or information. If you tie your fortune to the stock market, you had better buckle your seatbelt. Consider the dot-commers who thought that they had it all sewn up at twenty-something. Then they watched as suddenly everything came unraveled.

Take comfort in the likelihood that someday you'll be bumped up to first class, find an extra shrimp in your cocktail or get that perfect parking space right out front. And someday, maybe I will hear my mother say to me, "Robert, you have found yourself the most wonderful boyfriend!!"

(6/15/01)

HELP WANTED
(CONTINUED)

1. Falling

The parched earth beneath my feet has split wide open. Today, I have fallen beneath the terra firma and become imprisoned in the crevice of depression. I lack any means to scale the steep walls from this depth.

Outside the window of my small apartment, it is a warm, sunny, pleasant summer afternoon. That is normally enough incentive to drive me outdoors and somewhat lift my sagging spirits. Today is also the paramount summer holiday, July 4th, and it seems that the whole city is in a celebratory mood. The cheerful sounds of the crowds, the fireworks and the smell of barbecues wafting through my apartment window only emphasize the contrast with my gloomy state of mind. I heard it once said, "Don't you feel that everybody elsc is out having a good time except you?"

Today, I strongly feel this way.

This depression has not come on suddenly. It has been developing for months, and has seemed to deepen drastically in the last three days. I haven't been able to shower, shave or consume a decent meal. Dirty laundry remains unattended. Housework is neglected.

Very disturbing dreams have haunted me for weeks. I wake up several times during the night and find myself incredibly saddened. In these dreams I am angry. I try to hurt people. Feeling caged-in, I want to run away, but get stuck in parking lots or lost on city streets.

Now, as the lure of bright summer days reaches its apex and beckons all city-dwellers outdoors, I sit alone inside my small apartment. Fully awake and lucid, I am drawn to record the words that can best express my considerable anguish. KC sits at my side as I pour these words into my computer keyboard. I try to analyze the reason for this depression. The need to talk to someone is overwhelming. Those few confidants with whom I would most like to speak are not around. I hesitate to call certain other friends or family members. I fear shame if I follow this compelling instinct. It would expose my somber weakness to those who view me as strong and well adjusted.

I wonder how I got to this point. Why am I so alone right now? In retrospect, I should not have allowed myself to forego social plans for this holiday. I could rationalize that it is just happenstance: many friends are away for the holiday, I did not make appropriate effort ahead of time to be included in others' plans, or perhaps, nobody thought of including me in theirs. For this I am sad and regretful. But is that the real root of today's worsening depression? Somehow I know that the true cause is far greater.

For the last several weeks, I have repeatedly found myself in tears. Many complications have entered my life recently, but this time I have become completely overwhelmed. It is devastating to my ego that I seem unable to resolve my troubles.

Following the incident with the police beating and arrest in Key West, my therapist counseled me for the six weeks remaining before my departure for Boston. I recognized the urgency of our twice-weekly sessions. He witnessed first-hand my impulsive reaction, and foretold of the sharp negative emotional impact I could expect in months to come. I heeded his warning, but felt confident that my sheer determination to inoculate myself against this implosion would prevail.

Two days ago, I met with a Violence Recovery Counselor here in Boston. Ever since that meeting, I have only felt more agitated and forlorn. As I sat there in his office, I became restless and uneasy. Although his words were meant to comfort me and to validate my feelings, I nonetheless left there feeling worse. Our meeting served to help me to understand the role I had unwittingly been thrust into by the circumstances emanating from March 30th. It provided the opportunity to voice my raw emotions openly in a safe setting. Admittedly, just two days later, I cannot recall his exact advice, other than his validation of my strong emotional reaction,. I concede that this session was only a start, but at least I have taken the first step.

Whatever the cause, I only wish I had a cure for the sickness I am feeling at this very moment, that could instantly stop the all-consuming pain. I am angry and disappointed for not being able to conquer this depression by myself. Many friends and acquaintances on whom I thought I could depend for their assistance and support have let me down lately. I truly question whether my friends are really friends. Am I being avoided by others because I require a special understanding that they fear they are unqualified to provide? Or maybe I am completely at fault for this predicament because of my own habit of maintaining a steely façade. Does blindness play an important part in my isolation? Perhaps it does to some degree, but I do not want to place all the blame on this disability.

Obviously, it is more than just that, or the result of any single incident, that brought me to this place of desolation. The therapist in Key West saw my intense reaction as a result of cumulative stress. The incident of March 30th was the catalyst that finally broke my spirit. His observations have always seemed very astute; therefore I place a great value on this analysis. But even my awareness of this does not change my current situation very much. If a long grieving process is required to rebuild my self-esteem, ease the pain, and eventually restore some of my former strength, then what do I do in the meantime? Life goes on, troubles continue to mount, and I fall further and further behind in my goals. Time does not halt for anyone to accommodate a period of recovery.

The feeling of loneliness is perhaps the hardest thing for me to bear. On days such as this, I wonder, "Where is my support network?" – persons with whom I can be totally candid without feeling shame. I recognize that it has been my own pride, which demands that I only allow others to see the strong part of me. Due to this nature, I am especially vulnerable to feeling alone. If I cannot maintain a demeanor of control, I will instinctively choose isolation. This obstinate behavior results in perpetuating my tumultuous despair.

It is devastating for me to accept my inability to escape temporarily from this misery. Not long ago, I was able to get on my bicycle and go for a ride, or put on my running shoes and fly over the pavement. I was once able to make spontaneous plans and board an airplane for a distant location. Or I could get behind the wheel of my car and go for a drive into the country, to marvel at nature and leave my troubles at home. This freedom has been lost with the advent of total blindness. Knowing that my isolation cannot be overcome by the simple means that were once readily available to me is a source of great bitterness and frustration. Such imposed restraints are major sacrifices for me; not all people place the same high value associated with these liberties as I do. I feel incapable of relating adequately to the sighted the magnitude of these freedoms, so often taken for granted.

I will never again be able to walk alone in the woods, sail out onto a lake, stroll along a deserted beach with just my thoughts, hike solo up a mountain path, wander in and out of art galleries, or immerse myself in an exploration of a remote urban neighborhood. Such moments of solitude were especially important to me. Loneliness now equates to a deeply-resented sense of confinement.

The ultimate surrender of control was manifested by the incident on March 30th, when it was maliciously stolen from me. Not only was I physically harmed and totally disillusioned, I was thrown into a holding cell, without my cane, and I was forced to submit to incredible fear and humiliation. Alone and helpless, I felt no humanity existed to touch my world. Concrete walls enclosed me in a new definition of darkness so thick that I can never sufficiently describe it. My cries of anguish bounced back at me, returned unheard by another human heart.

2. Reflection

Now, three months later, I routinely busy myself in an effort to distract my mind from the emotional pain. A rational analysis of my obsessive-compulsive behavior reveals a harmful tendency. I impulsively demand that I bring my body to a place of absolute exhaustion through physical exercise. My schedule is rigid. The rest of my week is strictly planned around the time devoted to this twice-weekly activity. Each workout consumes the entire afternoon, as I must allow for travel in both directions. Travel is long and arduous, in that I must catch a trolley and then walk several city blocks, finally to get to the hardest part of the journey: making my way through a crowded shopping mall.

I somehow find that once at the gym, I am in a safe sanctuary. I do the same full-body workout program each time. At each isolated exercise, I work the heaviest weight I can endure, repeating each set to the point of absolute failure. Only when my muscles can no longer repeat the motion, do I move on to the next machine. Even then, after the last set, I berate myself for not being able to do more. The result of this extreme approach is incredible fatigue and muscle ache.

Well beyond a healthy determination to stay fit and attractive, it occurs to me that I may be aiming to project an image of brute strength to compensate for the weakness I feel inside. Could this be a valid revelation?

Admiration by others of my outward appearance of physical strength may compensate for my low self-esteem and personal feeling of inadequacy. A different reflection on this behavior may also be indicative of wanting to impose pain on my body as a form of subconscious punishment. I am disappointed in myself for my inability to handle current affairs.

Accepting this theory, will I allow myself to change? Likely not. I have found something that can satisfy my hunger for control, and acquire tangible results. Compliments may be the perfect food for my bruised ego. Yet I recognize the self-destructive component. Wearing myself out to the point of extreme exhaustion, I chance injuring myself. Self-loathing may be the root of this unhealthy obsession.

Similarly, I have recently become aware that lately, I submit to chance, as I never did before. When crossing the street, I enter into traffic with a more careless attitude. After all, even with great effort to avoid catastrophe, it happens anyway. I have come to believe that I possess little control over events.

I defer to the inevitable whims of the universe. I am tired of fighting just to get through each day, and I am tired of being blind. I am tired of always seeking solutions to endless problems, and I am tired of being a victim of others' choices and actions.

In lieu of a professional psychoanalysis, I delve into these postulations with the hope that I may reason my way out of this crevasse.

As I sit here on this summer day, I refuse to concede that this excessive behavior purposely seeks admonition or self-destruction. But rather, through the on-going gloom and fatigue, I tempt chancing injury and totally succumb to the reign of fate.

17. Facial Issues

"Feel my face," says my new acquaintance. I am being offered access to information through my fingertips that my blind eyes cannot perceive. This invitation is an intimate gesture, in order to level the playing field, so to speak. The person with whom I am conversing is opening up to me, either to assure me that I am not speaking with some grotesque creature, or to be kind by trying to make me feel comfortable. I acquiesce, more out of courtesy, than to divine the person's features. Society teaches us that the face we present to others reveals something about our character. I usually use this opportunity to convey that I place less value on physiognomy than on the information already imparted through our prior conversation.

Facial features are superficial. Some angelic faces can mask a most demonic character; likewise the plain and ordinary face often fronts a deep, honest and wonderful soul. Unfortunately, human culture has always equated beauty with goodness. Commercial advertising and religious iconography reinforce this message. Have you ever seen a Renaissance painting with angels whose faces are less than those of ideal human form?

If told that I have a handsome face, I graciously accept the compliment. Then, I usually encourage the flatterer to look deeper, so as to see the true person behind this face.

Faces are only masks. Genetics may have blessed some individuals with the gift of good looks. But a wise person should discern that beauty could deceptively conceal an unattractive soul. Many people go to great lengths to enhance or make improvements on their natu-

ral inheritance, while forsaking their inner being.

Allow me to explore other meanings of
"face" and "mask." I spent a lot of time reading
the dictionary, which as a linguist, I find both
enlightening and entertaining. This may sound
oddly nerdish to many. But please recall that I
teach conversational English to immigrants.
From dozens of definitions, I have extracted a
few which are relevant to my message:

FACE
(noun): "Outward appearance; value or standing in the eyes of others; prestige, self-assurance;
confidence. A façade."
(verb): "To confront with complete awareness.
To overcome by confronting boldly or
bravely...in a resolute, determined manner. To
confront, an unpleasant situation...with resolution and assurance."
(Idioms):
ON THE FACE OF IT: "From outward appearances alone."
SHOW (ONE'S) FACE: "An artificial or deceptive front."
MASK: "A face having a blank, fixed, or enigmatic expression...often a trait that disguises or
conceals one's real personality, character, emotions, or intentions."

Since the loss of my eyesight over five years
ago, I have worked hard to project a strong and
confident image. People often commend me for
my bravery, admire the appearance of a successful adjustment, and my outward upbeat
demeanor. When I write for publication, I try to
maintain this positive, informative and entertaining aspect in my work. Last month I wrote a

column called "People Who Need People." I was very reticent about submitting this column, as it was a deviation from my previous writing style. I thought it might be too serious or intense to put under my byline. But I submitted it anyway, and, in turn, received a great deal of positive feedback.

I would like to maintain an upbeat attitude in all my work, but I cannot always use amusing anecdotes to express my message. Once again, I feel the need to present a rather serious topic, and delay the column I intended to submit this week.

It's no secret that life is quite a bit more challenging when trying to maintain a sense of normalcy and dignity without sight. (Consider the idiom: "saving face.") Yet, I attempt to make my situation a learning experience for me and to remind others that each one of us faces our own unique set of circumstances.

"Why the long face?" you may ask.

Recently I have been beset by a myriad of personal problems that have overwhelmed me, putting me in a state of depression. In the past, I would go for a run, a bike ride, or get into the car for a quick escape. I knew the problems would still be here when I returned, but I would face them feeling refreshed and reinvigorated. Now those means of respite are no longer an option for me.

Pride can be an adversary when trying to maintain an image of strength while feeling weakness within. Anyone can understand how hard it is to put on a good face when feeling despondent inside. One thing I felt I could control was the information I could keep private. But with sadness written on my face, there has been no hiding my emotional distress.

I frequently sit at the computer and write what I feel. Some of this may be too controversial for publication. Other writings are strictly private. Some I use as a form of self-analysis. When I was feeling particularly blue last week, I wrote a long essay on depression. Upon completion, I noticed some intriguing revelations about myself. For instance, I realized that the weaker I feel inside, the more compelled I am to project a strong physical image. So I spend extra hours at the gym.

Writing and physical exercise can be great forms of therapy. But let's face it, when you are down in the mouth, sometimes you have no option other than to keep a stiff upper lip, grin and bear it.

(7/15/01)

My Dog Went Home Without Me

On the first Saturday following July 4th it was another in a string of hot, sunny days. I took KC to the park to play fetch. His skill in this area has always been unparalleled, and I know it is an opportunity for him to show off. I repeatedly threw the tennis ball way out into the open green space. As expected, he would return within moments with the soggy ball clenched in his jaws. Tirelessly, he would drop it in my lap, demanding another round. After one hour, I noticed that he was panting heavily from the excessive heat. One hour is not unusually long for KC to play in the hot sun, but I insisted he return home to cool down. Even though I always carry a bottle of water for him, I know that when he feels the need, he would find a puddle near the drinking fountain to wallow in the muddy water. I wanted to avoid this.

Back at home, KC flopped onto the cool kitchen tile floor in front of his water bowl. He kept taking occasional sips, but he was having trouble catching his breath. Throughout the evening and overnight, I was aware that KC was still having labored breathing, even in his sleep. I hoped it was just congestion. Do dogs get colds or sinus problems?

The following day, I had plans to go canoeing with friends. I was concerned about KC's continued symptom, and felt uneasy leaving him alone for many hours. But, as it was still extremely warm outside, I hoped that a day of quiet rest inside would mitigate his difficult breathing.

All day long, I felt anxious about my best friend. I returned home early that evening to find that KC was still having difficulty breathing. As this symptom had persisted through another night, I became even more concerned and felt it necessary to have him examined by his veterinarian.

On Monday morning, standing in the exam room, I was greatly outnumbered by friends and medical personnel. They all strongly advised that KC stay overnight in the hospital for observation, as they could offer no conclusive explanation for his breathing difficulty. The tenacious terrier in me came out as I dug in my heels. I strongly resisted acquiescing to the advice. My insistence to let him come home with me was strongly opposed by the group in the exam room. I desperately wanted to cling to my main source of serenity in these turbulent times. But I finally relented, despite my obstinacy and uncomfortable feeling. It would be selfish of me to deny KC anything that may be in his best interest.

As much as I wanted him with me, I accepted that I must do whatever is best for him. I was confident that he would be released by the next day. It seemed to me like a minor obstruction in his nose. I kept asking the vet whether he might just have a cold. Wouldn't a hospital stay be an overreaction?

I had a panic attack when I returned home from the veterinary hospital and realized that I was pressured to give him over to them against my will.

July 11th...

He has now been in the hospital for three days, diagnosed first with mild heart disease, and now with some sort of pneumonia. But the diagnosis keeps changing and I cannot get a clear prognosis from anybody.

It seems that everything I cherish in this world is slowly being taken away from me.

July 14th...

It has rained every day of this week since KC has been in the hospital. I visit with KC every afternoon. During today's visit, I heard the thunder from the frequent summer storms and requested that they close the window. (Few things in this world have ever frightened KC, but thunder has always caused him to tremble.) I maintain my confidence that, despite his medical diagnosis, we will soon be reunited at home.

July 18th...

Only twice in thirteen years has my dog gone home without me. The first time, several years ago, I found him waiting for me at the stoop of my building. He had tangled with a dog fifteen times his size over a tennis ball, and, for the first time in his life, conceded defeat. I doubt it was fear, more likely humiliation, that prompted him to make a hasty exit from the park and run the entire block back home, leaving me alone and bewildered.

The second time, I must ask him whether I should meet him at home, for now he lives somewhere else.

Yesterday I had to lay the body of my dearest companion, KC, under the earth. Mark and I placed his small frame in the wicker basket, which had served as his bed over 12 years ago, when I first brought him home at six weeks of age. Alex had used that basket for packing his belongings from San Francisco, when moving to Boston in 1985.

I had never had a puppy until KC came into my life in January, 1989. Alex had known how to house-train puppies from previous experience growing up in Panama. He directed me in this process. Until KC was housebroken, he had to sleep in this basket with his stuffed toys, in a corner in the bathroom. I vividly recall how he cried and yelped all night, and I was tortured listening to his anguish. KC made it clear that he wanted to be with us in the bedroom. He was confused by this sudden separation, after being coddled all day long. Alex had loved him so very much, but respected that I was KC's only true Daddy. Alex has since passed away, gone for eight years now.

Two days ago, I was once again tortured while listening to him struggle for breath. Mark stood by my side while KC lay across my lap. Mark held an oxygen mask over KC's nose, yet he continued struggling to inhale. His body was working so hard to fill his lungs. I felt his rib cage expand and contract to take in air. He did not cry. He was in his Daddy's lap, and I tried desperately to comfort him. I knew it was inevitable what I was being forced to do, to relieve him of his suffering. I cried relentlessly while stroking his tortured body, and kept whispering softly into his ears. In my incredible anguish, I requested that the doctor present give him even more morphine to comfort him, while I spoke gently to him. I told KC that we were in bed and were going to go to sleep; I told him that we had had a busy day at the park playing fetch; I told him that he had run around all day in the grass, under the warm summer sun. I thanked him for obediently guiding me to the bench. I kept telling him what a good boy he was, and how much I loved him. And now it was late at night and we had to go to sleep.

This was at 5:15 in the afternoon on Monday, July 16th. My tears fell like the summer rains onto his heaving body, but I made great effort to keep a calmness in my voice. We sat for about 45 minutes like this. Eventually as his eyes were closing from fatigue, I asked Mark to hold him up to me so that his face would look into mine. I wanted him to see my face one more time. My dearest KC was then laid back in my lap, and I stroked his bony torso; I scratched his ears. I kept speaking softly to him. I felt him fighting to cling to life, while his entire body struggled to inhale.

I eventually realized that the time had come when I must let him go. It was the hardest thing I ever had to do: to allow the doctor to give him that final fatal shot. My heart was shattering, as I felt his body finally relax. The life left his small body, as it lay stretched out across my thighs. Within seconds he was gone. I continued to stroke him with my left hand, while my right hand rubbed his warm head. My tears fell on his soft fur like the continuous rain showers we had had for the last seven days.

I had let him go home for the final time. Again, without me.

For the previous week, while KC was in the hospital, I had prayed like never before. I asked God to let KC stay with me for several more years to come. I do not know if God answers such prayers, but I asked everyone else to pray as well, especially those with more faith than I had in this power. My prayers were not answered.

Once again, something was taken from me: perhaps the most precious earthly gift that I had ever received. I was devastated. He was so important to me. Particularly at this time when I have lost so much recently, and felt his existence was my only comfort. I had been growing more distrustful of the world and people around me for some time now. I knew I could depend on KC. At least I believed I always could. But, alas, another lesson was in store for me. I was already ravaged by despair and cynicism. And this week I learned that there is always more that can be lost. Even when you think you lost everything else, there is always more to lose.

I was angry with God. I felt that I had never before asked God for very much. I always felt that I did what God had expected of me. I tried my hardest to fill my role in this world. But none of that mattered at this point. Life's cruelty knows no bounds. I pray that I do not lose belief in the goodness and wisdom of our Creator. I am shaken at our human ignorance for not understanding why horrible things go on in this world. I quickly put together a few words to bury alongside KC:

July 16, 2001
KC IS LOVE!

You saved my life. I am sorry that I could not save yours.

You were the greatest gift that the Universe has ever sent to me. I was blessed to have you in my life. Now the Universe has taken you from me. You were so much a part of me, that I am not whole without you.

You taught me so much. You brought so much happiness to many others as well. We are all richer for having had you in our lives, and are all much poorer now that you are gone from our daily lives.

I will always keep you in my heart.

Some say that I am eloquent with my words, but I could never express the feelings in words, that are in my heart today.

I do not know where your soul has gone after leaving this earthly existence, but I know that you were pure love, and deserve to be in the highest echelon of Heaven. I pray that there is a God, if only to know you, and to reward you for all the beauty in your soul.

I love you so very much, and always will for eternity. You were the best friend that I have ever known.

PEACE.
PEACE.
PEACE.
PEACE.
LOVE AND PEACE,
Rob

After Mark printed this out, I added some words that were lyrics to a song about Vincent Van Gogh: *"The world was never meant for one as beautiful as you"*

I signed my name and Mark wrote a few lines on the paper, as well. We sealed it in plastic and laid it on his cold, lifeless body in the wicker basket to be buried.

People call me with condolences. Somehow, I feel they think of me as just another person losing his beloved pet. I want to express that there was something so extremely special about my relationship with KC that it can never be compared to another relationship. I appreciate their words, but no words can comfort me right now.

"He had a good life."

"You will always have beautiful memories to keep."

"You had to let him go, he was suffering so."

"You will find the strength to get past this."

"Every day it will get less painful."

"He will always be with you."

"We are so sorry for you, but you have friends to see you through this."

"You are strong."

I cannot accept these words of comfort as more than mere platitudes. Although they are all said with the best of intention, I do not feel better. I do not want to hear these words. Nobody can know the pain I am feeling. Nobody can understand the void in my life right now. I appreciate their concern, but I do not want to hear them, so I must graciously listen, and thank others for these words.

I have already related how I would sometimes depend upon KC to get me back home. Whether in Key West, Boston or anywhere else we traveled together, he always understood the concept of "home". He knew it to mean our refuge, the place where we could securely lie down together and shut out the rest of the world. When he departed and left me alone in this realm, I constantly asked him to answer my one question: "Do you want me to follow you home this time?"

Apparently KC touched many lives. He was well known for all the reasons I have previously stated.

A week in the hospital was going to be expensive, particularly in light of my financial situation this summer. But I never considered cost when it came to providing KC with whatever he needed. In fact, I directed the hospital staff to use any measure to save my friend, regardless of cost. I had planned to work out the financial arrangements afterward.

But among the many condolence cards I received, I found a shocking surprise. I did not know how to react. On the second card that I received from the staff of Phinney's friends, there was a note that assured me that I need not proceed with making the financial arrangements I had planned. An anonymous donor had stepped forward and paid the entire medical costs. At first I felt awkward, accepting such an immense gift (the total bill was many thousands of dollars). I have always recognized my responsibilities, and this cost was one I had fully intended to meet. Eventually I was convinced that I should graciously accept this generous assistance.

Still uncertain about how to react, I took the advice of a friend, and sent a letter to the anonymous donor. The letter was evidently so sincere and touching, that it was widely distributed. As a result, this letter generated contributions to the Phinney's Friends program of nearly $34,000. Additionally, it will be printed in an MSPCA magazine, which could generate even greater interest in the program and other generous donations. Indeed, witness the enduring power of my beloved guardian angel, KC!

DEAR KC [5]

July 25, 2001

Dearest KC,

I solicit your advice, as so many have done before.

You had been my link to a better past. When you first entered my life in 1989, I was successfully fulfilling social and professional ambitions. But, shortly afterward, things drastically changed, and I was no longer chasing the same rainbow.

During the phase of my life which followed, your companionship was the only continuous element. Through the last decade, you saw me through so many losses and calamities. As the journey took many unforeseen twists, I came to rely on you ever more greatly. You depicted pure goodness. And now, at the dawn of a new decade, I am inclined to wonder if there is any such thing remaining in the world.

Since we were recently parted, I have become afraid to love another earthly being ever again. I fear being subjected to the pain of loss such as I currently feel. In the past, when I was overcome with despair, I always snuggled up to you as a reliable source of comfort and serenity. But now, feeling more devastated than ever before, I am without your solace. Ironically, it is the severe loss of your presence that confronts me with the very need that you so faithfully filled. My arms ache to hold you, to feel your small body push up close to me in the chair or on the bed as you often did, which allowed me to reconnect with the universal peace which dwells within us.

There is no familiar place left within my world where you were not once present to accompany me. Even when I traveled without you, somehow I still felt the link over the spatial distance. Today, my ventures out into the neighborhood alone, only bring me to a place of sorrow. Over our time together, my habitats have become your territories as well. So, now, wherever I go, your absence is conspicuous. When I scurry back home to conceal my pain from the world, I put the key in the lock, and before I turn it, I realize the emptiness on the other side of the door. You were the best part about coming home. I reveled in sharing your joy at each reunion. Now the front door opens to a vacant set of rooms. Tears instantly fill my eyes. Anguish is with me everywhere I go.

Particularly after losing my sight, I counted on you to take me back home. This afternoon I attempted to take a walk over to the park. This green acreage was your favorite open space. It had belonged to you. The route along Beacon Street toward the park entrance was no challenge, but as I entered the driveway, I became confused finding my way to the path. Eventually I found the walkway into the park. As soon as I sat down on this turf, with the warm July sunshine on my shoulders, I felt so lonesome without you. I quickly rose to leave. Heading back toward home, I shuffled slowly down Beacon Street, so aware of missing your lively pull on the leash, and your assuredness. I wondered how I would find the front stoop at the entrance to our home without your guidance. All through my sightless years, I relied on your assistance as I requested that you "Take me home."

Have you gone home to the place from

which we all originated? If you are home, perhaps I should be there as well. As your life slipped away from this earthly existence, I let go of the leash that bound us together. I wonder if I should follow you home now. Are you waiting there now for me as you so often did before?

Every tumultuous event that I had worried about prior to your illness now pales in comparison to my current torment. Now I know what it is like to lose the one I loved most of all.

Did you know that, for 12 years, I always suffered severe separation anxiety during business travel that kept me away from you for more than a short period? When we were apart for even longer, in order to reduce my anxiety, I would not allow myself to think about you at all, for I surely knew that it would only bring on longing. I always dreaded having so much distance between us. Now the distance between us cannot be measured in miles, but in worlds, or realities.

This morning as I lay in bed, the phone rang. It was David, one of our first volunteers to help me with you after I lost my sight. When David had worked at the MSPCA, he walked you a few mornings each week.

David always adored you, and both you and I grew to trust his medical instincts early on, long before he became a veterinarian.

I had called him last Monday, in tears, after receiving the latest news on your condition. I wanted to speak with someone that you and I knew and trusted, and understood our special bond. I was fortunate to have kept in touch with him, as several years have passed since he went off to vet school. I knew his advice would be wise, humane, and compassionate for both of us. David volunteered to speak with your doctors for me on a professional level, and then returned to me with his advice. I respected his medical opinion above anyone else. He phoned me back very shortly with the advice that I dreaded to hear, but it was genuine and sincere. I would never have let you go, had David not advised me that it was the only real option left for us.

David called me this morning as I lay in bed. He was at work and had only a few moments to speak, but he wanted to check in with me. He provided some words of comfort. He listened to me sob for a few moments, and pledged to keep in touch with me. His words sounded wise and loving. And then, for the first time since your departure, I actually felt your presence there in the room with me. It happened some time during my phone conversation, and remained for a few moments following the call. It was comforting to feel you there with me. I called you over to me for our "morning hugs." That's when you let me know that you are still with me, and have not ceased to exist. What joyous relief!

I hugged the pillow as I would hug your warm body, shedding a few tears. I miss you so incredibly!

With my inner turmoil and pain, how can I write my columns? How can I teach my students to speak the English language? I can't seem to get back on track. I can't be social. I can't enjoy leisure.

I recall the many times taking you to the Charles River Esplanade. You loved the fresh open space to display your agility. You could always garner attention from the passersby.

On many sunny weekend afternoons, when nobody else seemed to be in town, I would go with you down there to sit in the warm sunshine and play fetch with you or listen to the live music. Last week I went down there solo. My emotions swelled up when I was suddenly aware that I was in this spot without you, my most dependable little friend. When I needed the company of a friend most of all, there was no one around. I feel your absence at the parks, on the street, and in the house.

I do not even know what "home" means to me any longer. I await a message from you, my dear companion.

Please send me your wise guidance. I am so lost without you.

KC! I need to hear you! I need you to show me where the path is. KC! I need you to show me the way home!

KC, you were my summer day. Without you, there can never be another summer day.

I will always love you.

Dad

18. Good Scents and Nonsense

The sweet fragrance of basil pervades my living room. Unlike in Key West, my Boston residence has no earth other than potting soil. The two flower boxes, which I maintain outside my living room windows, are my only personal bit of land under the open sky. For the last three years, I have been growing herbs. (I discontinued my extensive colorful flower garden on the fire escape after losing my sight.) Now, summer breezes filter through the basil plants carrying their subtle fragrance into the open windows.

I have frequently been asked if my sense of hearing has become more acute after losing my sight. But no one has ever inquired whether my sense of smell has become heightened. As with my response regarding sound, I recognize that olfactory senses now fill a larger role in my perception of the world around me. My remaining senses have not improved; they have merely adapted to fill the void left by the absence of visual input.

Scents (odors, fragrances, aromas) have become another resource for guidance. They can provide information about my location and orientation. I may be enticed in a desirable direction, or warned of a place I best avoid. For example, odor is useful for locating the trash receptacle behind the building. On the other hand, the same rank stench may inform me that I have unintentionally wandered down an alley while searching for a street.

It's been said that many men determine whether a garment needs to be laundered by sniffing it, whereas women actually look to see if the item is soiled.

Nasal memory is very effectual. Aromas can

instantly stimulate the recollection of a long-forgotten moment or a subconscious memory. There is probably some connection here to the popularity of "Aroma Therapy."

I love burning incense and fragrant candles in my home. But, as a blind man, I must be especially cautious of open flames. This may sometimes constrain my cooking ambitions. Fear engulfs me when I smell something burning in the building. Admittedly, I have learned the hard way to keep plastic containers or wooden utensils away from the stovetop.

I admire cooks who can identify spices merely by fragrance. Lacking this skill makes my use of spices rather a shot in the dark. Besides, those spices remaining in my cabinet are so old that they have lost their distinctive fragrances and flavors. They should have been retired long ago.

Two friends of mine (a married couple, both blind) are very keen and entrepreneurial. Each has extensive backgrounds in social work and diversity training. Kurt had been a very talented chef in Chicago. Since their union, they have combined their skills. Their latest endeavor employs their talents for a unique approach to cooking. The concept for this project (a cookbook and accompanying video) encourages people to create food with more emphasis on the appeal of under-utilized senses. I envision this project will ultimately emit the sweet smell of success.

Some restaurants lure customers by venting cooking aromas from their kitchens onto the sidewalks. I often forget that I need to eat until the aroma of food fills my nostrils. Likewise, after a full meal the exciting new aromas of a passing tray of food can re-stimulate our senses, thus we forget how satiated we are.

Some foods smell better than they taste. Even non-coffee-drinkers comment on the rich aroma of freshly ground beans.

I always indulge in the bouquet of a glass of wine. Without trying to appear pretentious, I afford myself the luxury of a first immersion in a two-part sensory experience.

Last week, a security guard escorted me through a crowded shopping mall. He reeked curiously of too much cologne. Was it a cover up for a missed morning shower? More likely, he was the victim of the "Perfume Ladies" who ambush unwary passersby with the pounce-and-shpritz attack used in upscale department stores. I have witnessed signs in Leather Bars: "No cologne allowed beyond this point." The raw natural funk of skin/hide blends with smoke and alcohol to create the intended atmosphere.

In an odd parallel Political Correctness has banned wearing perfume in certain public places, in order to respect the air rights of the scent-allergic.

There are more ranges of aroma than there are colors in the light spectrum. I envy dogs their naturally broad nasal intelligence. They can detect a treat in a pocket or backpack from yards away. For the forgetful human, dogs may be useful in locating your private stash. (Just be certain that your hound is not a narcotics agent.)

As with color, the perception of odors is individualistic. Some people like the smell of skunks. It has been explained that if one component of this odor is undetectable (perhaps by a genetic defect, as with color-blindness), then a skunk's odor is identical to the smell of rubber.

Filmmaker John Waters incorporated scratch-and-sniff ("Odoramaä") into his craft to add a new dimension to the art. But due to human folly, carnations bred for new color variations have subsequently lost their subtle fragrance. Breeders must now try to correct this unforeseen consequence.

Nature is the ultimate divine expression of what humans refer to as "art." We are embraced through our known and unidentified senses. The fragrance garden in San Francisco's Golden Gate Park should serve as a model for an AIPP (Art in Public Places) exhibition in the development of Key West's newly acquired open public space.

Sometimes it may seem that life really stinks. So we should take every opportunity to stop and smell the roses – but just watch out for the thorns!

(8/1/01)

You Were My Summer Day

August 11, 2001
There will never be another summer day.
Regardless of what the calendar suggests, or prevailing mild
    weather conditions,
It matters not what annual holidays are nearby,
Nor can seasonal events or vacation destinations define summer
    ever again.
Summer once stood for adventurous travel plans, leisurely
    bicycle rides,
Benign air temperatures, sparkling shorelines, and green grass.
Puffy white clouds resembling mountains of cotton billowed high
    in a clean blue sky.
Simmering asphalt sizzled under the first splashes of sudden
    rainstorms.
Lightning spontaneously streaked across expanses of sky from
    unpredictable sources,
Thunder rattled the windowpanes.
Flower petals painted the earth. Tree leaves deepened in color
    as the weeks passed.
Fashions adjusted to bright warm days; living was casual.
Outdoor enchantment beckoned us to abandon our enclosed
    spaces.
And what we called "summer" never lasted as long as we wished –
Even when we were young, and time passed more slowly.

Four months offered time for things to grow and adventures to
be embraced.
It was a time to fill photo albums with sparkling images and
smiling faces.
Summer was the time for me to walk just for the sake of it.
Mellow afternoons passed languidly. The sun was in no rush to set.
I would throw a tennis ball as far as I could, only to find the ball
returned to me in seconds, slimy with his saliva.
Balmy evenings, extra sunlight extended outside activities
beyond the six o'clock news. Dinner times and their settings
were flexible. That all once meant "summer" to me.
There is no more sunlight in my life. It ceased to enter my eyes
years ago,
Lately light has ceased to illuminate my heart as well.
I am sad.
But even if I someday get over being sad, I can never envision
another summer day.
Sad is a state that I did not enter into willfully.
Sad did not have a well-defined border over which I
crossed –
It was more of a permeation deep into my soul.
Like a sponge, I absorbed forlorn emotions and became bloated,
Then tears streaked down my face like small salty rivers with
nowhere to flow.
Melancholia enshrouded me like a steel gray fog, it pervaded
my being, destroyed my sense of joy and power.
I am paralyzed. My creativity can only express pain.
Any other personal skills are now trapped in a locked trunk.
The horizon has vanished into an empty space.
My guts have been ripped open and my insides quiver with anxiety.
The "blue" of a summer sky is only a word that now describes
my mood.
I am lost with no one to take me home.
I do not even know what "home" means to me any longer.
I await a message from my dear companion, KC, but I am yet
to feel his wise guidance.

KC! I need to hear you! I need you to show me the path!
KC! I need you to show me the way home!
KC, you were my summer day.
Without you, there can never be another summer day.

DEAR KC [6]

August 17, 2001

Dearest KC,

How did it happen that you had become so much a part of me? We were so linked in body and spirit that our identities fused. So, when I buried you one month ago today, I buried a part of myself. I do not feel whole without you.

It may seem a paradox, but we reflected each other and complemented each other as well. You enabled me to know myself better by tapping my inherent wisdom. Humans tend to overlook what is closest to them. You reinforced my own fortitude, a trait in which you excelled. You were the tenacious terrier and I the pragmatic person. Together our attributes merged to create a strong unified team with a broad scope.

Now, I confront a new challenge without the benefit of your loving support: a cancer diagnosis.

This morning, my visiting nurse needed me to retrieve something from the hall closet. I extended my arm across the clutter and inadvertently brushed my hand against your Sherpa bag. A shock of emotion caught me unprepared. My eyes filled with tears and my insides rumbled with a stinging anxiety as I crouched in the hallway, just beyond the view of the nurse. Similar episodes frequently have sneaked up on me ever since you and I were parted.

I have agreed to a regimen of chemotherapy, against my gut instinct. Perhaps my consent to this treatment may be just to appease others, as presently I am more inclined to reject medical advice and follow you home, wherever that may be. Yet, in my emotional upheaval and utter distress since your departure, I have yielded to the urging of others, at least until I can see clearly once again. I mindlessly follow the procedures prescribed for me. If I think too much about it, I will either go insane, or decide to follow my instinct and abandon this regimen.

The last time I experienced such a strong intuition was the day I allowed them to admit you to the hospital for observation. I did not want to leave you there. Some vague instance of fear told me not to let you out of my arms. All the others present around me claimed to know what was best and most rational, so I was pressured to concede. I never brought you home again alive after that horrible day. I still wrestle with my conscience whether or not I should have followed my own instinct, despite arguments for following the course set by others.

I voluntarily gave away my control in that situation and will never know if I did the right thing. In that exam room, on that day, I believed that if I could have taken you back home, I could have healed you with my love and will. Doubts regarding my decision to relent still plague me often. I believe in more than medicine; I will never know if I did the right thing that day by leaving the hospital without you. Others still argue that it was the only wise choice. But like you, I honor intuition more than outside opinions.

The counsel from the others was probably best. You might have suffered more by not receiving all the medical care and attention; yet in the end, I am alone, and I will never know truly what you went through.

Did you question me for leaving you in the hospital that day? Would you have supported my desire to take you home with me, or would you have agreed to stay for the medical treatment? Do you feel that I betrayed you when I conceded to the strong convictions of those with whom I fervently opposed? Did I do what was best for you, or for me, in the end?

I wish that you could speak to me right now. Each night, I go to sleep hoping you will come to me in a dream or a vision with the answers. Please find some way to reach to me, and provide me your wisdom in this time of anguish and need.

Yesterday was the one-month anniversary of the saddest day in my life. I had to suppress my thoughts of you until evening. I did not want to break down in public, so I concealed my emotional distress until evening, when Lora came to visit with me. Lora has been a good friend to us both for six years, since starting as a volunteer with Phinney's Friends. She is a wonderful and sensitive woman who loved and appreciated you as much as anyone could. She had witnessed your light, and the intensity of the bond between us. Last evening, we cried together over your departure, but also marveled in your exceptional being.

Somehow I am sure you can hear me speak with you. You know what is going on in my mind and the important decisions I must face. Yet, this time I realize that I must learn how to live without you. Your presence in previous times enabled me to develop strategies with confidence. Now I am at a loss as how to reason clearly. And sadly, I can't find the wisdom to provide me with the guidance that I crave.

I grieve continuously over your departure. My sorrow is not an act of self pity, in that I want you back for my sake alone. Rather, I deeply regret that I cannot give you more years of the love and adoration here on earth that you so well deserve. I wanted more time for both of us to be together. This is what I cannot come to terms with right now.

What, if anything, will the passing of time change? The lesson I learned came with too high a price: love is eternal. And I know you will always be part of me as I am part of you. I love you.

- Forever, your Dad

19. No Just in Justice

"*JUST* because I said so!"

"*JUST* a spoonful of sugar helps the medicine go down."

We were probably mere tots when we first heard the word "JUST" in such context. Back then, the world was simpler. Ever since that time, authority figures in our lives have often used this word to evade answers and avoid details. As adults, this word is still used to pacify us, simplify, or to sell something.

Often interchangeable with "simply" or "only," the advertising industry thrives on this word:

"JUST ask your doctor for a prescription!"

"JUST enter and win!!!"

"JUST like new!!"

"JUST use our product and look twenty years younger!!"

"And it's all yours for JUST $19.99!!!"

Why are consumers so easily convinced that one can have the physique of a 25-year-old body builder by using home exercise equipment for *JUST* ten minutes a day?

"And it can be purchased for JUST three easy payments!" (Easy payments for the seller, perhaps, but not the buyer.)

Others are seduced into believing that incredible weight loss can be achieved by *JUST* one pill each day, or one can purchase 12 CDs for *JUST* a penny. When roped in by such promises we are assured that we can cancel at anytime *JUST* with a quick phone call, or *JUST* by returning a post card. *(They still have your credit card number. These post cards get lost in the mail or toll free numbers lead you into a tangled maze. But the charges JUST keep appearing on your monthly invoice.)*

"JUST stay on the line and a customer service representative will be with you shortly."

Such telephone service operations try to pacify us constantly with this calm recorded voice that repeats this message between musical intervals for hours on end. As the minutes tick by, they are hoping that you will JUST give up waiting in frustration. Most of us eventually do.

Telephone menus request that we enter the appropriate number to move through a convoluted maze of pathways. After many such exhaustive telephone odysseys, I have often found myself being asked, "*JUST* enter the 14-digit account number" that is printed on an invoice. This is not the place I want my exhausting journey to end, as I am blind and this number is not visible to me. Then I must go back to start at the top menu (if provided this option) to try to find another path that will ultimately lead me to a real human.

Sales personnel tell me to "JUST call me over if you need assistance." This presents a challenge, as well, as my blindness precludes me from locating the whereabouts of the well-intentioned, but flighty employee.

Technical writers for product manufacturers liberally pepper User Manuals or Assembly Instructions with the word "JUST." This leads to a lot of head-scratching, furrowed brows and self-doubt about our own intelligence quotient. Personally, as a blind man trying to operate in a mostly visual world, there is no such thing as "JUST." I receive advice or instructions where "JUST" is frequently used, without the realization that simple tasks for others are intensely more complicated for me. Details and logistical problems exist which a sighted person normally would never stop to consider.

People tend to overlook that getting to a place is a lot more difficult than "JUST" taking a cab. Even if I trusted the cab driver to get me there by the most direct route, and to tell me the accurate fare on the meter, I still need to locate the way from the curb to my destination. Before me still lies the challenge to find the entrance, and navigate a labyrinth of corridors and elevators past invisible signage. It recalls the entangled web of the telephone menus.

I am instructed, "JUST get at the end of the line." Even if the line is not one of those velvet rope mazes, I still need to locate the last person in line. When the line moves forward without my awareness, others get behind the person who had been ahead of me, while I stand there foolishly taking up floor space.

Please excuse my cynicism. We are all wary of the word used in these contexts:

"JUST call me any time." (Expect to get a voice mailbox.)

"JUST a moment, please." (A moment is an undefined period of time.)

But imagine a blind person hearing:

"JUST sign here."

"JUST call the number on your screen."

"JUST ring the buzzer next to my name."

"JUST get off the train at Kenmore station, then JUST go upstairs to find Bus #13."

Americans have readily adopted this word. Ask any pedestrian for directions, and count the number of times you will hear the word, "JUST." Politicians and military spokesmen rely on the ignorance of the public. "JUST" is used to simplify government budgets and deceive us regarding military operations.

A comic once used the line – "How to be a millionaire: JUST go out and get a million dollars."

E-mail marketers spam us to death convincing us that "this is no joke." They create a mirage of easy wealth. We should believe that our debts can vanish or huge fortunes will appear JUST through their simple schemes.

As citizens and consumers, are we really so easily duped when confronted with this word? I suspect it has maintained its effect because we first heard it from our parents before we learned to question authority.

"JUST" can also be a very callous word:

"JUST get over it!"

And, I suppose, that's JUST the way it is!!

(8/24/01)

"There are times in our lives when we all need a respite from turmoil and grief. Seek that place in your soul where peace always dwells."

The Wisdom of KC

20. How Leisure Suits You!

It is said that on the East Coast, when a new acquaintance asks you what you do, they are referring to your profession. Whereas on the Left Coast, they anticipate a response regarding what you "do on the weekends." The question is too ambiguous if it has a different meaning based on your geographical location.

Many of us define ourselves by our career. The most well-rounded individual would have difficulty describing him/herself as an artist/inventor/philosopher; one would find it even more difficult to decide which to categorize as vocation, hobby or recreational activity. That which earns the monthly income may not necessarily be the criteria. The independently wealthy and the involuntarily impoverished may both view themselves as investors or poets. Fortune may be the bottom line which distinguishes the profit from the prophet.

Our capitalist society divides us into demographic market segments. Individual identities are lost to economic, marital status, race, educational level, age or sexual orientation. Re search analysts collect such data to sell as a commodity to retailers and public officials.

Didn't you ever want to be selected as a Nielsen family, just so that your choice in TV viewing would vastly influence the entertainment and advertising industries?

Let's get past the job/career/profession label for now and focus on leisure activities. As both gardening and singing can fit into either category, what one chooses to do, either for income or for an outlet, says something about who one is. As a sighted adult, art and design were both my selected vocation and recreation. In accepting the notion of the talented prodigy, perhaps certain skills and masteries are predetermined.

Since losing my sight six years ago, I have had to re-evaluate my personal meaning of "recreation." Accepting the notion that recreation is defined as the way we select to use our leisure time, it appears that some people are either activists, while others are more like spectators.

I have always craved physical activities, ranging from biking and hiking to running or skiing. I was never big into contact or team sports, unless the contact was with nature and the team was for camaraderie (not competition). Even when I could adhere to the idiom, "keep your eye on the ball," I never excelled at tennis or racquetball.

Sight loss has severely limited participation in some favorite activities. I can no longer throw the cross-country skis into the car to go for a peaceful, solo jaunt through freshly-fallen snow that may have blanketed the woodlands overnight. Nor can I hop on my bicycle to catch the awesome sunset over the Charles River Basin. Sure, I miss these freedoms, but I am certainly grateful that I did them while I could.

Noting what others do for recreation, there are many things I would never choose to do, even if I could (for example hunting or car racing). For leisure activities in which I do partake (such as attending theatre and concerts), I do not receive the full content of the presentation. Missing the visual aspect of the stage action, I pay the same price for a seat, just to hear the dialogue or soundtrack.

Are some activities more esteemed than others? Is it nobler for a person to be artistic and creative, like a musician or sculptor, or to be intellectual, like a philosopher who works on searching for the meaning of life?

I have never viewed eating or shopping as a particularly exciting sport. This is good in that it is healthier for both my waistline and my wallet.

Boston provides a summer season rich in free, live outdoor musical entertainment. Truly, the best things in life are free, or at least need not have a huge price tag. I would rather drink margaritas, while dressed in shorts under the sun, than sip fancy cocktails in a tuxedo in a plush nightclub. Too many visitors to Key West consider drinking as a recreational sport. I enjoy a nice buzz, but it is less fulfilling when inebriation diminishes my awareness.

For me, reading (books on tape) occupies most of the time that others spend watching television. When I ask people if they read a particular novel, I often hear, "No, but I saw the movie." Most times, I had not even known that it was ever made into a film. Besides, the book is almost always rated better than the movie version.

I am not a snob about TV, but most programs being shown today really do suck. Additionally, I cannot follow the visual action on the screen. The popularity of "Reality TV" totally baffles me. These insipid productions cater to the most vicious ungamely and unflattering traits of human nature.

Adaptive computer technology has given me back the ability to write. I find it as a form of vocation, recreation and therapy.

So are my meditation, fitness activities and violin playing. Writing is a process of recalling what is already in my heart.

Sightlessness has made board games, cross-word puzzles and video games too much of a challenge. Even when using my Braille playing cards, I think it is more work than enjoyment. Inaccessibility to print or cyberspace makes it difficult to keep informed of musical artists and public events.

As a compulsive worker, I find it difficult to be a man of leisure. I must always feel busy. So, with so many entertainment options beyond my scope, I must redefine how leisure suits me now.

(8/17/01)

Cancer in Pisces

Since earlier this year, I'd had a foreboding premonition. Exactly two weeks after KC departed, the test results confirmed my suspicion. During the astrological period of Cancer, I had been undergoing a series of diagnostic probes on a swollen lymph node in my neck. The conclusive findings did not surprise me; I had anticipated the confirmed Lymphoma diagnosis. My last "Dear KC" letter briefly referenced this latest calamity.

As I was already in a state of shock and intense grief from the sudden loss of KC, I was somewhat dulled to any new assault that may come my way. Nothing else could have upset me more than had KC's departure.

I have been crying over his absence for several months now, but have recently discovered that KC is still in my life. The void of his physical presence is just as painful as ever, but I do take some comfort in the faith that his spirit still dwells around me. And in contemplating my newest circumstances, I felt it was reasonable to seek his guidance. I have always revered his ontological insight, and, since his love and wisdom is still available, I meditate in his presence. KC may not live here as before, but he has certainly not abandoned me.

When the diagnosis was confirmed, the oncologist presented only one treatment option. She outlined the standard protocol used for this type of cancer. It has been proven effective for the last twenty years. The doctor and her staff assumed that I would readily submit. Yet, my lugubrious mood and fragile emotional state painted a very muddled and dim vision of my future. Hence, I hesitated to embrace willingly the prescribed procedures.

Although I have always strongly acknowledged metaphysical forces at play in the universe, I have never placed much credence in the astrological zodiac. The widely accepted portrayal of the typical Pisces profile describes one who is artistic, creative, poetic and inclined to allow problems to work themselves out with little interference. I must concede that I accurately exemplify this characterization. (At least I formerly had.) Suddenly, I face the advent of cancer. Our Western medical culture decrees a purely-scientific approach, one that disavows any intangible alternative systems of remedy. My inherent Piscean laissez-faire attitude called for serious review.

I had a dilemma: if I planned to consider chemotherapy, a final decision was required promptly. Treatment would have to commence as soon as possible. Thorough scrutiny of alternative options (which included doing nothing) had to factor in my plan to escape Boston by mid-November for Key West. I did not have the luxury of time to mull over my course of action. Any delay of the start date for this 3-month treatment would adversely impact my own timetable.

After an ominous start to my summer, I was strongly compelled to maintain my plan to depart from Boston at the arrival of the cold weather in November, leaving my misery behind. But, facing a serious affliction demanded full attention. My state of depression handicapped my normal sense of judgment. Lacking emotional stability to make clear and rational decisions, I settled on a strategy to move forward.

KC seemed to advise me to call on the counsel of three close friends. I contacted each one, requesting that they come to visit with me individually, to discuss this urgent matter.

On three consecutive evenings, I presented my quandary. I updated each on my medical condition, and related my intense state of depression. It was necessary to stress my strong compulsion to flee, and my dread of the prospect of many months of unpleasant medical treatment. I wanted each one to understand my ample personal reasons to forego prevailing medical advice. The concept of poisoning my body with toxic chemicals disgusted me. Enduring the predicted drastic side-effects conflicted with my waning fortitude. My fatigue from the previous adversities impeded my ability to wage another battle. Rational thinking seemed temporarily beyond my capacity. I felt paralyzed in confronting the entire issue alone under these conditions.

I respectfully solicited the opinions and suggestions of these trusted and compassionate friends, hoping that fresh viewpoints would provide clarity. The three whom I had selected to consult were all of very different character. One was my health care proxy. I had chosen her for this role because we shared a common perspective on spiritual views. The second counsel was a devoted friend with a very rational scientific and pragmatic approach to life. The third confidant was a man closest to my age that I believed to be very sensitive, loyal and supportive. His vision of life was one of conventional religious faith, in light of human frailties.

I petitioned their opinions with deference and open-mindedness. Each evening, I arranged to meet with one person alone. First I talked, explicitly depicting my situation, carefully describing every factor that I felt needed to be considered. Then I yielded to their ideas and perspectives. I assumed the role of diplomat between my own clouded mind and the sensibilities of rational objective intellect. Indeed this was a very pragmatic approach for a Pisces. Ultimately, I found the answer that I was searching for by integrating three empathetic and logical opinions with my own instincts.

As a result, I went forward with the medical advice of my oncologist, and immediately proceeded with treatment. Privately, I retained the prospect that I could revise my plans at any time, as dictated by altering personal factors. I also reserved the option to consult further with professional therapists and medical counselors. I was committed to avoid a total commitment. Strict adherence to this regimen would secretly remain an option for me; I gave myself permission to quit at any time. From the very start, I had envisioned a compromise from the doctor's formal protocol. But, it was best that I keep this to myself for fear of external pressure or reprimands.

To avoid any further delays that would disrupt my long-term planning, I prompted the medical team to get me started as quickly as possible. This allowed me no time to adjust to the inevitable unwelcome intrusions into my normal routine. I forfeited any hope of attaining a comfortable sense of stability in which to heal from the previous wounds. Weekdays rapidly became dominated by therapy, blood work, medical exams, chemo treatments and monitoring new pharmaceutical prescriptions (ordering, inventorying, labeling and maintaining medicines, which can be particularly difficult without vision). In order to mitigate the side-effects of the chemotherapy, I required a visiting nurse to take blood samples and give me injections several times each week. My weekends became equally touched by many of these same invasive demands. The result was a growing sense of anguish.

For the first six weeks, I experienced less physical discomfort than I had anticipated. Despite the new complications in my life, I just accepted this temporal reality. But quite suddenly, the cumulative affects started to wear me down – both physically and emotionally. From the very beginning, I had entered into this from a point of suspicion and reticence.

This new burden only aggravated my existing turmoil. The effects from the toxic doses started to diminish my strength, inhibiting my ability to keep physically fit through this period. I was growing more miserable each week. By mid-September, I tapped into my network of support. With the assistance of others, I reinforced my personal conviction, and prepared myself to complete the chemotherapy. KC's spiritual presence inspired fierce determination. As the weeks passed, seasonal changes enabled me to focus more clearly on the approaching date of departure from Boston.

Nearing the end of the three-month course of chemo, I found my will was strong enough to reveal my intention to my oncologist. I informed her of my decision to bypass the radiation therapy segment. This deviation from the protocol was highly unconventional. I was braced to confront boldly the anticipated objections from the oncologist. With KC's power to guide me, I set my plans to emerge from this period of darkness.

My convictions had strengthened over time, so it was easy to remain adamant. I needed to recapture the ability to make decisions and determine my own fate. This step was important for me to reach. Taking control over my life again was vital. It was a greater benefit than I might have received from submitting to the will of the professional medical team. Accepting full responsibility for the consequences, I placed higher value on the fact that I was finally fighting back on my own terms with a renewed sense of self-confidence. Regaining empowerment was a very necessary victory.

21. Call of the Riled

The baby wailed at the holiday dinner table. If I had acted this way, nobody would remark, "He's so cute!" Impulsive outbursts are a privilege afforded only the very young. I felt very sad that evening and wanted to cry as well. But adults must adhere to rules of social convention. Shrieking out loud would have been vulgar and inappropriate.

Everyone fussed over the three-month-old infant. Undoubtedly, he was worthy of the attention. However, my only direct contact from across the table was the assault to my ears.

Recently, in times of despair and anguish, the advice given by therapists and close friends is to unleash unabashedly intense emotions, and to dismiss my reticence to call out for help. (Personally, the last part has been my toughest challenge.)

Rosie sits on the front porch of her little house in Key West every afternoon, just watching the world go by. She chats with every passerby. Her only complaint is that the temperature occasionally drops as low as 70 degrees. One day, as I strode by, Rosie offered to assist me past a particularly unfriendly stretch of sidewalk. When I politely declined her offer, this sweet elderly woman proclaimed, "You're an independent old cuss!"

This summer, several situations brought me to my knees in the privacy of my home, and I loudly vocalized my emotional and physical distress. I screamed until my vocal chords ached. Sound carries easily through the courtyards between units in this densely-occupied 4-story building. I became slightly annoyed that not one neighbor in the building responded with alarm.

Ironically, when my music is audible to my upstairs neighbor, the local police bang on my door. Life is indeed a journey. We go from total dependence in our early years, toward a degree of independence. We may travel back to that state of dependence occasionally, such as in times of illness. Eventually, we resurrect ourselves as independent adults. Should we live long enough, we ultimately end up back in another state of dependence.

When total blindness radically altered my life at age 37, I found myself in the uncomfortable situation of being dependent once again. It should have been the prime of my life – when all my freedoms get to be expressed fully. Adulthood carries the responsibilities of one's choices, but what a small price to pay for independence! Now, survival includes creative solutions, support networks and the reluctant abandonment of privacy. Secrets are laid bare when relying on others to read your mail, assisting in making purchases and being privy to personal possessions.

I diligently work on being more independent in my day-to-day life. The advent of technology and electronic gadgets have restored my ability to write, communicate, maintain records and schedules, take notes, do home banking and stay informed. But dependence on technology is a double-edged sword. When it fails us, we face turmoil. Bemused by the shock of others during a power outage, I am usually unaware the lights have gone out until I hear the chaotic reaction of my neighbors.

We have embraced our personal computers, digital devices and wireless phones. But with all this technology, the most valuable component may be the straightened paper clip that I use to reset the PC when it crashes, or to dislodge a jammed disc drive.

Wireless telephone companies entice us to buy a certain number of minutes each month for a fixed price. We feel obliged to use this allotment completely. As a result, people feel compelled to keep in touch by phone more frequently now than ever before, perhaps for the most trivial reasons. Maybe it's just to kill free time or to keep tabs on those in our lives. Some fear missing out on a social event or a bit of gossip. I think many use their phones from a public place JUST BECAUSE THEY CAN!

American society has made great strides in accommodating its citizenry by recognizing diversity, including physical limitations of many individuals. This is a slow cultural evolution, with yet a long way to go. I appreciate the direction in which we are heading.

Still, I have little choice but to seek assistance in finding public restrooms or making a selection from a restaurant menu. When I realize that I can wait no longer to request a bathroom escort, I still face the awkwardness of what lies ahead. (Braille signage that identifies the restroom is usually a small plaque in proximity to the door. The proprietor trying to comply with federal law may overlook practicality. Who would want to run their fingers up and down the walls of a corridor to locate this identifying marker? Such action may be hazardous and frequently embarrassing.)

Engineering designers fail to consider that a blind individual will likely become disoriented in the spacious handicapped stall, unable to figure out the door latch or even locate the placement of the toilet paper roll. Once finding my way out, I must locate the sink. It is almost certain to be placed as far as possible from the automatic hand dryers or paper towels.

In my quest to be as independent as possible, I have needed to abandon some pride, suppress anxieties, learn to trust others and schedule my time to fit with their availability.

Baby monitors may free the diligent parent from the anxiety of being out of hearing range from their precious infant. Someday, the kid will figure out how to turn it off to acquire a little privacy.

Let's be grateful for our interludes with independence.

(10/1/01)

22. Taking the Fall

As a bi-latitudinal dweller, I am an unbiased observer of my two adopted hometowns. I note similarities as well as distinct regional contrasts.

October has always been a favorite month of mine. It occurs in the only season that has two official names. (Does "Autumn" sound more pretentious than "Fall"?)

The season is ushered in by an equinox – how democratic! Many (mostly female groups) revere this occasion with a variety of particular rituals. I must admit that I do not understand the reason for this specific gender/astronomical relationship. Perhaps someone can clue me in.

In northern latitudes, I view October as the only noble autumnal month. November follows with its campaign of sleet and slush to herald the approach of winter's snow and bitter cold.

How beloved the full Harvest Moon! It appears bigger and brighter than any other moon of the year. I remember it casting its opalescent light in old, rural New England graveyards, and reflecting softly from the slate roofs of the Tudor-style houses in my Boston neighborhood.

Autumn had always been a favorite time for vacation. Summer crowds have gone back to work or school. I would take extended weekend road trips through the New England countryside in order to marvel at the scenic foliage. TV meteorologists provide daily reports during the weather segment, complete with maps pinpointing regions of *peak brilliant* colors throughout the month. Now, as a blind man, I feel sadly sentimental when I hear these reports.

Indian Summer is the term used to describe the warm spells that follow the first frost. (Probably some Pilgrim connection here.) Weather reporters are eager to forecast the first Frost Warning. It is regarded as their exclusive domain in the news department. There is the friendly "frost on the pumpkin," or the more ominous "Killer Frost." The latter demands residents to take plants inside or pick the last ripening tomatoes. Many suburban gardeners can be spotted in their nightgowns, under the silvery moonlight in a frenzy of activity following this dire warning.

Autumn is a season of Harvest Festivals and County Fairs. The Topsfield Fair, just north of Boston, is the oldest and one of the more renowned of this tradition. The most celebrated event is the contest which awards the cultivator of the largest pumpkin. This year's winner broke the previous record by entering a pumpkin that weighed in excess of 1200 pounds. (I wonder whether they do a drug test on the obese squash to detect any illegal steroids.)

Signs are posted near orchards to allure leaf-peeping tourists to "PICK YOUR OWN APPLES." After a long afternoon of manual labor, they end up paying more for the same size basket of apples than it would have cost them at a roadside farm stand (where they could also have purchased the fresh local cider).

As a relatively new resident of Key West, I have recently become aware of the less conventional events and festivals of this season. Proudly, many are done in the name of humanitarian fund-raisers. I wouldn't be surprised to learn that there is an event that rivals the great pumpkin weigh-in; perhaps one for the heftiest or hairiest drag queen.

It is a time for charitable events in Boston as well, with walks and footraces every weekend to fund food pantries and disease research.

Up and down the coast we say farewell to summer. At Harvard Square's OctoberFest, amidst the ivy-covered walls, huge crowds gather to celebrate with lots of beer, crafts, international foods and music.

In mid-October, the Charles River is the site of the biggest two-day rowing event in the world. Buff college male and female crew teams flock to the Head of the Charles Regatta, dazzling throngs of spectators lining the shoreline.

Fall fashions make the scene, perhaps to compete with Nature's seasonal pageantry. I recall driving home from work past spectacular fields of wild goldenrod and purple lustripe, surrounded by trees ablaze in crimson and orange foliage.

The season certainly invites all to show one's true colors. Bright maple leaves in New England sparkle under the sunlight as sequins and feathers festoon Key West's own frivolous Fantasy Fest under the palm trees. The Town loves pageantry and is far less Puritanical than the "Land of the Pilgrims." Key West recognizes that sexual pride is part of our culture, from ferocious female infatuation to lusty leather-clad libidos. Unfortunately for me, erotic display is a visual pleasure beyond my realm.

The blazing colors of the northern forests coincide with the flaming and proud colors that adorn the Key West festival, which leads right into Halloween. (I have heard Halloween described as the Gay National Holiday. EVERYONE is welcome to appear in drag!) Many northerners love autumn for the crisp cool air. They seem over-eager to rake leaves and ignite the first log in the fireplace. My house clutters up with various sweatshirts and jackets to suit the vast temperature fluctuations from 35 degrees in the early morning to 75 degrees by mid-afternoon. How is one expected to accommodate such manic weather? Despite local climate, Fall commences the new season for musical and theatrical calendars.

Leaves crisply crunch under my feet calling me to complete my business in Boston, and prepare to flee before the snow flies. Already, the anemic sun and chilly north winds forebode Fall's final formidable ferocity. Although I no longer witness colorful October transform into gray November, I sense the bleakness creep into my soul. I am lured to my home in the lush lower latitude.

(10/14/01)

Aggressive Mail

Americans are constantly under the assault of mail aggression. It no longer just clogs our letterboxes; it now seeks us out through cyberspace and deluges our computer hard drives. Ironically, as a blind man, printed material stuffed into my mail slot is useless clutter, but I can access my e-mail without sighted assistance.

The Delete key can more readily help me to weed out junk e-mail (spam) than the hand sorting method required for the mass of material hand-delivered by the postal service (snail mail). For that process I require human intervention. If all the paper mail was junk, I could just put a garbage can in place of my mailbox and eliminate the middle-man (or woman). It would surely save a lot of time. But for those few pieces of mail that are necessary, albeit not always welcomed, I must collect my daily delivery in a canvas sack until a friend or volunteer can sit down with me and separate the chaff from the wheat. Often the grain left behind is of the bitter variety: invoices, bad news, nuisance paperwork, etc. I fill many bags with the recyclable remnants.

Considering that the bulk of hand-delivered mail is throw-away, and a major portion of the remaining mail is bills or bad news, I dread the tedious task of plowing through the mail with a sighted friend. It is wise to attend to this task every seven-to-ten days in order to pay bills when due, or reply to timely paperwork. As it is, if my mail delivery is delayed because it is forwarded, or if it sits in my house unopened for too long, I still suffer the consequences of receiving information too late. I am frequently read invitations and notices of events long past their scheduled date. Not that I get many printed invitations!

But I do despise the aggressive mail. As I alluded to previously, the management of the snail mail is something I must endure at the convenience of a friend or volunteer, which may often extend beyond a weekly routine.

In early October, a significant letter sat unopened in my canvas bag for several weeks, as I awaited sighted assistance to "do the mail." When that day finally arrived, there were several items I shuddered to hear read to me. One piece in particular lay among the unsorted, sordid mass of paper. When this particular letter was finally read to me, I received quite an unwelcome surprise. It was from the prestigious Miami law firm that, last April, had agreed to represent me in seeking a just resolution to the Key West Police brutality incident of March 30th.

In May, I had left Key West for six months, only to face a barrage of unfortunate events. But I was relieved to feel a sense of comfort and confidence that any attention to this unsavory matter on my part could be deferred until my return to Key West in the fall. I felt assured that the situation was in good hands.

However, the letter contained an unexpected turn. I was informed that the law firm could no longer pursue the case for a variety of reasons. This meant that I had to start from the beginning to seek a fair resolution to this ordeal. It meant back to square one for me. I shuddered at the prospect of revisiting a haunting and traumatic situation.

I wish I had received this bad news via another means. It only served to reinforce my dread of the aggressive mail that lies dormant in my canvas sack waiting to assault me.

23. Local is Where You Stand

It has been stated, "All Politics is Local."

I contend that political philosophy is formed, not only by where you stand (figuratively and literally), but also the proximity of your heart to your soul. Personal issues shape each one's political profile.

I grew up in the suburbs of New York City. My parents had fled city life for a private house in the quickly-developing rural landscapes of Long Island. Post-war growth expanded these outlying communities into densely populated counties.

Suburbia was a great place to grow up. We had private backyards, and quiet neighborhoods in which traffic flow rarely interrupted our street games. Dozens of other kids lived within a small radius. Trips into Manhattan exposed us to some of the world's greatest cultural institutions. Come our teenage years, we discovered that the City offered everything that the suburbs lacked.

Our suburbanite parents left the mostly Democratic strongholds of the City to find themselves in a region run by a strong Republican Political Machine. Parents were pushing strollers, driving station wagons and attending PTA meetings. Naturally their politics were tied to leafy family-oriented communities.

In the movie, *Priscilla, Queen of the Desert*, I cherish the line that describes the suburbs as serving the function of keeping "them" (rednecks) out and keeping "us" (queers) in.

Our origins may determine where we stand today: regional, urban, suburban, rural, family and religious tradition.

As a childless adult, suburbia has little appeal to me. I prefer urban life, which offers more access to cultural institutions and ethnic diversity. I enjoy urban neighborhoods where one patronizes local proprietors. City parks offer greater opportunity for social encounters and interactions. (When driving through suburban neighborhoods in midday, I was amazed to see the only signs of life were hired landscape workers.)

Among gatherings of parents, the topic of children frequently prevails. Although never a parent myself, we still share similar concerns on many like issues. My real estate taxes support public schools and institutions for child rearing. I do not get the tax deductions that parents get, but I recognize that our society is shaped by subsequent generations. Hence, I care that values such as tolerance and environmental appreciation are family issues. It affects everyone that today's youth respect laws and are politically astute.

When I was young, I believed in our generation. We marched for peace, espoused liberal social and humanitarian ideals, protested nuclear energy, smoked pot, and embraced environmental conservation. I presumed that when we attained more political power, upon reaching legal voting age, all these issues would be properly resolved. But somehow, a new wave of conservatism suddenly swept into office. This has always disturbed me.

Adults choose causes by urgent issues directly affecting them personally, and the ones they love. Their financial status is often a factor. As life alters our status, matters tend to shift in importance. Sometimes we get involved in political causes that we may never have foreseen. Soccer Moms, whose previous political battles may have focused on dangerous traffic intersections, can become dedicated environmentalists overnight when they learn of a planned toxic waste dump nearby. (NIMBY!)

When I lost my sight, I felt obliged to learn how to be a good blind citizen; it meant joining the appropriate organizations and taking a stand on issues that affect the visually-impaired community. Now, I expend time and energy dealing with the local Department of Public Works, expressing my concern over safety and accessibility issues (which are easily overlooked by average pedestrians). Examples of this include safe crosswalks. To comply, the town often installs audible crosswalk signals that get drowned out by traffic noise. (I also question why driver's education omits national White Cane Laws, which requires drivers to yield to blind pedestrians in the street, and also the illegality of blocking designated crosswalks.) I gratefully acknowledge strangers who occasionally come to my rescue in the asphalt jungle. I feel further obliged to take up the cause of equal accessibility in both real space and cyberspace.

Have my civil rights and obligations been altered by blindness? I wonder whether I would qualify for jury duty. Lawyers would argue that I am incapable of visually evaluating presented evidence. If so, isn't it ironic that the symbol of justice is the lady with the blindfold holding the scales and the proclamation, *Justice is Blind?*

Yet, I qualify to be a blind eyewitness. Two blind friends recently were called upon to be legal witnesses to an official document signing, in the presence of a notary public.

My local recruitment office never gave me a copy of the "Gay Agenda," of which I have heard so many conservative politicians speak. (Perhaps it is not printed in Braille.)

Doesn't *Gay Republicans* seem like an oxymoron?

How do some people claim to be apolitical? Shouldn't everyone care how his or her tax dollars are spent? Some vote merely by their pocketbooks. And, as we are all citizens of the same planet, can we ignore global politics and international civil rights? Fundamentalists and radical viewpoints rarely represent rational thinking. Ours is a complex, pluralistic society.

College students, DINKS, dog-owners, disabled, parents, business-owners, laborers, retirees, tenants, property-owners, minorities. . . chances are, that during the course of life, we will identify with several of these groups. So, doesn't it make sense to elect a government that is fair to the needs of each?

Don't waste your vote.

Don't believe everything you hear.

Don't enlist in a cause merely under pressure of others.

Don't elect single-issue candidates.

And, don't trust me. I'm just a self-righteous, liberal newspaper columnist.

(11/2/01)

24. Six Calendars

Rip van Winkle slept for 100 years. He awoke, startled at how the world around him had changed during a century of slumber. At least he was well rested. This gave him an advantage in adapting. Of course, changes did not occur as rapidly then as they do in current times. I personally wake up each day knowing that the future has crept up on me over the last six years, while I was pre-occupied. I was not sleeping; rather I've been very hard at work. I had to face many unforeseen tasks, but it still feels like the reverie is far from over. (Did you ever wake from a particularly vivid dream in which you were hard at labor? When you woke, you felt anything but rested! That's how I feel most every day.)

Much of my time has been occupied adjusting to this new world of darkness. I have come to view my life as B.B. (Before Blindness) and A.B. (After Blindness).

Every year, as a gift of appreciation for my financial support, I receive a calendar from an environmental organization. I have not been able to see the beautiful natural images on each page of the last six calendars. Yet, I proudly hang it to display my continued connection with this movement.

Time has not stopped on my account and time lost can never be recovered. Irrational fears of Y2K have come and gone. We have entered a new Millennium and witnessed startling political firestorms. Since 1995, how many weather events have already been dubbed "the storm of the century"? The human species has vastly inflated the earth's population, while hundreds more species have become extinct. Many great and revered individuals have departed this world.

Broadway has reminded us that 525,600 minutes is only one way to measure a single year. The contents of the swollen female bellies I saw in 1995 are now boarding school buses. To put a good spin on the fast pace of time, I just remark that we do not get older; instead they keep making more and more young people. To my friend's delight, in my mind's eye, nobody around me is aging.

People compliment me on my good adjustment. But I do not feel it could ever be adequate. Things are further complicated as the rules keep changing: area codes, zip codes, tax codes and dress codes. Styles, fads and overnight sensations have passed by without my notice. I feel so un-hip regarding new musical artists, actors, movies and other forms of popular culture.

Staying up-to-date and well informed is now much more difficult. Finding that there are now people more to the political Left than I am has been a surprise!

My time is filled with re-learning how to achieve daily tasks and how to be better organized. It is very fatiguing. (It takes more concentration to do laundry in the dark.) Focus must be extra-sharp, and I must always remain more alert to my environment. I am very conscious of making embarrassing blunders in public. Intuition sometimes proves more valuable than information.

I have had to learn the idiosyncrasies of adaptive technology on my computer. (Look Ma! No mouse!) My good friend is a rocket scientist. Even he cannot use my mouse-less computer.

Trade shows that I attended in the early nineties, gave me a preview of future products,

214 • ROBERT MICHAEL JACOBS

gadgets and appliances. Now these electronic marvels line store shelves. You may have acquired a DVD player, while I learned the meaning of DVS (Descriptive Video Service). I drown in a pile of mystifying remote controls. I missed out on the dot-com craze. I never downloaded music, porn or stream video from the Internet. I still can't hack online chat rooms.

Six years of new products are unfamiliar to me. For example, automobile designs, scooters and computerized gym equipment that beeps. Product packaging provides a new level of frustration. Childproof containers may as well be adult-proofed. I only buy toothpaste with the flip top, just to avoid the mishap of losing the cap. It seems that all fresh fruit now bears sticky labels that I cannot locate until I find them in my mouth.

Memory fades with time. How can I refresh my knowledge of names or identify the composers of popular classical music themes? I cannot read the liner notes on the CDs, so I feel insecure speaking about many musical subjects. On the other hand, I can excuse my mediocrity while playing the violin, as I am forced to play only by ear.

I must contend with high prices, as I cannot browse for sales or cut coupons. I pay whatever I am told. "Today's specials" are not always made known to me. I receive one benefit here in Boston: I get a fare break on the mass transit system.

Overall, living is now viewed with a different slant.

Over one decade ago (circa 5 B.B.), I was an upwardly mobile yuppie. I made a rather propitious financial retirement investment in a Biotechnology Sector Fund. At the time, I only expected the possible financial rewards of putting faith in this emerging science. Now the odds have doubled on a favorable return for my investment, as these once upstart startup research companies are on the cutting edge of the medical frontier. Their successes may either provide me financial security, or better yet, return hope for reintroducing the light spectrum into my brain.

(11/16/01)

SECTION THREE

Pale, Skinny and Bald

The travails of the last six months, in the northern latitudes, have left a detrimental effect on me as a whole – outwardly on my appearance, and inwardly by psychological upheaval. Having left Key West last spring a bit battered and bruised, but buff and bronzed, the months in Boston chiseled away at my chiseled physique. Due to months of anguish and chemotherapy, I paid the exacting toll of too many troubling episodes. Although I devoted as much energy as possible to maintain mental health and athletic conditioning, such efforts were severely thwarted by the ravages of toxins and stress. As I struggled to stick to my compulsive fitness regimens, extreme fatigue and anxiety constrained my ambitions.

By the last chemo treatment at the end of October, my hair was so thin that I chose to take a razor to my scalp. Shaven heads are fashionable again (as my Dad had predicted back during the long-hair styles of the 1970's). The first tactile feel of my own bare skull seemed strangely foreign. But I foresaw that once the chemo poisons had cleared my body, my hair follicles would reawaken, and the Key West sunshine would witness the restoration of my natural cranial covering. And, hopefully like Samson, my emerging hair would parallel enhanced strength.

Despite my dedication to continue with weight training at the Boston gym throughout the entire treatment period,

I was finding it an ever-increasing challenge to grapple with gravity by pushing iron skyward. As my blood was growing thinner, I faced the familiar weight-training machines twice each week. To my disappointment, I found that shortness-of-breath and faintness had replaced the natural high I had once received from the rush of adrenaline and endorphins buzzing through my body. Additionally, the arduous travel between home and my downtown gym was exhausting. By the completion of each workout, I sat in bewilderment as to how I would summon up the physical and mental energy to get my fatigued body safely home again.

(Without the incentive to get home to KC's joyous greeting at my front door, I often would just sit a while before evoking the strength and courage to find my way to the subway. I searched for reasons to loiter downtown until rush-hour traffic would subside.)

In spite of my best efforts and high motivation, I grew more anemic along with the dwindling autumn sunlight. As a result, by November, my muscle tone and my skin tone had notably faded.

My southern home would welcome back a physically and emotionally diminished resident. I held no illusion that I was running away from many of the problems that had beset me since earlier this year. In fact, my return to Key West would re-arouse many quiescent issues that I had left unresolved last season. I also carried the new anxiety of what it would be like living there without my canine housemate. But, a change of environment was in order so that I may endeavor to climb out of the dark, cold crevasse into which I had fallen in Boston. The warm sub-tropical sun lured me upward, lifting my spirits. My renewed resolve enticed me to rebuild my previous healthy (albeit superficial) façade. This seasonal re-settlement demanded a new local gym membership. I was eager to establish a revised weekly schedule that incorporated some sun and leisure time.

The natural life force from Key West's clement weather conditions inspired me to reconstruct what I had lost. A dormant vigor would re-awaken from setting my sights on more noble objectives than those dominated by medical concerns. Emerging from the shadows of the summer storms brightened my demeanor. So had the certainty that KC had stayed with me as my Guardian Angel.

I was determined that "pale, skinny and bald" was only to be a temporary condition.

25. Doctor Knows Best (?)

"You need to stay overnight in the hospital. Low blood counts make you very susceptible to infection. You could die within 24 hours."

"I'm not staying here!" I responded adamantly to the doctor. "I'd rather die at home. Besides, there are fewer germs at home than there are in this hospital!"

I had just spent two hours in the ER waiting room, amidst coughing, sneezing strangers, who perilously populated the air with malevolent microbes.

(More people pick up illnesses in hospitals than from anywhere else. In one extreme case, I know of a woman who was admitted for a broken leg. She caught pneumonia in the hospital and died.)

I feel that some doctors think that the "DR" before their names stands for "Don't Refute," and the "MD" stands for "Minor Deity."

My oncologist acted so self-assured and aloof. She was revered by her colleagues, yet, as her patient, I felt she overlooked the total picture. She knew her specialty, but she never really sought to know *me*. Healthcare should encompass more than chemistry, formulas and statistics.

During my treatment period, the doctor ignored many factors that were making me feel miserable. When I spoke of dizziness and shortness of breath, she expressed little concern, as they were not congruent with the statistics recorded on my medical chart. Disregarding emotional issues and physical limitations also compounded the peripheral impact of the treatments. Doctors sometimes neglect to understand the experience of the patient.

Lora's husband, David, is a cardiologist. Two weeks ago, Lora felt exhausted, had high fevers and swollen glands. She asked David for medical advice. He calmly responded, "Just get over it. There are no treatments for viral infections."

Last week, when David exhibited the same symptoms, a fellow doctor prescribed an antibiotic. David recovered quickly, enduring far less suffering than Lora had.

On the first day of my treatment, I was sent home with a sheet of lengthy instructions and various medications to combat side effects. No accommodation was made for my blindness, which barred me from reading the instructions and the labels on the pill bottles.

Emotional stress often makes the treatment seem worse than the illness. Lab tests alone cannot measure quality of life. The results are meaningless when the individual's unique circumstances are ignored. This is tunnel-vision. Even a sightless patient can see this.

My doctor resented being challenged by me. Contrary to her medical advice, I had made a personal decision to skip the last segment of the prescribed therapy. This seemed to cause some contention between us.

During scheduled appointments, her beeper constantly interrupted the flow of our conversations. She responded to each call with urgency. As a result, I felt that my questions and concerns were never fully addressed.

I soon had developed a prejudice against her. Perhaps she viewed me as a difficult patient. But it is wise to avoid an adversarial relationship with someone authorized to stick needles into your skin and small metal instruments into sensitive body orifices.

Mutual respect between the doctor and the patient is a crucial element of success.

On my final visit, she gave me the most thorough examination in months. Before she left the room, I attempted to be diplomatic, so as to mitigate any misunderstandings between us. I openly explained the rationale for my decision. She seemed to appreciate my candor. My frankness may have reduced whatever contention had arisen between us. She also may have gained some more respect for me as well.

Some doctors' attitude conveys the notion that the patient is totally ignorant. My first visit to a new doctor inspired him to give me a lecture on the basic axioms for maintaining good health. I listened patiently. Despite my maturity and healthy appearance, he talked down to me as if I were a young child from a Third World country.

I've spent enough nights in hospitals to know what goes on after the staff doctors leave for home. I have observed negligence and disrespect. Most patients will agree that a hospital is no place to get rest. Recovery is hampered by lack of a sense of well-being and trust. Stress and anxiety are harmful.

Doctors may resent well-informed patients. My accumulated knowledge results from personal experience, medical consultations and reliable resources. Important decisions are hardly whimsical. Rather, they are based on diligent research and anecdotal information. If I feel that I should defer my own judgment, I enlist the opinions of friends, therapists, clergy and family members to provide objectivity.

Today's patients sit for hours in cold waiting rooms, told that the doctors are running far behind schedule. The same excuse is always given:

the office is short-staffed on that day.

Several years ago, I stayed in a renowned Boston eye and ear hospital. One would presume that the staff would be sensitive to the special needs of the blind. Instead, I was confounded when issued a standard set of instructions, spoken rapidly in a thick accent, advising me to use the RED "nurse call" button on the TV remote control. Before I could speak out, the nurse was gone. For two days, I blindly had to navigate the slippery floor of a flooded bathroom until housekeeping finally responded to my pleas.

But, in that same hospital, a Pain Specialist had the insight to acknowledge that medicine extends beyond medications. He understood the connection between stress and pain, and prescribed a private room so that my beloved canine companion could be on the visitor list. This made all the difference in my recovery!!

(12/1/01)

26. Winter Weather Refugee

I was given a lucky break this year: mild weather lingered into the autumn months. Only a few short cold snaps punctuated the season, just enough to reinforce my determination to flee before the snow flew. At any time, the Canadian border would open, and the floodgates would release the bitter-cold air into New England. I waded through the crunchy piles of leaves that assemble at the base of my front stoop like an angry mob. The crisp night air already carried the foreboding smell of fireplace smoke. Signs pointed South for a timely departure from Boston.

I haven't always been a Winter Weather Refugee. As a matter of fact, I once loved the cold winter. The freshly-frozen lakes lured me over with my figure skates, before the hockey players tore up the smooth surfaces. I welcomed heavy snowfalls, which temporarily softened the city's hard edges and spread a clean white quilt over the grimy streets. Sunlight glinted through long icicles that clung like crystal stalactites, to the eaves of the mansard roofs. Snow dusted the red-brick bowfront buildings and lined leafless ivy vines.

I enjoyed cross-country skiing along the sidewalks, thumbing my nose at automobiles stuck in snowdrifts; or gliding along the Esplanade beside the snow-blanketed summer picnic grounds that buffered the skyline from the frozen river. Tracking through beautiful snow-laden forests combined the sensations of tranquillity with healthy exercise.

Following three years of college in Rochester, NY, where it snowed daily and the sky was gray from October through May, I came to Boston on a January day. The sunlight sparkled off the snow and, despite the cold, it seemed balmy in contrast to my college town.

"What a concept!" I thought. "The sun can shine in the wintertime. . .Let this be my new home!"

And for fifteen winters it was, until I went blind.

Suddenly, the beauty of winter eluded me. As I had to relearn navigation on these new terms, snow became an additional obstacle. The chill lost its charm. Ice became something to slip on, not to skate on.

I felt SAD – Seasonal Affective Disorder. In order to survive blindness, I would need to re-locate to a winter climate where the weather did not confine me indoors with condo fever – the urban equivalent of "cabin fever." Every venture outside had become a tiresome ritual of pulling on layers of clothes, and selecting which pair of gloves I would risk losing that day.

I sought a climate where clothing could be an accessory, like jewelry, not a necessity to shield bare skin from the elements. My search for a livable American city, where daily stress would not be compounded by cold climatic conditions, brought me to Key West. I had never been here as a sighted person, but one winter here convinced me that it felt right.

My friend, Mark, accompanied me this year on my southbound journey. We had both mentally prepared for the inevitable airport episode: "Nightmare in Miami." Sure enough, flight delays and missed connections made the travel demons proud of their work.

Mark stayed for 10 days to help me get settled. We cleared the yard of debris, set up the computer, and worked on a few home projects.

Of course there was the perennial pilgrimage to the K-mart to stock up on a season's worth of household supplies. This retail jungle could ensnare one for days. As Mark ran through the crazy maze of aisles, I was left alone with the filling shopping cart and the horrifying thought that if the store were suddenly evacuated, I would have no chance to find an exit.

I was bewildered that this mega-store appeared to lack any rational layout of merchandise placement. Why did I knock into a stack of Cheese Whiz™ in the soap aisle? Ask for bug spray and ant traps and you will be directed to the "cat aisle" and told to look next to the vanilla wafers.

The automated self-service checkout registers also disturbed me. The kind, female voice announces the item's price, and a mean, male voice orders you when to start packing a new bag. I envisioned this automaton slavemaster standing over a cowering lady robot.

Resettlement requires appropriating many hours for setting up phone and internet service. Mark commented that mileage points should be awarded for each minute kept on hold by customer service personnel.

Since adopting the travel pattern of migratory fowl, each season demands readjustment. It takes time to reacquaint myself with the spatial dimensions of my home environment, or risk bruises to both body and ego. Each returning season requires me to relearn the appliances and identify the supplies stored in cabinets and under the sink.

I have lived in Boston for 20 years, and therefore retain visual memories of the city. In Key West, I use mnemonics to memorize the order of the streets from north to south and east to west. (The retail storefronts may change, but fortunately they do not rename the streets each year.)

I have less fear of being felled by a falling coconut in Key West than by being impaled by a homicidal icicle, unable to cleave to its eave in Boston. So, it was for safety sake and mental health that I became a Winter Weather Refugee.

(12/8/01)

Back Around to Square One

Lest any reader get the impression that my experience last spring with Key West law enforcement officers was an isolated incident, it should be noted that the local newspapers still regularly report accounts of the pugnacious propensity of the police. Apparently, the penchant for excessive and unjustified use of force against residents and visitors by several rogue officers have sullied the reputation of the entire force. Their predilection for violent tactics has blackened the eye of the whole department.

Currently, many months following my run-in with the lawmen, there is a significant amount of litigation outstanding against the city, mainly for alleged abuse of authority and unwarranted brutality by pugilistic police personnel. I am hardly alone. It seems that, if someone has a new complaint against the cops, they should get to the back of the line.

Meanwhile, since my receipt last October of the odious letter from the Miami lawyer, who had initially agreed to represent me, I have been left without any legal representation. Diane, the woman who had originally connected me with the Miami law firm, remains concerned about my predicament. Together we set out to find a new judicial advocate to take my case.

Some personal acquaintances advised me that I should just drop the whole thing. After all, the incident is now behind me, I lack the financial resources (unlike the City) to stage a legal challenge, and it would be a painful ordeal to submit myself to the judiciary process. It has been argued that I should cut my losses and accept that my yen for justice is too idealistic. Additionally, some claim that my well-publicized incident has already initiated beneficial changes to police protocols. Was I the canary in the coal mine? Due to the rash of citizen outrage, Florida State Prosecutors are currently investigating allegations of corruption and unwarranted police brutality in the City of Key West. Now it almost appears that my own complaint could be clumped together with all the other candid public clamor.

Despite this well-intentioned advice, my principles will not allow me to "just accept" the unjust, outrageous ordeal and forget the incident without a fair resolution. No one has yet been held accountable for the battering and indignities to which I had been subjected, nor for the others who have suffered from similar situations. My terrier-like tenacity compels me to be proactive in pursuit of moral rectitude, for reasons that extend beyond equitable compensation. It may be unrealistic to expect appropriate financial reparation or otherwise, yet, there is a broader issue that must be considered.

Last March, as I lay sprawled across the floor of that jail cell, injured, in shock and in severe pain, I lost something more than my freedom for one afternoon and evening. I lost touch with all practical reality, entangled in the snare of the most hostile nightmare imaginable. Nothing seemed to make sense. Even to this day, it often feels as if I still cannot completely awaken from that repulsive reverie. Many months of counseling and introspection have enabled me to recognize that my memories accurately reflect the events of that day. In turn, I wonder how I can ever again feel a sense of peace and security.

Nine months have now passed. My final destination on the road to wellness is not yet in sight. It won't be visible until I feel assured that a fair closure is on the horizon. Until the city government of Key West genuinely perceives the full scope of the incident, and is willing to acknowledge fault and responsibility, I can never feel that anything has been truly reconciled.

On the legal "Yellow Brick Road," I find myself back to Square One. But this time I am not entirely alone. Diane's continued concern about my situation has prompted her to assist me in my search for new legal representation. I face the same obstacles that I did last spring: few local attorneys are willing or eager to litigate against the city or the police department. Their reasons are understandable. Such bold maneuvers would risk retaliation. In many instances, local lawyers need the city's cooperation in order to practice. Few would jeopardize the good graces of the politically powerful. These lawyers would be labeled as antagonistic. Consider the difficulties their practices would encounter in the future, if they were to request police officers or government employees to testify as witnesses on behalf of their clients.

My legal superheroes would need to have the testicular fortitude (cojones [sp]) to grapple with government officials. These crusaders must cherish the values rooted in Truth, Justice and the American Way. Ultimately, my search must land me a suitable lawyer to lead a suitable lawsuit; the right one will have the courage and will to help me seek a just resolution.

Through Diane's assistance, I have located a startup law firm interested in hearing my story. Eager to meet with these gentlemen, I requested Diane forward them the contents of my legal file – the documents and evidence relating to my case. We set up a meeting. I anxiously walked the several blocks from my home to their nearby office. We talked casually and became acquainted. Then, I detailed my account of the confrontation with the cops. Next, we called Mark, back in Boston, on the speakerphone so that he could personally relate his witness testimony. As Mark and I had rarely discussed the concise details in private, I was as eager, as were the lawyers, to hear it from his vantage point. For the most part, our stories squared, allowing for vastly distinctive personal perspectives.

So far, I had managed to keep a cool demeanor, while emphatically stressing the horror of the incident and its lingering impact. Then one lawyer read me the four reports filed by the officers involved. Prior to this meeting, I had never heard first-hand these official statements and charges. As each false accusation against me contained in the reports reached my ears, I became increasingly unnerved. I could not believe what I was hearing; I became frantically disturbed. So much for keeping my cool demeanor!

Unable to continue to restrain my rage, the fabricated accounts I was hearing totally unhinged me. Whether it was a visceral reaction to the assault on my integrity, or the resurgence of dormant anger, is still uncertain. I was embarrassed at my loss of composure in front of the two lawyers, and apologized profusely. What type of impression would they have of me if I projected myself as such an emotional cripple?

For fear of risking my credible image, I desperately attempted to stabilize my emotions. I felt impelled to rebuff the charges and insinuations. In response to this gross defamation of character, I was convinced that an impromptu physical demonstration was in order. Using my cane, and the office furniture for props, I staged a dramatic reenactment of my actual motions from that hot afternoon so many months earlier. (A constant concern for me is whether it is even possible to impart accurately the experience of a blind person's perspective to sighted individuals.) They respectfully listened and quietly observed my presentation. Did my passionate performance successfully illustrate those physical movements, which were so misrepresented in the police reports? Had my fervent re-creation adequately conveyed my sense of pain and injustice to this audience?

I felt very comfortable in the presence of these two gentlemen. They seemed to understand me and expressed empathy for my situation. This meeting provided me with a very positive feeling and a renewed sense of hope.

At least the ball is rolling again after being stuck in the muddle for so long. Where it will lead is still a great uncertainty.

Undoubtedly, this ball of harsh and irritating yarn will continue to unravel. Stay tuned.

27. The Secret Gardener

Ten years ago, I could never have foreseen myself tending an invisible outdoor garden during the month of December. Even as a young boy, I loved to make things grow. My parents allotted me a small, shady section of the backyard. It took great effort to make anything thrive there other than moss. Years later, I claimed a sunnier location to raise a crop of cannabis.

In Boston, I found apartment living rather confining for propagating plants. They adorned every window, but only the hardiest ones survived the meager light from the northern exposure. Without access to an outdoor plot of land, I eventually extended my horticultural endeavors to the fire escape. Each spring, I would expand my lofty botanical zone with additional potted plants climbing the steps to the story above, suspending more bird feeders and enlarging the herbal annex. Finally, it resembled the Hanging Gardens of Babylon. I'd sit outside tending to my myriad of colorful coleus, blossoming begonias and jubilant geraniums. Passersby called up with compliments.

When I lost my sight, I could no longer maintain this menagerie. Even my indoor plants suffered from oversight under my oversight. As plants never vocalize their needs, I would forget to water the unseen vegetation. Dead leaves crumbled to the floor. Outside, the abandoned flowerpots now collect snow in the winter, and host weeds in the summer.

Moving to Key West enabled me to become the proprietor of a few square feet of real estate with a year-round growing season. I reveled to create a tropical sanctuary. So what if I couldn't see what I sowed?

During my absence, the trees form a leafy canopy, blocking out the sun. Each season upon my return, I must trim back the prolific palm fronds. I love waking up to feel the morning sun on bare skin, and absorb its vitamin D, as I consume the rest of the vitamin alphabet orally along with my coffee.

Last month, I ventured outside to inventory the survivors of the summer storms and insect infestations. They earn a special place in my heart for their fortitude.

My first task was to tactually remove debris by raking my fingers through the clutter of dead foliage. Last year, this uncovered a beautiful orchid clinging to a piece of driftwood. I tacked it to a post to display its many blossoms. I misted it daily. One day, a professional gardener marveled at the hanging orchid. On closer inspection, she assured me that it would never die. Amazed that I had unearthed a rare and hardy variety, I eventually understood that she was telling me that it was silk. It appears so real that admirers need not know its true false nature.

My friend, Mark, climbed the Schefflera with my Ginsu knife to reclaim more open sky. Intent at overcoming his tree-climbing phobia, he hacked away at an offshoot, but the mother tree angrily tossed him groundward. *Thud!* Suddenly, Mark lay moaning on the ground.

"Are you alright?" I inquired, as I prayed that he hadn't crushed any of my precious plants.

Determined to add some spice to the yard, I filled a planter with herbs. Sadly, I drowned them with love (I over-watered). Basil boldly survived, but poor Rosemary succumbed to root-rot.

I've developed a special love for my Hibiscus. Perhaps it stems from sympathy.

The first year that I planted her, she bloomed with gusto throughout the season. But last year, Hibiscus was hurting. Slowly fading away, her strength was being sucked out of her at a snail's pace. She was unable to yield even one blossom, becoming a pathetic remnant of her former vibrant self.

I returned this season to find her tenaciously clinging to her shredded foliage. Drastic measures were called for. She had been ravaged and decimated by a devious lover. The sneaky snail population, concealed by day under my wooden deck, was my rival. My affection was nurturing, whereas their romance was consuming. These ravenous Romeos only lusted for her luscious leafage. I couldn't allow the snail terrorists to savagely seduce my beloved flowering plants. I felt her fear. She was shaking like a leaf. (Her sister, Ginger, hadn't fared too well, either.)

Retaliation meant chemical warfare. Once my ruthless rivals had been identified, the solution was simple: snail bait. Had they targeted the protrusive Schefflera instead, things need not have come to this. But, these snails were barking up the wrong tree.

This over-the-counter product was readily available. It is against my nature to take such severe action against nature, but it was clear: *the escargot must go!* I once cherished the snail shells I collected on Rockaway Beach; now their garden-variety cousins were held in very low esteem.

The bait was set like an irresistible midnight buffet on a cruise ship. That night, when the floral allure beckoned them to their nocturnal nosh, the snails greedily consumed the toxic hors d'oeuvres.

The following day, Mark collected the remnants of the snail militia: over 150 troops. Their demise was a tribute to their gluttony.

I speak with Hibiscus everyday to assure her that I will always love and protect her.

Today she showed her gratitude by presenting me with one huge, fragrant blossom.

Regarding the snails' tale: their fatal foe was not the formidable feast, t'was bewitching beauty that killed the beast.

(12/15/01)

2001: A Space Odd To See

Tomorrow is the last day of the year 2001!

For the past four decades, 2001 loomed on my horizon as the "futuristic epoch." As an avid reader of science fiction through my teen years, I had entertained dozens of speculations and conjectures of a brave (or shattered) new world (and beyond). 2001 represented the start of the next new era. The Third Millennium would be a time when humanity would either realize its greatest potential as God's creation, or would have become misguided in its struggle and effectuate the demise of Earth's blend of resources, biologies and civilizations. Idealistically, I dared to believe the former, yet intuition told me that the latter was the more likely scenario. But so far, we are still here. However, it remains a valid argument whether or not modern humanity has progressed very much in building a better world for all its inhabitants.

Year 2001 is about to complete its minuscule allotted segment within universal time. As so, it was just another numbered year, another 365 days to group together under the same numerical banner. The number is merely a surname, which serves only to distinguish this twelve-month span from those similar periods that preceded it, and from those to follow.

A new calendar year traditionally prompts us to pause in retrospection on the previous 365 days, to summarize and evaluate. Perhaps because we humans need to stop on a regular interval for review. The human mind can only focus on time in relatively small doses. Too many days grouped together would be troublesome for us to give each 24-hour period an adequate account. One day is not more important than the previous or the next, although any single day can be far more pivotal and affect those that follow; yet each 24-hour period contains the same potential in the larger scheme of time.

One day remains in this calendar year. I believe that a set of 52 weeks is arbitrary, and really does not indicate the completion of anything other than an artificial marker of time. Still, I am drawn to write an epilogue (epitaph?) for 2001. I feel compelled to pause and scrutinize highly significant moments that have come to pass since the year had begun.

Personally, I cannot view this span of time as ordinary. This calendar year seemed an aberration, far too eventful. It leaves me more rattled and disturbed than any of its predecessors. An equitable survey might reveal similar grievous devastation among many others as well.

I wish that many of the events of this past year had never happened – especially all in such a small dimension of time. Many occurrences will haunt me from the present forward.

There were certainly some successes to mark this year, but sadly, it is the losses that have been so overwhelming. Optimism has suffered severe collateral damage. Despair and grief reigned. Any single misfortune from the many that I could recount would have been enough to trouble me deeply; but the continuous stream of catastrophes wore away at me like relentless crashing surf against a rocky shoreline. Does any specific event overshadow all the others? Or, perhaps, is there some esoteric cosmic connection among them? From this place in time, it remains a dark mystery. Should I have learned something vastly enlightening from these constant blows, in that it all had an ultimate purpose? I confess that I am too blind to see whether a broader scope may someday resolve this riddle.

I curiously search for a connection between these incidents. Can I even place the initial origin of the turbulence? If there is any link, it might predate this calendar year.

2001 did start out rocky, but the early technical problems that I encountered could not have foretold the subsequent traumatic events. Actually, the frustrations with technology I had endured in January were merely a continuation of the string of hardships and impediments, which I have faced since losing my eyesight.

Interwoven among my published Blind Snow Bird columns, I have recounted several incidents that have defined these last twelve months. Their cumulative affect has considerably weakened me. Previously, I had regarded myself as strong and resilient. But now, that self-image has been altered.

As the new millennium began, I envisioned a potentially exciting fresh venture. Embarking on this new endeavor, I strove to be a more widely-published writer. My vision was rooted in a socially-motivated goal to extend my message to permeate the broader culture. Previously, my ESL tutoring only touched a small number of lives. Now I had been granted the opportunity to reach large numbers of citizens through the printed media. This did not diminish the importance of my one-on-one work with new Americans. My ESL tutoring aimed to strengthen their language skills, so that they could seek an easier road to happiness and accomplishment. I felt well-qualified to assist others achieve a future of successes and prosperity. After all, I had also been struggling to overcome obstacles to initiate a fresh start in life.

Had I not undertaken my latest enterprise, I fear that the tragic events of 2001 may have ultimately destroyed me. Instead, I should be grateful that this year only left me in tatters; in retrospect, I survived to accept and resolve to overcome the travails.

As the year opened, I had just begun my third season as a winter resident of Key West, the fourth year of my flight from the dark and cold of New England winters. Two years prior, I had acquired my own home here. This major move was aimed at achieving an easier life for an extended season. I reasoned that a longer period spent in the Key West community should result in a greater sense of stability, and expand my potential for finding peace, comfort and happiness. Now, upon review of the year about to end, that dream may appear elusive. I continue to struggle to find meaning amidst the emotional pain. Without KC, this home feels empty and lonely.

On the thirtieth day of March, I felt a quake that would reverberate aftershocks in all the days to follow. It was an event that set the stage for impending trauma and emotional upset, which left me unprepared to manage what lay ahead. The events of that day have already been documented, so I need not recall them here.

How much destruction to my foundation occurred from that incident to make me so ill-prepared for the unforeseen events that were to follow – many still to be resolved? I literally and figuratively had my legs kicked out from under me on that day. This massive blow strongly diminished the fortitude necessary to guide me through the crises yet to come. Each attempt to rebound from the casualties that followed was more difficult. When I needed strength the most, the reservoir appeared to provide inadequate resources to fight or face the situations.

Last spring, upon my return to Boston, I continued to suffer the lingering affects of March 30th. It had been left unresolved. I thought that I could release it for a while, so that I could rebuild my damaged person. But it wouldn't go away, nor allow me to get back on track. Once I understood this, I sought continued professional counseling and support. Only an active plan could enable me to accept, and hopefully repair myself from the damage.

The stirrings of other events were interfering with my recovery. Financial and health problems further impeded my attempts to rally. I felt very alone despite the support of a few close friends. By early July, I recognized the depth of my depression. Amidst this emotional breakdown, I began to compose a document called *Depression*. It was my belief that I could best write from a point of intense turmoil. I still believe that the sincerest hard-edge feelings can only be expressed most vividly when the pain is a sharp blade against the surface of our being. To this day, I cannot go back and reread the raw emotions expressed in the words of that document. And just three days following this course of writing that so poignantly journaled my deep despairs, I endured the beginning of the most terrifying situation of the post-March 30th period. When I sat down on that fourth day of July to chronicle my state of desolation, I truly believed that my life could not sustain another tragic blow. But, as if to be tested, I was about to encounter even greater upheaval. Inevitably, the Blind Snow Bird columns reflected the dark shadow that hung over me.

Last July 4th KC, the most beloved, loyal and dependable figure in my life, sat beside me as I started to write this personal document, *Depression*. It became an on-going journal written as a flow of consciousness to satisfy two urges. Primarily, it was a therapeutic means to release all the intense emotions which were seething inside of me. In this exercise, I also believed that, in its review, I might be apt to judge my present state from an external vantage point. Over the weeks that followed, I continued to add further reflections of the changing situations. At one time, I felt this document might eventually become a suicide note. The storm clouds continued to gather. I was rapidly losing faith in human support, and acknowledged that only KC would stay by me in the most turbulent of times. But suddenly, even KC revealed that he was also subject to the workings of a cruel and chaotic universe. KC exhibited signs of illness that I first believed were minor. But I was about to face my greatest loss yet.

It rained every day that KC was in the hospital. I was totally distraught when I looked back at the pain expressed in my writing from the previous week; I realized that the crevasse beneath my feet still had the power to pull me in even deeper. KC succumbed to his health problem in only eight days. As long as I had KC in my life, I felt that I could somehow confront any challenge. Perhaps I was deluding myself, but in retrospect, this was not far from the truth. I had sustained many losses and affronts over the preceding twelve years, yet I always had KC there to sustain me and draw me through each crisis. From the loss of my partner, my health, my career, my sight, my independence, my sense of dignity and financial security, I could always ground myself in his existence and an intangible connection to the universe as a whole. But without warning, he was gone. I was left alone with nothing but fallible humans and a vague notion of the Higher Power of God. While I struggled to maintain my belief in God, I started to feel that God had stopped believing in me. With no warning, I had to decide how to continue my journey into a frightening future alone.

I have already chronicled the turbulent events that followed. They colored my writing and mental health for the months to follow. My sadness clung to me, from the streets of the city to the privacy of my home.

My condition prevented me from making any decisions, particularly ones of great magnitude. Yet I was soon expected to make major choices regarding medical treatment. I would have selected to defer any decisions, but this was not an option.

On September 11th I was halfway through my course of chemotherapy. The state of anguish and siege, which had previously seemed to be mine alone to bear, suddenly became the burden of the entire nation. My own familiar sense of despair and jarring emotional upheaval were now pandemic. As if my string of misfortunes were a harbinger of a grander devastation, the world outside my own immediate realm plunged into a similar state of trauma. Now my personal troubles were but a microcosm of the global crisis that struck us all by the terrible events of that infamous day. Until that morning, I had almost felt that I had a monopoly on pain, then a bolt of lightening struck at my country, and one man's worries and crises were drowned out in the din of a louder collective cry.

As the world absorbed the shock of the terrorist event that broke the reality of so many, destroyed lives and faith, I sunk deeper into my morass of sadness and loneliness. Anger and panic were never far from the surface. As others watched the horrifying visuals on television of the ruthless demolition of New York's Twin towers, I could only visualize the nightmarish images. Personal accounts came to me via many sources. I felt even sicker. (I had many connections to the event, as it was my hometown, and I saw the rise of these towers thirty years earlier.) It seemed that our whole society was being crushed under the same despair with which I had recently become so familiar.

As November approached, I feared the move back to our home in Key West without my best companion.

Just as I had anticipated, the grief has been almost impossible to bear. I cry every day, and call out his name and pray for his presence to rescue me from my melancholia.

I work feverishly to stay busy pursuing larger goals, even if only to distract myself from this situation. To my amazement, I have managed to write once again in the lighter, more humorous style that I had developed previously. But too often I am crushed under the weight of personal emotional disaster. I continue my sessions with the therapist. Resolution to my daunting situations still appears remote.

28. Homecoming

Home is where you complete the circuit. It's where you start the day, and hopefully where you will end the day. You've run all the bases and landed at home plate. Congratulations! Collect your $200, you've completed another lap on the Monopoly board and avoided bankruptcy along the way.

Home is a place for renewal. It's your personal space to rebuild your fortitude, to face another sunrise again in 12 hours. Home should be a refuge for peace and security, providing comfort and stability, when you need to shut out the outside world. It is where your music plays. You can talk aloud to yourself in privacy, dress up or dress down completely; feel free to drop any pretense, to bare it all. Hang out and let it all hang out. You have the home court advantage. It's the place to entertain in your own personal style.

People who work at home get to wear their bathrobes and fuzzy slippers on the job. They can postpone their morning shower, manipulate their own schedules and enjoy their private diversions.

"Home" often trademarks superior or desirable quality. Think of home cooking, home-made or home spun. There are perhaps more songs, poems, phrases or sayings about "home" than anything else other than "love" or "rainbows."

Coming home, going home and leaving home – all are significant events repeated over the course of life's journey.

Home has been an endearing concept throughout human history, from caves to condos. It is our nest, the place to hang our hat, collect life's souvenirs, surrounding ourselves with cherished belongings and beloved companions: friends, plants or pets.

In art school, I produced a mixed-media scrapbook to illustrate the spontaneous home environment that I had created. I was trying to convey that we subliminally design private sanctuaries at home that reflect the workings of our mind. It is often bewildering to learn what people select to collect; we cannot always understand the peculiar personal fascination others have in their collectibles. It's usually not for their items' material value or aesthetic content. I've known people who collect bottle openers, swizzle sticks or anything portraying their favorite farm animal. Well, you know what they say: "One man's meat. . ."

My art project was an exercise in self-revelation. Currently, I find that writing expresses subconscious thoughts and perceptions. I can best write what is in my heart when I am at home. There is a mysterious connection between our heart and our home.

After I became blind, I recognized the necessity to reduce clutter. I inventoried my knick-knacks. Most were originally displayed for decorative purposes. But many tchotchkas held sentimental value. As it is especially difficult to dust the surfaces around these objects, I needed to minimize what remains on display. I have a peculiar attachment for two small pieces: an onyx puma and an onyx turtle. They confront each other on an antique mahogany tabletop. They had to stay. I feel some subconscious metaphor that connects them. Sort of a yin-yang thing; each represents complimentary manifestations of animal nature.

If our home reveals our true character and taste, how comfortable are we within our exhibit gallery? Do we feel the need to remove from sight some of our photos, posters, objects d'art or adult toys when certain people come into our home?

Coming home is also returning to the month called January. The annual cycle of time is renewed. We commit ourselves to resolutions, as the earth begins another revolution around the sun. Universal time and human activity are synchronized.

Year 2002 is a palindrome. It's the first one since 1991, and the last one until 2112. We may recall the last one, but who will be around to observe the next one?

With the new year as a metaphor for home, we re-enter our front door following a 12-hour absence, flop into our favorite chair, and announce, "What a terrible/wonderful day!"

So it is for the year. We first pause to look back, and then we look forward to a new year/ day. We proclaim a similar summary of the previous 12 months/hours.

"I had a pretty successful and productive day/year" or "Thank God this day/year is over! I never thought I'd get through it!"

But in spite of it all, we almost always do. Time requests we stop to review and renew; reassess, refresh and plan home-improvement for our soul.

Recently, while walking home, each time I came to one of the three major intersections along the route, something unusual occurred. Frequently, a car dashes through the crosswalk nearly knocking me down. On that day, Karma came barreling down the street instead. At each precise moment, someone approached and offered to help me across the intersection. Most often, when in my greatest need, no one is around or willing to stop and assist. Perhaps that day I was projecting some aura. Or possibly sometimes life just evens out. If the previous day/year sucked, maybe the universe will be kinder to us in our next go-round.

Cheers to those good people we encounter along the way!

We accumulate a lot of drek on our trek around the track. Wipe your feet on the mat and Welcome Home.

Happy New Year!

(1/4/02)

The Wicker Chair

I'm back again in the familiar, wobbly wicker chair. Surrounded by a sea of soft cushions, I am shielded from the rough rattan surfaces. Last April, I occupied this special seat for six one-hour sessions.

Today, sitting beside and slightly forward facing me at a right angle, is the man who witnessed my spring meltdown in the weeks following my confrontation with the Key West Police. He sits to my right, once again, as I fidget slightly. Following a half-year gap, Dan awaits my first words. How clearly does Doctor Dan recall my mental miscarriage? I had attempted to keep an email correspondence with him during my summer absence, but the barrage of personal tribulations precluded me from maintaining any regular interchange.

Now, sitting within four feet of this therapist, I need to update Dan regarding the string of calamities that had followed our last session six months ago. All the turmoil has affected my present state of mental health. Where should I start? I know it would take most of the first several sessions to share my interim tales of misfortune, but I desperately want us to resume at once any progress we had previously achieved. However, since those sessions, the picture has become far more complex!

I like Dan. He has always made me feel very much at ease. Emotions are easy for me to express without reserve in his presence. His apparent intellect, gentle manner and pragmatism, comfort me with confidence. We would talk. What did I hope to achieve? Answer: a renewed sense of strength and a path to peace. Am I "expecting" too much? We spend a great deal of time clarifying mutual definitions of the words we use. As a writer, concise communication is paramount to the exchange of concepts and representations. I make great effort to avoid letting semantics cloud the real issues.

As so many troubling situations are still fluid, I constantly need to keep him informed. I value his calm, rational feedback and his appraisal of my state of mind.

A sense of stability and sound reasoning has seemed too sparse in my life recently. I fight to tread turbulent waters. The tides are unpredictable, sharks lurk nearby and my baggage has been pulling me under. Dan plays the role of my life preserver until I can once again feel securely grounded. Without this weekly fix, I would remain adrift in this sea of uncertainty. I suppose that I maintain hope that the cushion beneath my butt might serve as a floatation device.

As it turned out, Dan has been facilitating a support group for cancer survivors. I arranged my weekly appointment schedule such that Dan could transport me to this meeting immediately following my therapy session.

Admittedly, I have a poor history of dealing with support groups. In the past, I have always instinctively rebelled against the collective consciousness expressed by such a gathering. I despised anyone else's whining other than my own. In retrospect, I even felt hostility toward other attendees who had fewer than five major problems going on simultaneously in their lives. However, with this particular cancer survivor group, I could not feel that I fit in for other reasons. Unlike the others, my cancer was of very little concern to me; it was in the past. And I never truly thought about it until I listened to the discussions among these individuals. I even felt a little shame that my experience was not nearly as devastating as those of the other attendees. (Yet, I stayed with it, and even somewhat participated, until other circumstances precluded me from attending the meetings. Frankly, I was a bit relieved.) But I am not yet ready to give up the wicker chair.

29. Crossing Duval

"May I ask you how you knew that the light had changed?" asked the man who had just observed me navigate the busy intersection of Southard and Duval.

"I didn't." I responded honestly. "It just felt as safe a time as any to scramble for the opposite curb."

Many who see me blindly travel around town inquire about my source of information. I attribute my mobility skills mostly to intuition and some very subtle clues. Crossing Duval is always a risky venture.

"A blind man walks into a bar. . ."

Sounds like the beginning of a joke, doesn't it? When I am that blind man, it often does turn into some sort of comical scene. Walking into a bar can be painful (unless I manage to find the door). Key West is in no short supply of Public Houses of every ilk. Nearly every other threshold on Duval Street leads into a drinking establishment.

"The band will now take a break. Drunks may feel free to ramble among themselves."

Scott, the construction worker, sidled up next to me and initiated conversation. After mentioning that I write for "Celebrate," I asked him if he ever reads this publication.

"No" he responded, "But I once lived in San Francisco."

I understood his intimation. He further added that he didn't read much of anything. (Many people claim not to read newspapers, as "news is depressing." It disturbs me that some people choose ignorance over information, especially as I envy the ability to access printed material.)

I often wonder if drunken barflies really understand each other's slurred conversations. At the Parrot last weekend, I was sitting comfortably at the bar. When the band finished their second set, I got up to walk outside. A garbled phrase caught my ears. It sounded like "Grayf'l Dead." I asked the source if she was saying "Grateful Dead," as I have always been a dedicated Deadhead. Her vague reference lacked much discernible information, other than that a Dead sound-alike band was playing somewhere in town. Further details were as sketchy as her enunciation. I exited the bar.

Within moments, my ears drew me in the direction of Duval Street. Familiar tunes and flashbacks from the '70s led me to an open doorway. I walked up a ramp and found a place against which to lean. Clueless as to my location or whom I was listening to, I did agree that they performed a very convincing mimicry of the late Jerry Garcia and company. I turned to face the music. A woman beside me offered an available barstool. I asked her the name of the bar. She looked around for information.

"I think the bar is called *Budweiser*," as she read a neon sign on the wall. I found that I was sitting next to another tired and drunken couple that had just driven down from the mainland for a night out. Weekends abound with such visitors with vague origins. They can name five states in which they have lived over the last two years, but they cannot recall how many bars they have patronized since five o'clock that same afternoon. The following dawn greets them in old cars and vans parked in the Sears parking lot. Fortunately, most elect not to drive back north after their night of revelry.

Last night, upon leaving the coffee shop

where I had attended an informal gathering of writers, the familiar sounds of the Dead-like band once again filled my ears. I asked a fellow meeting member to accompany me in the direction of that magnetic sound. We walked toward the compelling source of rock and rolling. Feeling my way up to the bar for a couple of beers, I inadvertently brushed against a woman. She started cursing me out in a LOUD obnoxious dialect, a cross between Revere, Mass. And Canarsie, Brooklyn. There wasn't an 'R' sound to be heard. I responded in the same tone, as I assumed it was her only known mode of communication.

After paying for the beers, I suddenly felt a tug on my arm from the direction of the boisterous, bellowing broad. A soft voice was pleading an apology for her previous behavior. I wasn't even certain if this was the same female, as this new voice was sweet, absent the trashy dialect. She insisted on buying beers for my companion and me. I declined her offer and accepted her apology with little concern. Within minutes she followed us back to our table with two fresh brews, suddenly becoming our best friend. She dragged me toward the dance floor, colliding me into furniture and annoyed patrons. It was easier just to oblige than to protest.

When she wasn't hanging on me or playing with my friend's long hair, her booming voice could be heard over the music and the crowd, loudly abusing some other poor schnook. She alternated between personalities, like the changing colors of the traffic signal at the busy intersection.

I frequent many predominately-straight hangouts for the live music. But I feel lost amidst lushing ladies, yet equally as challenged in finding a prize amongst guys when drinking beers with the queers.

Is it the intoxicating tropical climate or the bountiful boozing that makes crossing Duval such a treacherous traversal?

(1/11/02)

For Pause

"Where is KC?"

It was bound to be something that I would confront when I moved back to my Key West neighborhood. I had just endured four months of such inquiries in Boston. The most upsetting of these queries came on the day I resumed my ESL tutoring, two weeks after the loss of KC, and the same week of my confirmed cancer diagnosis. In the wake of ten years of tutoring, this past summer, I had been working with a student who seemed to be my greatest teaching challenge yet. I have taught a broad spectrum of skill levels, but my current student was having an exceptionally rough time. My patience and abilities had always extended to the measures required for each student, as no two students have ever shown to have the same needs. But, for some reason, the summer of my greatest discontent found me working with an extremely nice middle-aged man who just was faced with more difficulty than any others I had tutored. Never before had I been unable to rise to this challenge. And as much as ever, I intended to achieve my teaching goals in spite of everything else in my life.

But that day arrived when my student entered my home and looked around. Immediately he noticed KC's absence. (This is testament to the magnificent presence my 10-pound companion always emanated.) Instinctively, my student asked the anticipated question; I choked. Unable to calmly respond, I tried to dismiss the subject. He persisted with this line of inquiry, despite his severe communication deficiencies. Clearly, he was concerned and bewildered. But I could not bring myself to vocalize an answer regarding the missing four paws, so I kept trying to divert his attention, and move into our lessons.

It was not just my inability to answer this specific question on this particular day. My paralysis, it seemed, extended to my capacity to resume my regular tutoring for the remainder of the season. I managed to get through that day's arduous session. But it was apparent to me that I hadn't the patience or fortitude to maintain the standard for which I had become known and admired. Ironically, just two weeks earlier, while KC was in the hospital, I had been the recipient of an award from this agency for recognition of my long and devoted service. I felt greatly honored and as committed as ever to continue my work.

But on that day when my student asked me the first question I was unable to answer, I realized that I could not meet the challenge required for an indefinite time to come. Reticently, I called the agency the following day and explained my situation. Although it was clearly accepted with the greatest of compassion, I felt another blow to my self-esteem. Looking back at it with what I now know, I also contend that if the grief hadn't usurped my teaching endeavors, the cancer treatments eventually would have done so.

On every other occasion when KC's absence was noticed, I was able to relate the sad news. But what I dreaded more than anything else, was the follow-up question in which I was asked if I would soon get another dog. Although I recognize that the inquirer's intention was benevolent and caring, I shuddered at the use of the often-used word "replace". I assumed that everyone should know better than to suggest that KC was "replaceable". Depending upon my current mood at receiving this question, I might vary my answer from polite, to admonishing, to curt. Besides, I adamantly insisted that I would never again have another dog in my life. My reasons were many, and if I felt the need, I would enumerate them:

"It would be unfair to any dog, as they would always be compared to the best;"

Or, "I could never stand going through such a devastating loss, ever again;"

Or, "I feel unfit to provide another dog with the love that I had for KC."

Fully aware that I would be subjected to the same inquiries and comments once resettled in Key West, I decided on an approach that would abruptly terminate any further questions. I carefully selected my words for the response of the inevitable question:

"The only way that I could ever envision another dog in my life is if KC were to place blatantly such a dog in my path. And I would be certain that it was clearly an obvious action of his purpose."

With all honesty, I truly intend to adhere to this vow. Having fully established confidence that the spirit of KC is still present in my life, I know this to be the most sincere reply I could provide.

30: Chicks and Cricks

In primary school, I was taught that four seasons comprise a single year. A revised definition for 'season' has altered that axiom. My Key West 'season' begins shortly after the last leaf on the tree by my front stoop in Boston surrenders to the forces of gravity and wintry winds. 'Season' ends around the time that the first lilac blooms in the Arnold Arboretum. Given this new equation, nearly four years have passed to coincide with my fourth "season."

Over this time, my view of Key West has evolved. There have been certain revelations, but Key West still exudes mystique.

I should have gained enough sophistication by now to have debunked the prevailing urban legend that once you are a resident long enough, the insects do not bite. If this is true, I sing the Snowbird's lament. This rule may only apply to year-round residents of the Rock. Perhaps my northern blood is still rich enough to entice thirsty flying parasites; alas, they do not pass me by for some red-blooded tourist.

This season, I immediately noticed something was definitely different in my neighborhood. I keep my windows open at night to let in the fresh air. A new audible component caught my attention: Crickets. Had I just never noticed them in my previous seasons in Key West? Not likely. Contrary to most people, I find chirping crickets to be somewhat disturbing. (It can probably be traced back to a childhood phobia that I developed at sleep-away camp in a rural setting. I cannot recall the relentless summer song of the little buggers in my suburban backyard.)

Things began to make sense once I also noticed the forlorn tone of the sad serenades of the sexually-unsatiated insomniac roosters, crowing mournfully for the missing hens. I hadn't given much thought previously to the mysterious disappearance of these bothersome birds. It had taken me two seasons to accept these foul, foraging fowl as neighbors. They would run amuck, strewing mulch over the pathways, accompanied by the high-pitched peeps of their ubiquitous broods. Somehow with their departure, the frustrated melancholic males were left behind. Now, more than ever before, Key West's night air is filled with the calls of horny cocks.

I cannot explain the sudden absence of the chickens. But theory has it that as annoying as they were, they dined on the insects, to include the now abundant crickets. Over the last two months, I have only encountered one squawking hen – and this was over by the courthouse. I considered that her presence in that location suggested that she was seeking a restraining order against the ambushing bush roosters.

Greg, of the tree service I had hired, informed me that the coconut trees in my yard were abundant with produce. I was exhilarated to learn that there were ripe nuts in my palms. I asked Greg to retrieve the precious tropical produce. Last year's experience, using every sharp implement in my toolbox, taught me that it would be a tough nut to crack. This is an unsafe occupation for a blind person to attempt. Last season's episode left me all cut up, just to inhale a rancid odor from the big bean. My hard work and pain only yielded a foul fruit. This year it would be different. The nut had been harvested right off the tree. Retrieving all the sharp tools previously employed to achieve this task, this time I included the all-purpose Ginsu knife. With far less personal damage, I managed to achieve my goal.

I feasted on the kosher milk and meat combination for nearly a week. It was the sweetest homegrown harvest in which I have ever indulged. I still await the appealing bananas from my tree to embellish my breakfast nook. Meanwhile, the alleged Papayas remain far out of reach. This is all so exotic for a boy from New York!

Now after four years, I am a more seasoned seasonal resident. I have learned the necessity to reduce systematically, the SPF over my first month of making tan while the sun shines. However, I still wind up with a one-sided tan (frontal) for lack of alternating my solar exposures. I have also noted that locals do not easily tolerate large temperature and weather fluctuations. A deviation of 5 degrees from the seasonal norm is like breaking the law. Most assume Key West is Camelot.

During 'season,' the weather usually does abide by this unwritten law. Most weeks, the TV meteorologist can take a vacation. The news stations can show re-runs of the previous week's forecast, and few would be any the wiser.

Warm winter weather was my primary draw to Key West. I find it odd that so many locals and tourists stay in their refrigerated (air-conditioned) rooms and eat in refrigerated restaurants. When I wake up to a sweet, sunny 72-degree morning, I resent the loud hum of nearby air conditioners drowning out the sounds of nature. The noise also pervades the night air, after the daytime temperature falls. Why not open a window?

Aren't the night sounds of loud and rowdy

roosters, crickets and the occasional catfight worth the fresh florally-fragrant balmy breezes?

As for me, if I could learn to tolerate the clattering cluckers, I suppose that I will come to accommodate the clicking crickets.

(1/18/02)

Deputy Kevin

Sometime around the early-Passover season of 2002 (Jewish Holidays never come "on time;" they are either considered "early" or "late" each year), I found myself asking the traditional rhetorical question, "Why is this night different from all other nights?"

This line was not being recalled in the context of the holiday ritual. Rather, my contemplation was inspired by an odd set of events which caught me off guard.

One evening, I had been having a beer in the front bar of a local hangout. Sitting on a barstool next to a tourist, we had been engaged in a lively and interesting conversation for nearly one hour. When my new acquaintance excused himself to leave, I decided to find my way to the adjacent barroom within the same establishment. As I am a familiar face here, the manager of the bar approached me and offered to assist me to my destination, up one step and through a set of swinging doors. We exchanged friendly chatter as he guided me to an available stool at the far end of the bar. This corner was the frequent location of a regular local patron, Kevin. A tall, relatively quiet man, he could always be counted on to claim the same bar stool as his domain. He was often so quiet that I would not know of his presence until I might inadvertently hit his rather large feet with my leather boot. Then he would sarcastically say something in response, and I suddenly became aware of his proximity.

On this particular evening, the manager who had escorted me to this spot, chose to give an explicit directive to Kevin. As I turned to order a beer from Billy, the bartender, I was unaware of their brief exchange.

When I eventually learned of the manager's command, I was a bit surprised and disturbed. The manager had insisted that Kevin make certain that, when I was to depart for home, I must be overseen being put into a taxicab. I clearly was not intoxicated, nor did I have the reputation to become so. It was merely an honest concern for my security.

Kevin had been deputized. He accepted this role like a military order and demanded my absolute compliance. When I inquired as to the purpose of such a sudden concern, Kevin remarked that "when someone makes the headlines" as I had, it should mandate an urgent response. He was referring to my much-publicized confrontation with the police during the previous season.

My immediate reaction was vexing – I felt somewhat offended. The reason for my resentment this particular evening was that I had been walking home by myself for nearly one year since the episode with the cops. I tried to point out to Kevin that this had happened over 10 months ago and this evening was the first time that anyone expressed such dire concern for my safety. I had appreciated the conveyed senti-ment by the manager and this patron, but I also felt annoyed. Why was there no such similar reaction immediately follow-ing the news headlines last spring? Irritation also stemmed from the feeling that I was being treated like a child. Unin-tentionally, this demand was further depriving me of my sense of control. Through my stated response to this sudden impo-sition, I clearly acknowledged the good intentions of both the manager and his deputy.

After the manager had walked away, I was constantly conscious of the odd feeling that my anointed bodyguard was keeping steadfast vigil. Kevin frequently spoke out to remind me of his surveillance duty. The declared limitations on my freedom as an adult were more of an obtrusion, nearly insulting. I began to take this all very personally, resenting the stigma that drew such unwarranted attention. Was I being unduly assessed as incapable of self-preservation, or lacking common sense to take necessary precautions? Despite their good intent, I felt this action had expressed little confidence in me; I was being viewed as a victim. Was I just being stubborn or ungrateful?

For the past year, in response to a high level of paranoia, I had kept a small knife on my night stand for a sense of security. I had also acquired a "rape whistle" to carry, after recently getting in the middle of a shoving match while walking down a crowded sidewalk in front of a notorious nightclub. When a female voice approached me during this scuffle, and identified herself as a police officer willing to drive me home, I refused her offer; partly out of mistrust and fear, mingled with doubts as to why she was more focused on me than on breaking up the rowdy, offensive mob.

Now, under the gaze of Deputy Kevin, I was becoming further annoyed with the feeling of repression as the evening wore on. I pointed out that I was not planning on leaving alone on that night. But, nonetheless, I felt pressured to submit to these intrusions. It was slightly embarrassing to explain this to the man with whom I had made arrangements to leave together.

After an initial flurry of headlines that followed the arresting episode, I was no longer front-page news. The only head lines were those creases on my forehead from anxiety. Nearly one full year had since passed. I was still struggling to cope with the lingering effects. Engaging therapists and lawyers, I had been evaluating all legal issues and ethical obligations. Although the events of the police incident still troubled me daily, they had become further entangled with a host of more recent personal woes.

The March 30th incident had become my own private hell, less of a community issue. The world-at-large turned its attention toward more current events; many were larger in scope and profoundly horrifying.

I continued to strive to heal and regain focus and control in my life (although destiny had appeared to throw many more punches in my direction). Albeit slowly, strides were measurable in my goal to reclaim a sense of normalcy. It remains unclear whether time was contributing to the healing process, or if I was just becoming more resilient.

But here it was one year later and the festival of Passover had come around again. Traditionally, it is a celebration of freedom and renewal. I had no desire to be on the table as the Sacrificial Lamb.

31. Blind Vanity

"Nice tie-dyed tee shirt!"

I had not known what I'd been wearing that evening, and couldn't tell from his tone, if his remark was sincere or sarcastic. Had I committed a major fashion *faux pas?* Ill-suited attire can be a casualty of choosing garments by touch alone. I was recently complimented on the fine color match of my tee shirt and sweatshirt. Pure coincidence, a lucky roll of the dice.

I stand and reflect in front of the full-length mirror. The glass gives me no feedback. It may as well be a blank canvas. I use my imagination to conjure up my image based on what clothes I think I chose. It helps that I had been previously sighted.

Once I arrive at my destination, whether it is a concert hall, theater, nightclub or restaurant, I am never certain if I selected appropriate apparel. Halfway through the evening, I often ask my companion: "What am I wearing?" or else, "What is everyone else wearing?" By then, it is too late to change attire.

Blindness and vanity are at odds. Adhering to the look in GQ or IM would be a difficult goal. But I am not overly concerned. I may be so out of style that it is seen as cutting-edge or Retro. When I need to shop for clothes, I must be in the company of a good and trustworthy friend. It is frequently assumed that the province of acceptable good taste is a gay male's domain.

I've traced back this phenomenon. During the development of the species Homo Sapien, the merging of two branches in the evolutionary tree, *Homo Sartoris and **Homo Epicurus,

*Sartoris: devotee of fashionable attire
**Epicurus: devotee of refined taste, particularly in food and wine

was responsible for the rise of Homo Erectus, and the lineage of gay DNA (i.e. Homo Sexual).

Historically, this emergence in human culture probably coincided with the Lascaux cave paintings, discovered in France. The paleolithic-era caveman who left us this archeological marvel was probably gay. He looked at the bare rock and thought the place needed a touch of personal décor. Hence, as the first Interior Decorator, he was an innovator in creating a very enticing vocation for sensitive young boys. Additional circumstantial evidence as to his sexual orientation is his chosen location: to display his artwork near the trendy vacation spots in the south of France.

Fifteen thousand years of design have refined accepted good taste. The only problem is that it gets revised at least once every seven years. Oddly, it appears that the commitment one has to one's stylish wardrobe happens to coincide with the average length of a "long-term" love relationship.

What has become known as "gay-dar" is a vital instrument in the operation of gay culture. (For the unfamiliar, "gay-dar" is a linguistic derivative of "radar." It is the subtle or not so subtle clues received through instinctive intuition to detect the sexual orientation of a total stranger.)

No longer is it accurate to depend on the stereotyped lisp and limp-wristed mannerisms. It has been replaced over the last two decades with a new stereotype: fashionable taste in clothes, accessories and hair styles, gym physiques, one's selected profession and the brand name on his underwear. A combination of these indicators is usually quite reliable. A sighted friend recently confided that it is getting harder to tell merely by appearances. As gay men are usually fashion frontiersmen, the trends seep into hetero culture. If the subject is younger than 26, he probably isn't even sure of his own sexuality. Another friend related to me that everyone in his theater group incorrectly speculated as to the sexual orientation of a cast member. All were caught by surprise when he introduced his (female) girlfriend.

Blindness has impaired my gay-dar dish, obscuring all visual clues. Clothing, looks and projected attitudes pass by undetected. When recently told that I had been getting "checked out" at the gym, it brought to my attention how clueless I could be. Missed opportunities. Instead of being informed of this afterwards, it would have been more of a service if someone had taken down names and numbers for me.

Eroticism, a blatant component of gay male culture, is a visually-dominated expression, as are drag shows. Sightlessness precludes me from fully appreciating many of this island's social and entertainment events.

Drag performances may be only one gay contribution to pop culture. But it has certainly found an audience here in Key West, where straight tourists flock to fill the seats. I suppose it is a novelty for many visitors to this exotic city. The visual illusion created by these queens of the stage is lost on me. Guys in disguise as theatrical icons may as well look more like Rodney Dangerfield or Buddy Hackett, but if they sound like Judy Garland or Billy Holiday, I can still be fairly entertained.

Projecting a false image is only a pretense. Vanity can also be very superficial. Pre-judgment based on images can be a mistake, a missed opportunity.

Many people are hesitant to approach me, as a blind man, because they feel intimidated or awkward. I attempt to convey that no one should feel uncomfortable around disabled persons. In my case, look beyond my cheap shades and battered cane and find the real man. I have no intent to present any illusions.

(1/25/02)

Karma

On the last Wednesday in January 2002, I was sitting across the kitchen table from my friend, Susan. We were sorting through my accumulated mail. The telephone rang. Dee, my social worker/case manager here in Key West, was on the other end. She had just received an odd request, which she wished to share with me. A friend of hers, Dawn, who worked for a veterinarian, had called Dee regarding an unusual situation. One of the doctor's clients had a female Yorkshire Terrier that died in giving birth. The 2-year-old Yorkie left behind two orphaned male puppies. As they could not nurse from the mother, they would require special hand-feeding in order to be weaned. Dawn was well-acquainted with Dee's nurturing nature and her reputed inclination for saving troubled animals. So, Dawn had approached Dee to inquire if she could possibly provide some support in this effort.

As I listened in awe, I couldn't determine whether or not Dee was asking me to play a role in this effort, or just wanted to convey this information for reasons of her own. But, I intuitively felt certain that this situation was a message from KC. It felt as if KC had intended for me to adopt one of these orphaned puppies. He had been witnessing my intense grief and loneliness over the last five months. His love and loyalty had survived.

As Susan sat across the table from me behind a pile of

unopened mail, I became overwhelmed with emotion. Tears came to my eyes, and I lost my voice for a moment. Something extraordinary was occurring. As Dee spoke, my mind went into a whirlwind of incoming thoughts. I could not focus on what Dee was saying, but it seemed apparent that I must interrupt her.

"Dee," I said, "I think this is a clear sign from KC. I am a little scared to say it, but I feel that I am meant to adopt one of those puppies."

By the time I hung up the phone, any doubts were erased from my mind. Susan witnessed my sense of wonder as I recounted to her the situation.

Subsequent conversations with Dee provided me further evidence that this event was preconceived in a metaphysical realm. After I had told Dee that KC expected me to adopt one of the puppies, she revealed that someone within her agency had since come forth and generously offered to pay the breeder for the puppy. This individual wanted to remain unidentified and had only come to know KC and me from our published columns in "Celebrate!" I was astounded, but not unlike my reaction when the anonymous donor came forward to pay KC's hospital expenses, I knew it was necessary to accept graciously.

For many years, particularly after losing my eyesight, I had been unable to accept gifts or assistance in any form. Ironically, this was during the period when I was most in need. But I have come to realize that the same acquired wisdom applies to *me* that I wrote about in "People Who Need People." The lesson I should have internalized is that giving is frequently far more rewarding than receiving; to refuse a giver is to deny their intrinsic role to manifest their fundamental essential benevolence.

Now, a very special puppy was conspicuously being placed in my path. Arrangements and logistical details were being attended. The breeder of the puppies was very concerned about their welfare, and revised her original notion. Despite her own grief stemming from her loss, she decided to raise the puppies until they were three months of age, in order to oversee personally their proper care and immunizations. Additionally, she was very anxious that the orphaned pups find homes with the appropriate recipients. Dee held many conversations with her, and was very convincing that this was all meant to be. Dee prodigiously related to the breeder how this puppy would fulfill its true destiny as my new companion. There could be no better life in store for the specially-selected Yorkshire Terrier, who the breeder had informally dubbed "Mister Personality." (Guess which other dog in my life had acquired this nickname by his league of admirers!)

It was essential that I wait about eight more weeks until I could receive this blessed gift into my home. A new sense of agitation took root deep inside me. My therapist had suggested that I was experiencing the anxiety of an expectant father, a view with which I could concur. I prayed that KC's plan would be fulfilled successfully. Once I looked ahead to this life-changing event, I kept worrying that something could go awry. After all, consider the record of my previous twelve-month period. I was too nervous even to speak to others of this anticipated occasion. Although it was difficult to keep silent, I wanted to manage my expectations so that I could not suffer another severe disappointment. In the meantime I would need to prepare for the eventuality.

I shared the prospective news with very few people, only those who truly knew that KC was capable of such a fantastic design. Mark sent me gifts from Boston for the puppy. This only made me more nervous that destiny would cruelly intervene once again. But I proceeded to make preparations.

I spent countless hours securing the yard. KC had once burrowed under the fence between my yard and the adjacent property when we first occupied this unit. It took me a long time to figure out where his cries of confusion originated. Immediately after I rescued KC from his plight, I bricked up the tiny escape route. Not that KC's curiosity would ever again allow him to make this mistake twice.

This young puppy would not yet be trained or sophisticated enough to recognize the potential dangers of his own curiosity. On the days prior to his anticipated arrival, I surveyed the yard for any potential hazards. The biggest chore I undertook was on the morning of his expected homecoming, Sunday, March 17th. I needed to secure the gap between the earth and the raised wooden deck, as I feared him nosing his way under the deck and becoming trapped in this enclosed space. Hours of sweat and labor eventually assured me that the space was as fortified as possible to prevent such an incident. As I worked in the yard under the hot sun, I spoke with KC, and prayed for the ultimate success of his plan.

When I finally reached Dee on her cell phone in the mid-afternoon, it was confirmed that they were both safely on their way, southbound through the chain of the Florida Keys (still several hours away). I finally felt a bit more relaxed, knowing that the puppy I was to name "Karma David," was close enough to be real. Remembering that I had no collar or leash for my new companion, I felt it was now okay to leave the house and seek them out along Duval Street. I did not know where I could purchase these items, so I set out for a particular retailer that I knew carried an eclectic array of merchandise.

As I walked into the store, I was greeted by someone who claimed to know me. She identified herself, and I was amused to learn that she was the wacky young woman who forcefully dragged me onto the dance floor three months earlier (the one I referred to in "Crossing Duval"). On this special day, she appeared sober and more lucid. I presented my dilemma, but the store was not stocked with the kind of items which I needed, nor could anyone present clue me in on where to find such supplies. When I told her that Karma was a very small puppy and that I would resort to finding a creative temporary solution, she suggested that I use a belt or a string of beads. My mind searched my house and I recalled my vast collection of Mardi Gras beads that hung on a hook in my bathroom.

I went home, intent on this new project to occupy the remaining waiting hours. Karma's first leash would be fashioned out of a product of Key West's ubiquitous symbol of celebration. This would appropriately suffice for now.

Approximately three hours later, I nervously waited in my newly puppy-proofed home. Time slowed to a crawl. I was too nervous to eat. It had been five hours since I had spoken with Dee by telephone. I paced my small living room (which is no easy feat for a blind man – without bumping into walls) like a typical expectant daddy in a maternity ward. At 8:30 p.m., the doorbell finally rang. I rushed to answer the call. Dee entered carrying a small nylon sack containing my new son. I backed into the living room as she released the precious cargo of the travel bag. I knelt down on the floor, and was immediately leapt upon by a tiny bundle of soft, furry joy. Karma fervently licked me everywhere with his little wet tongue; and I laughed and cried with happiness. It was like a long-awaited reunion of two parted lovers. Dee and her boyfriend stood by to witness an incredible outpouring of excitement and joyous passion from both Karma and me. These specially-appointed couriers could attest that this puppy knew me and understood that I was to be his daddy. Had KC instilled this message in him? Was this passionate greeting being relayed by KC through his spiritual progeny?

It is now one week later. I love Karma David incredibly. I also have learned a new definition of a word that I have used frequently before: "challenging." A blind man attempting to house-break a three-month-old puppy! Is it impossible? Not when one's dedication to the task is motivated with love.

Two days after this most memorable St. Patrick's Day, I sat down and composed the letter below to the anonymous gift giver:

Dear Friend,

Miracles cannot happen without the presence of angelic catalysts.

Being responsible for another precious living being is the greatest impetus to push forward through life's most turbulent challenges.

Recently, after a long string of tumultuous events, my vision became so distorted that the tasks of daily living appeared as a monumental obstacle for rediscovering peace and joy. Without enumerating these incidents, I assure you that the depth of my misfortune was uncanny. 2001 saw me through a period fraught with an incredible series of blows. The most devastating of all was the loss of my dearest canine companion, KC. Over the previous twelve years, KC had been there to teach me how to rekindle the fortitude that I would need to cope. I have written so much over the many years about his wisdom, and his innate ability to touch so many lives besides my own. Only KC could bring me peace or make me laugh when I had come to believe that nothing but misery lay in store for me.

It is not an exaggeration when I say that he saved my life. When I lost my sight, I was so distraught that I felt there was no reason to go on. But KC saw this and snuggled up to me to remind me of the vow I had made seven years earlier. In 1989 I had adopted him and promised to stay with him for all of his life. So, in 1996, when I was very sick and had completely lost my eyesight, he reminded me of this pledge. He was my incentive to find a future in the darkest of times.

The year 2001 literally and figuratively knocked me over repeatedly. Included among my losses was the greatest gift that the Universe had ever placed in my life. Two weeks after losing the special being that had saved my life, I faced the prospect of combating cancer. My depression was so severe that I could not cogently make the choices necessary to confront this new challenge. I spoke to KC and prayed for him to send me some of his wisdom. I grieved over the loss of his physical presence, but soon grew aware of his spiritual presence in my world. This gave me some comfort, but I still ached for our close earthly relationship.

I have no doubt that KC saw me crying out to him in pain, and he was able to do what he had done so many times before. He sought to gather all the finest components to bring light back into my life. KC selected you for your compassion and generosity to play a pivotal role in this Divine plan.

I write to you with my deepest gratitude and admiration for exemplifying the finest attributes of humanity. After a long period of losing faith in people and goodness, I have once again been enlightened that there are angels in our lives, who caress us in our worst of times.

Nothing I can ever write could adequately express my feelings of thanks – for your loving kindness and, in turn, the vitality that it has generated within my soul. Your benevolent act has awakened in me the will to survive and has inspired me to continue the chain of spreading hope and goodness to others.

On Sunday, March 17, 2002, Karma David came into my life. The boundless energy and exuberance of this puppy can only be matched by his instant sense of loyalty and remarkable expression of love. I am no longer alone. As he will forever be a part of my life, so will you for making all this possible.

I recognize that Karma is not a replacement for KC. There can never be a substitute for KC. I was not eager to get another dog, partly out of deference for KC, and a host of many fears. First, I was afraid to love ever again, as the loss brought on a grief as large as was my love, and I feared I could never endure such pain ever again. Additionally, I did not want to be unfair to another dog, as I feared the temptation to always compare him to KC. Lastly, I was reticent to make that vow again: to stay present for the lifetime of another companion.

But, KC allayed all these fears, as it was so clear to me that this set of circumstances was all part of his will. He heard how I was responding to queries about getting another dog: "The only way I would have another dog in my life is if KC, himself, clearly places this life in the path of my own journey." He also knew that I could only have another Yorkshire Terrier. And, it seems that is exactly what has occurred. I believe that only KC could have contrived such a set of circumstances.

It's not going to be easy as a blind man living alone to raise a puppy into adulthood, but I have learned that nothing of true value ever comes easy.

Karma and I thank you for bringing us together. It once again proves that only love can restore hope.
Sincerely,
Rob

Stand by Your dog ...

You can be certain your dog will always stand by you. KC certainly did, even from across the great divide. His gift of finding me a new companion was noble, putting aside any jealousy in order to help me rediscover faith.

Shortly after KC succumbed last summer, I was directed to a woman, also named Dawn, who was an "Animal Communicator." She had been recommended by the director of the Phinney's Friends program. I called Dawn last October with a sense of mild skepticism, but intense curiosity. Over the telephone, I relayed my well-prepared questions and several statements, which I wished to convey to KC. Dawn replied to my queries by assuring me that KC was safe and content, and that he had heard all the words and thoughts that I had been directing toward him since his departure. After this conversation with Dawn, I still was not wholly convinced, but I did feel a clearer sense of KC's continued presence in my life.

Now it is my turn to stand by my dog – this time that dog is Karma. I stand for hours each day on the sidewalk beside Emma Street while he loiters around in the grassy apron near the curb. Everything is new to him. I ask KC to send him some guidance in how a dog must learn some very vital behavior. As Karma stands up to his shoulders in the soft grass, I can feel that he is perplexed as to what I am expecting of him.

"Please, KC," I whisper softly, "Teach Karma what he needs to learn."

As I cannot see what he does during these outings, I am unable to know when praise is due. So I constantly speak to him and express my love, hoping that this will properly inspire him and eventually convey my will. Again, I am being forced to learn patience – this time while I stand by my dog.

A New Daddy…

"Karma, I am your Daddy, not a chew toy!"

There is so much for Karma to learn. But it warms my heart to hear once again the crunch of kibble at my feet. And Karma does love to eat!

Karma nibbles.

Karma nibbles kibble.

Karma nibbles Eukanuba kibble.

You can view Karma nibble his Eukanuba kibble.

You can view Karma carefully nibble the crunchy Eukanuba kibble at his kitchen dish.

Karma's kitchen dish of crunchy kibble keeps Karma busy contentedly nibbling.

Karma is happy.

So is his Daddy.

Web Defeat

Sometimes I think that a blind individual trying to navigate through cyberspace might as well be trekking around the far reaches of outer space. We have the technology, but our institutions lack the social imperative. I have previously recounted the difficulties of a blind man traveling public sidewalks, at an ATM, in a theater or a restaurant. As it is, physical environments are fraught with plenty of concrete barriers and obstacles. The less tangible ether-world of the Internet attempts to connect us all democratically to the information super-highway. Yet, the tangle of on-ramps, road signage and breakdown lanes have excluded some of us who would benefit from this access the most.

Now that conventional stationery and postal service can be substituted by an electronic mailbox, a checkbook can be replaced by on-line banking, and computer application software can simulate the essential purpose of address books, notepads, ledgers and file cabinets, the high-tech world has opened many passageways to the disabled. Unfortunately, computers crash for unknown reasons, cannot spit out cash withdrawals, and Internet sites are designed primarily for visual interaction. Adaptive technology to retrofit a standard home computer adds considerable financial burdens and incredible user complications. Gooey Phooey!!

True, it has opened many doors; unfortunately some

of the thresholds are impassable. These last several years have made me ever more dependent on this unreliable and mystifying means of reaching out to interact with the world outside my home. E-mail flies through cyberspace to bring me news, both good and bad, and allows me to stay connected with friends, family and business associates. But it has also opened the door to a deluge of time-consuming e-junk. Listening to e-mail newsletters is far more tedious than visually scanning those papers that clog our mailboxes and crowd our coffee tables. Accessing current news and listings via the Net is a far cry from reading the local rag in the corner coffee shop or perusing the aisles of the public library. It might be easier to catch the gnus (wildebeast) on the African plains than to catch the news on the Internet.

My first forays into the snare of the World Wide Web was several years back. Although my earlier career was as a professional computer application specialist, I barely tiptoed into the world of LANs and WANs, the forerunners of today's Internet. I had mainly thought of "servers" as waiters or waitresses and webs related more to spiders or duck feet.

Then, with the advent of blindness, my life changed suddenly with little warning. I needed more answers than ever before, yet the means to find them became vastly inaccessible and elusive. Recall my confrontations with health and legal issues. Consider my recent ventures into the world of publication, financial investment activity, ESL tutoring and medical research. Each warranted diving deeper into the murky waters of the swampy World Wide Web. I was the gullible rainbow trout chasing the fly and heading directly into the fisherman's net. Like the unsuspecting fish, I became ensnared by the invisible intricacies of the Web.

There is enough information out there to assist the courageous (or foolish) explorer, but too much information is as stupefying as too little (information). As I dangle precariously in cyberspace, I get too dizzy to find my way back home to Mission Control. And after I enter this mysterious, meandering maze, have I retrieved what I set out to find in the first place? Or have I just passed many irretrievable hours of my life in pursuit of the Cheshire Catfish of the data pool? When I do find a few tidbits of useful information, I need to clip it out and save it within my myriad of computer pigeonholes. What I stashed away and where I secured it is another mind-boggling mesh of memory matrices.

My e-mail must get sorted into dozens of encoded electronic mailboxes. Documents need to be assigned to reside among numerous named computer-file folders. Personal data, numbers, listings, directions, contact information, schedules and records get catalogued inside a computer hard disc smaller than a (tiny) bread box. Harsh lessons from the past have taught me to make frequent backup copies, which then also must be labeled tactically and tactilely in my physical realm. With ever-increasing crashes of the Windows interface, software applications shatter and leave me in an eerie silence. I then find myself picking out the splintered shards of fragmented files and licking my wounds – only to reboot the machine, reopen the windows and assess the damage.

The events of this past eighteen months have drawn me repeatedly to my laptop's keyboard. To avail myself of the copious amounts of information that cram cyberspace with almost everything a citizen needs to know, I waded into the Internet swamp. Then I mostly just waited. Search engines queried me for criteria. Yet, each one had its own protocols regarding key-word syntax. If I were fortunate enough to phrase my search correctly, it would sprint across the Web in order to retrieve speculative leads as to where I should wander next in my quest. I may sit and stare at the computer monitor for slivers of eternity, awaiting an audible completion of this task. (Staring at the monitor is just an old habit, as I have no visual clue as to what is being displayed.) The monitor may be staring back at me, anthropomorphically speaking, awaiting my response, as it assumes I am tuned in with the status of this task. Perhaps it returned with a message, but did not inform my ears. Perhaps it gathered hundreds of leads that I would need to sort through individually. Visually, this process may be rather simple. But, with ears for eyes, I often must audibly inspect each site to determine whether it is relevant to my inquiry. Then I encounter the tangle of sites with hyperlinks that either don't work properly or lead me in circular ramblings or down dead-end paths.

I may spend hours in this fruitless meandering, only to find myself back to where I began, hours before. It's a plain fact that most web site designers do not adhere to recommended established specifications set by organizations that publish accessibility standards. As a result, I find some web sites are usable and others are totally baffling. At times, my frustration level slowly mounts and leaves me exhausted and enraged. After all, I simply want to be able to shop on line, track reliable information resources or conduct business through the Internet, as can most consumers, seekers and surfers. But when it requires a sighted person sitting next to me to guide me through the maze, it negates the whole purpose of the Internet. I scream for independence, but my calls are clouded and diminished in the digital darkness.

"PC," as an acronym, has two current connotations: "personal computer" and "politically correct." Sadly, the PC as an appliance is not PC, in that it does not guarantee equal opportunity to all.

When I relate my frustrating forays into financial, government, retail or research sites to others, I am often encouraged to take up this "accessibility issue" with the appropriate institution or web host. As a sightless suitor, I am well-suited to cite many an unsightly site unsuitable for the excited sightless. If I could clone myself, I would surely have enough causes to keep a battalion of "Robs" busy. But, as there is but one of me to assert my quest for justice, I must select my causes with care. Life saps me of enough energy just getting through a week.

KC taught me that I must take some time to stop and sniff once in a while. And then he sent me Karma David to keep this lesson fresh in my mind. So when I find myself snagged in the cyberspace spider web, it's time to take a break, and rest my weary wings. And if the hungry Internet arachnid approaches, it's as simple as logging off (until tomorrow).

Alt, Control, Delete!!

The Jailor

HEADLINE: "EX-JAILBIRD TURNS JAILOR"

I'm sick of sick irony! This former Jailbird has now be-come the Jailor. However, the current situation is very unlike my own personal detention experience. In reluctantly assuming this role, my heart is broken from hearing the desperate cries emanat-ing from the holding cell in the next room. The major difference, in this case, is that I *love* the one whom I am forced to confine. There was *no* love last season, when I was the inmate at the county jail. Now, my imprisoned one is sad and confused about these newly-imposed restrictions on his freedom. So am I. The forlorn wails and pitiful cries are unsettling – and these are just my own! Karma David's vocal displeasure with this new arrangement is equally as unnerving.

Flashbacks of my incarceration over one year ago haunt me, vividly recalling the severe agitation this sudden, unexpected loss of freedom can evoke.

1. THE INSIDE POOP

When Karma first came into my life, I was told that he had already been housebroken. This proved to be untrue. I believed that I could accomplish this mission myself. This also proved to be untrue. As it has always been my natural inclination to be a problem-solver, it was characteristic for me to take this tact. But, following one month of discovering

Karma's post-processed kibble as little stinky presents on the rug, I finally recognized that, what I was finding present between my toes and on the soles of my sandals, was certainly not the sweet smell of success. Therefore, as in many previous situations, I had come to accept that I must seek outside assistance. Once this was clearly evident, I sought to find someone who could help me rectify this messy problem.

Karma's initial freedom to roam out back had turned my yard into his personal poop deck. I had tried to entice him to appreciate the allure of the earthy enclosed side yard, but he quickly learned to slip stealthily past me and bound up the steps to the preferable wooden deck. This cunning maneuver should have been an obvious omen as to his own inclination toward self-determination.

Progress was elusive, desperation mounted. Committed to apply any tactic that was suggested, I eagerly submitted to any advice offered. Along the fence, I liberally sprinkled droplets of a very foul-smelling product specially formulated to inspire doggies to do their duty. Then I would stand amidst the stench in the side yard with Karma on a very short leash for 15-minute durations at two-hour intervals, and immediately following any consumption of kibble. As I stood over him, I continuously fed him firm words of encouragement to promote productivity. I attempted to foster an affinity for the mulch surrounding the palm trees. The leash imposed forcible restraint to deter Karma from an immediate retreat to the wooden deck.

Alas, as it has been growing late in the season, the advent of summer weather brings high humidity and mosquito-drenched air. Every winged insect within miles swarmed to investigate the source of the new stink on the block. This made for a very uncomfortable climate for our frequent ventures, diminishing my patience and endurance. Despite generous applications of insect repellent, I still appeared to any species of bloodthirsty insects as an open bar at an Irish wake. Subsequent administration of topical antihistamine lotion to my itching, ravaged skin did little to mitigate my fear and loathing of these outings.

Conceding the requisite of sighted assistance was what led me to the current situation. But, even after conceiving a plan, successful execution is not guaranteed.

I solicited advice in seeking someone to assume the role of co-trainer. The word went out from everyone with whom I have contact. Slowly there were a few nibbles in my fishing expedition. Several initial attempts left me without success. These liaisons included: a local support organization, a con man that claimed to be a dog trainer and a seven-year-old girl from the neighborhood (whose motivation stemmed from her mom, who eagerly wanted the child to overcome her fear of dogs). None of these efforts resulted in success.

After recognizing that the bed was a safe zone, on which I could rely on Karma to keep clean, I was grateful that he was too small and fearful to dismount this soft, lofty plateau. The carpeted floor, an appealing place for him to unload, was in plain sight but just out of his reach. Unfortunately, this "safe zone" was only acceptable to him as long as his daddy was also present. When I left the room, yelps of angry protest were his method of manipulation. Was I to become hostage to this three-pound dictator?

Who would come to my rescue, where could they be found, and what course of action would be prescribed?

Eventually, I located the one person on this island who was reputed to have the skill and credentials to tackle this problem. His name came to me via several sources as a result of my networking. If anyone could handle this situation, it was Raul! He generously offered to meet Karma and me in our home. Raul was quick to size up my little furry housemate. He observed an intelligent and attentive dog with a daddy challenged to provide the constant vigilance such a task requires. The problem of a blind man, trying to enforce the necessary disciplines to achieve the desired result, was particularly enigmatic to Raul. But he appeared encouraging and optimistic, exhibiting a zealous interest in resolving this stinky issue.

Based on the premise that a dog will not foul his personal space, he suggests that I keep Karma confined to a small, designated indoor area for the next three days, aside from his outdoor interludes. These excursions will provide Karma his only opportunity to pee and poop. Under normal circumstances, after being observed doing his business outside, the dog is rewarded with limited house freedom (under close, visual scrutiny). But when taking Karma out for this purpose, even with a mere three feet of lead between us, I cannot track urinary conduct or ascertain bowel movements. Nor would I be able to catch him at the exact moment of inappropriate toilet activities in the house. Therefore, sadly, little Karma cannot be trusted to enjoy any unrestricted indoor freedom. So, constant confinement for three days is my best bet for having a housebroken housemate. I am to check back in with Raul at the end of the week with a report.

It is unfortunate that it has come to employing this draconian tactic, but teaching Karma the house rules of elimination etiquette has proven to be a task beyond my capability. At the advice of this renowned expert, I must defer to this counter-intuitive measure in order to regain the control in this new relationship. As nothing else so far has worked, this prescribed remedy has been nearly guaranteed to produce the results, which will, in the long term, be vital for future happiness. Karma must learn the real poop!

2. A SHORT PUPPY-DOG TAIL OF WOE

Day 1. . .

Several small cardboard boxes and a violin case are wedged beneath the bed frame and the floor. One larger box blocks the gap between the bed and the closet door. This contrived formation delineates the enclosed area containing Karma's puppy bed. The six-square-feet of floor space, created by this enclosure, defines my puppy's small indoor universe. Although well-stocked with toys and a water bowl,

Karma is certainly not pleased with this new arrangement. He is determined to let it be known.

The pitiful wails of sorrow and piercing yelps cut painfully into my heart. They are as sharp as his little puppy teeth, gnawing at me like his tenacious jaw whittling on a chew toy.

Day 2. . .

I feel compelled to flee the house, to be out of range of his mournful moaning. It is uncertain who weeps more – Karma or me. This is a very unhappy situation for us both. If I stay away from home for several hours, I will not be subjected constantly to his upsetting sounds of sorrow. Besides, he probably sleeps during my absence, reducing his own personal stress. I also need to find a respite from the stress.

Day 3. . .

"No walls can hold me!!"

Proud of his great escapes, it has now become a contest of wits between the Houdini puppy and me. Karma has now accepted my diligent efforts to wall him in behind obstacles as a challenge. As soon as the plush puppy penitentiary in the corner of the bedroom is further fortified to my satisfaction, he immediately goes to work to tunnel or climb out of confinement. Within moments, he arrives at my feet as I sit at my computer in the next room, as if to boast smugly, "That was a good try, silly human, but I outsmarted you again. Care to go another round?"

(I wish I had had him as a cellmate one year earlier.)

Day 4. . .

Concede defeat. I have reported in with the dog-training expert (Raul) to apprise him of the current status. The attempt to reform Karma's conduct through confinement lost its initial aim once he came to view this as a contest. Raul has since contacted his own gurus and has returned with no clear alternative solution. As I plan on returning to Boston in two weeks, where I will have dependable, voluntary round-the-clock sighted assistance, Raul suggests that Karma and I return to our previous state of détente. We should enjoy peacefully the remainder of our stay in Florida. He can see no reason to foster hard feelings through this battle of wills. Besides, if I could live with the small inconvenience of peanut-size poops for a short time longer, our mutual growing bond will suffer no long-term harm.

Raul was right. By this time, Karma has narrowed his preferred locations of inside misdeeds to only two distinct locations. If I tread cautiously through these zones, I can well manage the inconvenience without too much anguish.

It is clearly time to throw in the proverbial towel. Unlike, in the more literal sense, my surrender two weeks earlier, when I learned to accept that the bath mat was not destined to remain adjacent to the tub. Karma had developed an ardent fixation to employ it as a doormat for his puppy bed. At every opportunity, he would drag the heavy towel from the bathroom into the bedroom. This standoff also resulted in Karma's ultimate victory.

The $64,000 question is one without a clearly-evident answer:

How does a blind person, living alone, train a quick-witted, independent-minded puppy to be housebroken? Apparently, it is a situation that has never before been knowingly confronted, resolved or documented.

3. KC's Karma

Having demonstrated that I was willing to go to Mosquito Hell and back to achieve this mandatory goal, I accepted the notion that I was braving a new frontier. Failure was not an option. Nor could I decline the compulsory challenge, as it was clear that KC had confidence that this was only another hurdle which I needed to confront in order to make my life whole again. At every turn, I was reminded that this was all part of KC's scheme.

It seems obvious to everyone who knew KC that Karma is his spiritual progeny. Karma, like KC, is extraordinarily personable, bold, funny, clever and affectionate. Repeatedly, instances of Karma's behavior appear incredibly reminiscent of that of KC. And then, there is the phenomenon of the re-appearing toys. KC bequeathed these gifts to be passed along to Karma. In this instance, there were several playthings in which KC never demonstrated a great deal of interest, although playing was one of his outstanding talents. As if to bestow an inheritance from his spiritual father, these pristine items mysteriously surfaced from out of nowhere. Karma discovered these long-forgotten, misplaced toys. Karma cherishes them with abandon, knowing from whom they have been sent. Karma revels in the *Squeaky Muffin* and the *Daily Growl.*

Aside from enduring insect attacks, severe exhaustion and being diverted from my regular production schedule, I have the mixed blessing of being seen with the new, irresistible, adorable puppy every time I take him outside. He relishes the attention that is showered upon him. Likely, these constant distractions remain the reason why he does not relate going outdoors with going pottie. He always views these excursions as an opportunity to amuse and delight the pedestrians. I need to request constantly that the fawners refrain from this flattery.

Mark suggested I fit Karma with a sign (like "STUDENT DRIVER") that says "PUPPY IN TRAINING, DO NOT DISTURB." Perhaps this may discourage diversion from the true meaning of his outdoor mission. It is nearly impossible to find a quiet, out-of-the-way location to give us the peace to work on our lessons. I suppose that when he (if ever) gets over the glamour and magnetism, which is the "Curse of the Cute and Famous," he will be ready to attain the more noble ideals of his higher mission in life.

Chagrined, Shredded and Shaggy

Five months ago, I returned to Key West with a se-verely-diminished self-image: pale, skinny and bald. My literary compositions of the last 12 months have chronicled a summer rife with grief and despair, followed by an autumn of personal and national disaster. Boston's bleak, cold November winds and rains bade me farewell, as they seemed to reflect my weather-beaten soul. The absence of sunshine, combined with the impact of three months of chemotherapy had left me tattered and forlorn. I was eager to rejuvenate my spirit and my body in my warm, sunny winter retreat near U.S. Route 1's Mile Marker Zero.

Another winter season has now passed. The time has arrived to set my sights northward. As oppressive heat and humidity envelop my island home, a bright and sunny New England climate is reawakening the verdant life of a new spring season, presenting another opportunity for renewal. Mild ocean breezes and floral-scented air await Karma and me – some 1500 miles to the north.

Although the prospect of a satisfactory resolution to my legal woes has so far eluded me, I have restored my bronzed, buff physique ("shredded," in the slang vernacular of my gym buddies), and re-grown my hair. Two out of three isn't bad!

The refreshingly dry warmth of Key West's autumn

embraced me the week before Thanksgiving. Given the events of the previous year, I contemplated whether or not I had reasons to be grateful. Merely having survived the preceding events was ample reason for gratitude and celebration, viewing the most trying times of my life through the rear-view mirror. Visibility of what lay ahead remained murky on my present voyage, but I was still driving forward, not lying in some roadside ditch. Clashes with Fate had sideswiped me repeatedly. But, assiduously switching lanes as necessary and keeping my hands firmly on the wheel had set a cautiously hopeful course for the future. I would come to learn that KC had not abandoned me, successes and opportunities still maintained outposts on this journey.

On the first morning of this new calendar year, I awoke with a foreboding premonition. Now, in retrospect, I may have misinterpreted this intuitive sensation. I had become so accustomed to similar vagaries as being signs of trouble, that I immediately discounted any chance that it could be foretelling of good news. My prognosticators had become impaired from incidental damage.

Perhaps I really was due for a reversal of fortune in this New Year. The Universe could be set to swing the Pendulum of Fate in the opposite direction.

Come the end of January, certain rumors proved to be true. "Celebrate! Key West." for which I had been writing a column for the previous 52 weeks, was being sold. The new owner was from up north in Florida. The entire staff from the previous regime was suddenly locked out. This, alone, disturbed me. From what I heard of the "new" direction of the editorial focus, I was not interested in approaching them to continue writing my weekly column. Nor was I invited to do so, which was no surprise in light of the altered style of the alternative (now bi-weekly) newspaper. According to some fellow columnists, the new owner was looking for a "gay-er, fluffier" content. As my writing was not necessarily directed toward a GLBT audience alone, I would not fit in with the publication's new image. I have always prided myself in writing on issues of sublime substance, even if they were often cloaked in humor, irreverence and sarcasm.

As it was, for the previous three months, I had been casually seeking to identify a national publishing syndicate which could bring my writing before a larger readership. The timing of this change now seemed auspicious. I began my research in more earnest. Using search engines on the Internet to the best of my ability, and tapping into assistance from my friends and tips from fellow writers, I began networking. By the middle of January, instead of busily *writing* columns, I found myself busily writing e-mails to publishers *about* my columns. Upon reviewing the topical material for which many publishers were searching out authors, I noticed that my niche was unique. This became my selling point.

The search and research fully occupied my days, but I dearly missed writing. Then, I began to consider that perhaps I would be unable to sustain a weekly production schedule over several years without becoming repetitive. Further, it occurred to me that I might have been misinterpreting the meaning of this call for change. Upon reviewing a year's worth of work, I recognized that the topics I had been presenting had paralleled several personal concurrent stories, which had become the undercurrents moving me along. Coincidentally (or not?), the year I had selected to be a regularly published writer had been the most turbulent year of my life. There actually were several interwoven storylines buried several layers beneath the anecdotal columns that I had been producing. The flavor, style, texture, themes and mood of each piece were indicative of the abrupt hairpin turns along the sheer cliffs on which I had been traveling.

I chose to revise my ambition; I wanted to continue to chronicle these still-fluid stories, while simultaneously working to bring to the surface the backdrops of the previous columns. After all, I continued to experience the effects, and was yet to see how each subplot would turn out. So, this volume of work became my new project. It gave me back the chance to devote my time to writing, and maintained my grander objective of ultimately reaching a wider readership. Vigorously, I plunged back into writing, relieved to set aside the Internet struggles temporarily. But, my new endeavor would not lack trials and adversities.

The six-week period of Spring Break nearly gave me a Spring Breakdown.

When is an hour not an hour? When it is Happy Hour that goes from 11 a.m. to 8 p.m., all along Duval Street.

With the ubiquitous lure of cheap booze, daytime drunkenness among the flocking college crowd raised the pitch of abundant foolish and hazardous behavior. Although to some proprietors, the youthful tourist influx attracts a temporary boom to business, on the whole the City of Key West pays dearly in other ways for this scene. As do I personally, constantly mangled by drunken bicyclists, confronted by rowdy and disrespectful vacationers, and the need to navigate obstructions of vastly increased amounts of trash along the paths and sidewalks. Once again, the issue regarding short-term transient rentals within my gated condominium community becomes a hot-button political issue. Boisterous vacationers clash with the working and retired long-term inhabitants.

At one point, the rowdy, inebriated college kids upstairs were swarming in-and-out like bees around a hive. In a unit designed for a maximum of four adults, more than twice that number share the cost of a weeks rental, making their rooming as cheap as the booze. The dirt and the noise from the round-the-clock partying creates a disruptive environment in which to live and work productively.

As Spring Break season came to an end, Karma came into my life. Another, but far more welcomed disruption to a productive work schedule. Meanwhile, my Legal Lambada moves along in jerky motions, consuming time and attention, with no end in sight, as the temperatures continue to rise.

A Tail of Two Dogs

Mark had arranged to come to Key West in mid-May to help me return to Boston with the prodigious pup. Mark is well-acquainted with the stress I suffer during airline travel and the subsequent complications related to my regional transition. Under normal circumstances, it is a trying ordeal. But this particular seasonal migration would be especially worrisome, due to the transport of the first-time flyer in his carry-on travel bag. Mark was demonstrating compassion – whether he was sizing up the potential trauma to Karma or to me was not relevant. I graciously accepted his offered assistance. And along with this generous offer, also came a pledge to stay in my home for as long as necessary to help with the unfinished business of properly training Karma.

Many will attest to the fact that puppy training can be a full-time occupation. Constant vigilance and the establishment of mutual trust are mandatory. Mark double-teamed with his five-year-old Yorkie, Rocky, to undertake this task.

For a small bit of background, it should be told that Rockwell Joseph (Rocky) joined our extended biped/quadruped clan nearly five years ago. As it was quite apparent that Mark had fallen in love with KC at our first meeting, I felt it was appropriate that he expand his own feline nuclear family to include a Yorkshire Terrier. He had been boasting of KC with such passion for two years. One Sunday afternoon, I prodded him to scan the classified section of the *Boston Globe* so that we might visit a litter of newborn pups. I knew that once he saw the puppies, he would consider adopting one. And from holding one in his arms, it would certainly be a short leap to commitment. I secretly had planned on making this his birthday gift, once he had made the choice. It was clan destiny to even out the canine/feline ratio.

It was September 15th, the same date that marks the anniversary of the advent of my total blindness. On this sparkling late-summer afternoon, Mark drove KC and me to Concord, Massachusetts, where we arranged to meet a dog breeder and her brood. Two three-month-old pups remained from the original litter of four. The female puppy was playful and gregarious. She and KC hit it off immediately. At one point KC emerged from the woods with a five-foot tree branch in his mouth (he always was an over-achiever). This female puppy was hanging tenaciously on one end by her clenched teeth. Meanwhile, the male puppy, the runt of the litter, was very timid and lay quietly curled up in my lap. Most of the attention was focused on KC and his new friend.

Suddenly, Mark turned around to look back at me in my chair. He swears that he heard this little fellow call to him: "I can be a good dog. Please choose me."

Mark consulted KC, who strongly approved of this choice. So it was that Rocky came into our lives on the Ides of September. This memorable event further served to overshadow the previous association that I had with that inauspicious date.

On the day that we returned from Key West with Karma, Mark went over to pick up Rocky from his accommodations, which he refers to as *Camp Run-a-Muck*. No kennels for *our* best friends! This is a private home where a woman lovingly boards a menagerie of pets while their folks are away. All species of creatures share this den of diversity. (They appear to have so much fun there that they don't always seem very eager to come back home!) For two months,

Mark and I had anxiously anticipated the meeting of the new Yorkie cousins. Karma had never met another Yorkie, and Rocky had only known his mentor, KC. A joyous meeting was highly expected.

Upon Mark's return to my building, Rocky ran exuberantly down the hall to the door of my apartment, with his usual display of enthusiasm. Mark opened the door. Whereas Rocky would normally throw himself at me with abandon, instead he stood at the threshold and spied young Karma with suspicion. As Mark ushered him inside, it was clear that Rocky was quite miffed.

"Who is this impish little upstart sitting next to my Uncle Rob?"

For two days, Rocky gave me the cold shoulder, as if to accuse me of betrayal. When he finally warmed up to his cousin Karma, Rocky allowed me near enough to show affection. It took several more days before Rocky would approach me on his own.

Karma's sudden presence was a startling blast of high energy in Rocky's otherwise placid existence. The constant urging to spar and play chase by this little ball of puppy fuzz was somewhat of an intrusion on his serene lifestyle. Karma rocked Rocky's world. Yet, he showed tremendous tolerance – until Karma found Rocky's beautiful protruding ears to be an irresistible nosh on which to nibble. This constant pestering wore down Rocky's patience (if not his ears). He eagerly sought peace and solace from this endless hounding. Karma had not yet mastered mounting the couch, so Rocky found this to be his only place of refuge. Within days, Rocky came to recognize his vital role in the taming of the shrewd.

Rocky accompanied Mark on their frequent outside excursions. Rocky set an example for young Karma to view the outdoors as a preferable world in which to excrete and explore. By observing Rocky, Karma learned "doggy-see, doggy-doo-doo." Rocky had become the model for Karma, as KC had for him, five years earlier. Rocky showed Karma all of KC's favorite spots, and how to mark the exact places by lifting his leg to pee – or was this gesture a salute?

This sighted live-in human/canine teacher/tutor team worked diligently. The dedicated duo established appropriate boundaries and encouraged Karma to discern proper behavior. To our delight and amusement, Rocky extended his role to keep a watchful eye on Karma indoors, tattling on Karma when puppy curiosity drew him to mischief. Sergeant Rocky would blow the whistle by a loud vocal warning to bring the nefarious activity to Mark's attention. If anything, he may have been a bit overzealous in this capacity. If Rocky even *suspected* Karma of monkey business, he would let out a series of yelps. Poor Karma, naturally nosy and rakish, might have started to feel somewhat repressed.

It took this team only days to teach Karma the real poop, something that I was unable to accomplish over the previous two months. Mark and Rocky stayed with the task until Karma came to recognize the basic rules. Rocky was so happy to go home to his quiet, familiar suburban retreat to languor in a well-deserved respite.

As I was getting resettled back in Boston, volunteers were being organized from the MSPCA's Phinney's Friends program to continue reinforcing Karma's puppy dogma. Now, KC's legacy in helping to establish this wonderful social service organization has come back around to open doors for Karma.

All the recent distractions and complications certainly robbed me of time to devote to other matters. My regular working schedule at the computer has been nearly obliterated. Tending to the immediate situation of parenting a pup has disrupted production for the last several months. These have brought some of the busiest and most exhausting days of my life. But as I have always said, anything that is truly valuable in life usually is worth the extra effort.

"Rocky" cannot be spelled without "K-C." And "Karma" cannot be spelled without "M-A-R-K." Thank you, Mark. Thank you, Rocky. Thank you, dear KC!

COPS AND LAWYERS

Once upon a time, when I was very young, it all seemed so simple: there were Good guys and there were Bad guys. We learned to play games such as "Cops and Robbers" or "Cowboys and Indians." It was our first introduction to a paradigm of *Good versus Evil*. These childhood games presented us the concept, with an unspoken understanding, of who were the Good guys and who were the Bad guys. Slowly, a more enlightened consciousness crept into our educational system, and it was no longer acceptable to represent American history with such a slanderous ethnic bias.

On television, the era of the Western was soon to meet its demise. For nearly a decade to follow, the archetypal "Good versus Bad" models took on the characters of secret agents, superheroes and their antitheses, law enforcement detectives, Cloak-and-Dagger murder mysteries and international undercover political spies. The long-absent Native American character eventually resurfaced in an Anti-Litter Public Service Ad. A tear streamed down the well-defined face of the Native American as he stood by the side of a highway and ruefully observed the New American family, thoughtlessly toss their refuse from the window of their passing sedan.

A more enlightened American society was moving toward politically-correct values. Gender and ethnic empowerment rose through the increasing diversity of the American population, and thus redefined public social etiquette. Boorish behavior was equated with those who made sexual or racial slurs·

As Polish jokes became taboo and in bad taste, lawyer jokes proliferated. They even became accepted as fashionable and hip, edgy humor. Americans found a group that all could agree to dislike, without fear of condemnation or retribution. These professionals could even laugh at themselves. As far as I know, not a single lawyer has sued for slanderous, comic chatter. Perhaps, due to the current proliferating litigious climate within our culture, they have enough business that they need not defend their profession's reputation.

Over the last several years, our world has been rocked repeatedly by scandal. This has further undermined previous naïve notions of who were the Good guys and who were the Bad. Egregious behavior associated with "respectable" American icons exposed a new reality. The media (itself under scrutiny) were filled with reports besmirching nearly every element of society – raising moral and ethical issues about the shortcomings of our political leaders and political reformers, legislators and judiciary, clergy and religious leaders, government agencies and watchdog committees, teachers and educational institutions, scientific researchers and medical professionals, mothers and fathers and nannies, corporate leaders, industrialists and product manufacturers, social workers and their agencies, social reformists, law enforcement leaders and civil servants, brokers and stock analysts, sports heroes and entertainment superstars .

Stereotyping has become acceptable as long as it appears flattering; for example: Gays as leaders in the arts and arbiters of good taste; Asians as intellectually advantaged; athletic or musical prowess among African-Americans; women as more honest and pragmatic than men, etc.

Is it any wonder why we have all become so confused and cynical? Blind trust is no longer prudent.

Corruption is hardly a recent phenomenon. Kings and Queens have been losing their heads at the hands of the masses for centuries. Revolutions historically have toppled oppressive regimes. In more recent times, politicians and snake oil salesmen have both become measured with the same skepticism. Bureaucracies have long been viewed as self-serving. Can it be that just a few "bad apples" have been distorting the image of entire institutions or groups?

Since the unparalleled terrorist events of September 11, 2001, the public has been on a heightened sense of alert. The President came on TV and frightened many Americans with dire warnings of potential danger, and then told us to go about our lives as normally as before. His plan to protect the homeland included a designated color-coded warning system in order that the public may appropriately adjust its degree of paranoia. Concurrently, American citizens adopted a bunker mentality, while the spirit of patriotism soared to new heights. Meanwhile, individuals began to view each other with greater suspicion in the streets, malls, subways, airports, parks and stadiums. Anybody among us could be one of the new era "bad guys" – your fellow airline passenger, the recently-hired store clerk, your new neighbors, the taxi driver, and so on. Xenophobia and hate crimes increased drastically to parallel the new patriotic fervor.

Recent months have brought us a rash of corporate and church scandals, further rattling previous complacent attitudes and belief systems. A popular television business news announcer referred to the current flurry of corporate scandal, regarding massive accounting fraud as a "CEO Crime Wave". Top-level executives walked away from collapsing corporations with millions of dollars and quickly called their lawyers. Panic swept through an already nervous stock market, causing indices to tumble. Company, union and government pension funds lost immense capital value, virtually overnight; workers watched their retirement plans evaporate. The recently appointed Chairman of the Securities and Exchange Commission addressed the nation and quoted an old movie line: "I'm mad as hell, and I'm not going to take it anymore!" Then, this same individual assumed the role of policing the very industry (corporate accounting) of which he had formerly been a prominent insider.

As a powerful religious institution betrayed the confidence of the flock, the "faithful" voiced mass outrage. They collectively demanded Church hierarchy accept culpability for blatant negligence for deliberately ignoring the long-overlooked prurient and unlawful behavior of their clergy. Church officials called their lawyers, and responded with a claim of "charitable immunity" to protect their assets from litigation. Throughout the crisis, these powerful religious leaders continued to skirt any confession of wrongful conduct on their own behalf.

American news jargon has become littered with popular phrases: "perp walks," "defrocked priests," "insider trading," "corporate malfeasance," "suicide-bombers," "double-dip recession," "Axis of Evil," a new meaning to "nine-eleven" and "Ground Zero," "cyberscum," – and more every day. Religious fanaticism and global capitalism have exposed their seriously sordid sides.

Current events follow several decades of highly-visible courtroom dramas and congressional hearings, which had already tarnished societal fundamentals, presumptions, perceptions and conceptions. Yet somehow, the startling news items of our new Millennium appear to have far exceeded past revelations by breaking through previous inviolable, sacrosanct barriers. Church and corporate leaders denied accountability and responsibility for a tidal wave of criminal and immoral activities at the expense of the public. Compounded with the previous deterioration of trust, such exposes created an environment rife with massive cynicism.

In the past, when we were unjustly injured, we would run to the cops. Now, when we suffer from harm, we run to the lawyers, all the time maintaining our scurrilous image of the legal profession. But what is one to do when it is cops who have become the bad guys? Which lawyers are worthy of our trust? And what would motivate lawyers to take on the agents of law enforcement? Money or justice? Who is going to have greater credibility before a jury or a judge? In today's world of diminishing integrity, this raises even more uncertainty.

Given my unsettling experiences with each, I can say that at least the lawyers return telephone calls.

In light of these historical events, I became diverted from the basic intent of this segment. But the underlying theme seemed so appropriate to mention, as it creates a larger backdrop to my own drama that I could not resist.

Several months ago, I wrote of fighting the blight of the snail population in my yard; all the while a larger battle has been waged as I fight City Hall. The saga of my conflict with the Key West Police Department seems never-ending. Somewhere between the scale of the Snail Wars and national corporate corruption scandals is my own personal quest for justice and accountability.

In short, I present the current status of this ordeal below.

My new legal team impressed me as compassionate, ethical and pragmatic. Despite my initial visceral reaction (I shattered at our first meeting) upon revisiting the horrific details of the March 30th incident, both Warren and Joe genuinely expressed empathy for my outrage and disgust. However, as a start-up law partnership, they could not offer to represent me in the case on a contingency basis. They further raised doubts that a local jury would award a compensatory judgment in my favor that would exceed the costs of litigation. But these two gentlemen had won my confidence by their sincerity and sense of commitment, so I agreed to pay them on an hourly-fee basis.

Meanwhile, the City of Key West, as a defendant, had no such financial limitations – it runs on public tax dollars. The City employs full-time legal representation as part of its local government structure.

At the first meeting with my new legal team, we three developed a strategy. Our first tactic would be to notify the

City of Key West informally of our intent to sue. In this initial communication, we suggested that we were open to a judgment of an objective legal mediator as an alternative. This would save time and costs for both sides. Admittedly, although I craved justice and accountability, I took into consideration the emotional stress I would need to endure through a courtroom battle.

The City consulted with their lawyers. In response to our offer, City representatives gave us the impression that this was agreeable to them. We were requested to arrive at a dollar amount that accurately reflected the direct costs I had incurred as a result of the incident. In doing so, I would be foregoing any compensation for personal pain and suffering. Eager for an out-of-court settlement, we accepted their word in good faith, and scrambled to calculate this amount, complete with documentation.

For nearly two months that followed, I expended a great deal of time and effort to recall thoroughly all expenses, gather the amounts, receipts and documentation. When this information was collected, I submitted all figures to my legal team. And my hourly legal costs continued to mount. Upon completion of this arduous task, by any standards, the resulting amount was extremely reasonable. We were prepared to negotiate as necessary, but I also intended to request a formal apology, and to have the record of my arrest expunged.

We submitted the final dollar amount to the City's legal representative in compliance with our stated agreement. We awaited a response. Many weeks passed.

After enough time had passed for the City to respond, Warren initiated contact. The City official, who had originally accepted this measure as a compromise to litigation, informed us that the City was only willing to settle by an offer of a very small sum. Warren viewed this as a token action to rid them of this problem. I interpreted it as an indication that they had had no intent of keeping their end of the bargain, and had only been stringing us along. Such a move was only a delay tactic by the City officials to test our resolve. Their meager settlement offer could only be regarded as a "nuisance" fee to terminate this problem. In my view, it was an insult added to my injuries. It had become clear to me that their scheme had always been one of deception, and that any deals they would propose held no veracity. The City officials anticipated that I would either give up my quest in desperation, or run out of money to pursue further action.

All these delays had pushed the original incident further into the past. When it appeared that fairness was not of any concern to the city government of Key West in this matter, it came time to move forward with the strategy outlined at our first meeting.

We gathered for a second meeting. It seemed to occur simultaneously to both me and to Warren that, perhaps, some publicity would spur the City officials to reconsider their original (meaningless) gesture. Warren suggested that I call the owner of a certain local newspaper. This gentleman had been fighting a similar battle with the city, charging that he had been unjustly arrested due to his critical editorial positions regarding local politics. The owner/editor had aligned with the Miami ACLU (American Civil Liberties Union) to pursue litigation. Warren contacted the ACLU. Meanwhile, I also called Ginny, the former editor of *Celebrate!* for whom I had written my weekly columns. She was now working for another local paper as a reporter. Her new colleague, Tom, at this widely-circulated newspaper, had originally written the story of my incident in April 2001. Tom continues to cover the many on-going incidents and events involving the Key West Police Department.

Tom was very agreeable to report the follow-up story of my situation. In our conversation, Tom indicated that he recalled the original story very clearly. He suggested that we should hold off on publishing the update until we had word from the ACLU as to whether or not they would be providing me legal backing. He was well acquainted with our contact at the Miami ACLU.

Another month passed as the ACLU reviewed my case. By this time, it is May 2002, and I was busily preparing for my return to Boston. When I finally got a call from the representative of the Miami ACLU, this is what I heard: the ACLU could not take my case due to several factors. For one, the City's Police Department and its officers may be protected from the specific litigation I was seeking, due to the lack of existing judicial precedents. The Key West Police Department has no special directives for arrest procedures of a blind or otherwise disabled person. Since no written code of conduct for such a situation existed for dealing in a particular way with a blind person, the police could claim that no existing rules were broken. Undoubtedly, under testimony, the police officers involved would protect themselves with a false claim that they did identify themselves as they approached me, and that I resisted verbal warnings. Hence, they could further claim that my conduct warranted the excessive use of force which included knocking me to the ground and pinning me in place with the full weight of a man on my back. (They would be forced to account for the physical injuries I had sustained for which I had documented medical proof. Certainly, they would testify that the extensive degree of brutality I stated did not occur. Each officer would back up this story to protect one another.)

The second reason the ACLU gave for having passed on taking up my case was that, in conference, they deemed that my situation was not "ground-breaking" on the basis of legal principles, whereas in the case with the newspaper owner, there were clear associations with freedom of speech and other extant protected civil rights.

This decision was presented to me through a phone call by the ACLU lawyer who had served as our liaison. He explained their reasons in detail, but used legalese jargon such as "qualified immunity," and the like, which I could not, as a layman, fully comprehend. Even though he expressed recognition of the injustice I had endured, he cited judicial statutes, which would supersede the ability to claim violation of my civil liberties.

From what I did understand of his explanations, I challenged some of the logic and reasoning directly, although I knew it would be to no avail. All that I could do was to express my deep disappointment with their decision.

However, in light of the merits of my case, and the unique legal ramifications, the ACLU did offer to try to locate a local law firm that would agree to represent me on a contingency basis. Upon a subsequent conversation with Warren to discuss these recent developments, I learned that a lawyer in Miami had offered to take my case with certain conditions. This Miami lawyer would work with Warren and Joe, provided that I pay all the up-front legal costs to pursue litigation. Such costs would entail further investigation, depositions and filing fees. I would need to bankroll a retainer fund for $5,000 at the start, and was assured that the total estimated amount should not exceed $10,000. These costs would be deducted from the final settlement amount before the lawyers claimed their contingency fee. I indicated that this was agreeable with me, but as I was imminently leaving Key West, I did not take any immediate action. I knew that nothing would proceed without a personal consultation with the Miami lawyer, and a signed contract, which stated these conditions. It would give me a few weeks to consider more thoroughly this proposal.

Within weeks of my return to Boston in the middle of May, I was informed that my story was back on the front page of a local newspaper.

Blind Man Abused By Police May Sue
Will Police Officials Apologize
For Roughing Up and Arresting Blind Man –
or Will They Stonewall and Get Sued?

The newspaper owner, working with the ACLU on his own litigation against the City of Key West, brought my story back before the public eye. In light of this latest resurgence of publicity, and the public's call for the creation of a Civilian Review Board (recall that there is a growing list of litigants making charges of abused authority by the cops), the Police Department held a public meeting. A department representative candidly discussed immediate efforts to rectify concerns and take responsibility for past offenses. Warren addressed him directly, to hold him to this promise. Additionally, he informed the City's attorney that an impending lawsuit on my behalf was being developed for imminent notification. Warren then presented an offer for the City to reconsider our previous agreement to settle at the amount calculated and submitted to them months earlier.

Now I was back in Boston, busily readjusting, settling in, and concentrating on training my growing puppy. When I next heard from Warren in the middle of June, he informed me that the City's attorney concurred that the amount we requested for a monetary settlement is quite reasonable, and that he will recommend this course of action to the City Manager for his approval.

Once upon a time, when we were young, we thought we knew what we should believe. We were blind and naive; we could afford to be idealistic. Then we grew up and life happened to us.

Our eyes were opened, and what we saw did not match our preconceptions. As an adult, the time has come to reassess and make some difficult choices. We cannot just pretend to be Cowboys or Indians anymore.

DEAR KC [7]

June - October, 2002
Dear KC,

When I first began recording the words included in this volume, I could never have foreseen that the following eighteen months would
be so eventful. The stories wrote themselves; I
merely arranged the words. You sat quietly by
my side, while I scratched out notes for my first
few proposed weekly newspaper columns. Now
I compose the last segment to be included in
this collection. Karma sits (not always so quietly) by my side, and we can feel you watching
approvingly. Maybe someday I'll see this book
in print with my own eyes. Until then, I'll reflect
on the deeper meanings of all the experiences
chronicled within.

Does a story ever truly end? I once thought
so, perhaps if it were a biography of one who
has passed on. But, added to all the things that
you have taught me over the years, you have
now disproved this notion, as well. Your life-
story will continue indefinitely, through infinite
love and revelations, for all those you have
touched either directly or otherwise.

In a few short weeks, I will brace myself for
the one-year anniversary of your departure from
my immediate realm. Today is the first day of
Summer. As I look back on last summer with all
its turmoil and sadness, my greatest ambition is
to arrive at a new period of peace and serenity.
No single endeavor, no matter how consuming,
can rival this intense desire.

Safely back again in Boston, I can review
another strange season in Key West. As intended, I had ducked another New England
snowball. But, as it turned out, a record mild

winter melted into a record cold and damp spring to welcome me home. Doesn't this underscore the underlying theme of the previous pages?

I was so lost without you in Key West. You sent me Karma. He is very much like you in his character and personality; this has raised speculation that Karma is "the reincarnation of KC." Perhaps you picked the one dog in a billion that could fill your paws, or perhaps you put a lot of your spirit into him. I love and admire Karma so much that I will never assume that he is anyone other than his own dog, and he is surely your spiritual progeny. It was painful being in Key West without you. When Karma arrived at my home, carrying with him all your love and exuberance, I felt blessed once again. But he never made me stop crying for you! Time may heal in terms of dulling the sharpest pain, but the scar of your untimely departure will always remain.

Now, as I work to complete this book, others frequently ask what my writing is about. For many months, I could not provide an easy reply. Throughout the process, I did not know the exact answer; I just knew that I had a lot to express. Upon review, I clearly noticed a common theme kept reappearing. In the various columns and the interwoven storylines, issues of personal control kept bleeding through the lines. I had been waging a constant battle for dreams unattainable, and recorded the ebb and flow of my despair, convictions and fortitude.

KC, I have learned so much from you. As the source of my inspiration, your teachings have always been an element in my eclectic collection of compositions. Your soul reflected what truly lay in my heart, and helped me to come to know myself better. You must also be the enigmatic source of courage, which enables me to disclose publicly such personal experiences and introspection.

As I stop to assess the lessons of this journey, the syllabus appears to have been quite extensive. What have I learned?

• We should acknowledge wisdom that we might unknowingly already possess. It might have been acquired subtly from our personal experiences, or absorbed from those fellow travelers. Some answers we seek have been with us all along as "standard equipment" with our minds, but our nature is not to come to this realization until prompted by our hearts. I strongly believe that you, KC, were sent to me over twelve years ago to accompany me on my journey, and regularly arouse insights which lay dormant.

Many societies and cultures try to dismiss our natural inclination toward understanding the metaphysical realm. It takes initiative to accept that intuition and instinct tap known and unrecognized senses to access relevant information. How is it that dogs seem to know this by nature?

I tell people that when one finds himself wandering blindly, just keep moving forward. A source of information awaits your arrival. It may be as subtle or as esoteric as the sound of a distant trolley bell, a mild scent on the breeze, or a vague premonition. For me this lesson is both a literal truth, and a metaphorical guide by which to live.

• Be alert. People can look at something, but may not observe what should be obvious. The greatest lesson that I learned in art school was how to *really see*. "Looking" does not imply seeking the obscure, but becoming aware of the world around us. How well dogs practice this attention!

We should never shut out information, or immediately discount its inherent value. Too often it is easy to deny information for the nature of its outright appearance. Recognizing that which touches our soul through the corporeal senses, or more abstruse avenues, is the source of all our perceptions. And perceptions define comprehension. Comprehension directs our course of action.

Fear and trauma can cause a paralysis, detaining one's access to a source of guidance. The universe around us keeps moving. One can never resist being touched eventually.

Denying is easier said than done. Few knowingly choose fear. But, being timid could prevent one from acknowledging self-imposed restraints.

•Teach others what you know; ask about things you don't know. Share insight and knowledge to assist others. When this is done with no expectation of personal gain, a light is generated which will carry one through the darkest of times. To save one person from anguish, by imparting the lessons already learned along the way, one's own trials and triumphs will have served a greater purpose.

Never turn down a request for help, someday that plea will be your own. Acknowledge your own Karma.

All noble efforts will deliver some return. Points are not accrued by the balance of triumphs over losses, or the amount of control we appear to attain. Rather, the truest value is in how we evolve in our management of the inevitable pitfalls.

• It is never a certainty when we are at the bottom or the top of our game. Keep seeking higher ground; one never knows when a deluge will come along to sweep it all away.

In turbulent political and economic times, every technical analyst and professional economist is met with the same uncertainty that plagues us all. An expensive lesson gets disseminated across all borders: we are all mostly guessing. As the stock market plunges, the most common question seems to be: "Where is the bottom?" When it becomes apparent that nobody really knows much of anything, the "wise" confess to their ignorance. The refrain to the former question is something like: "Don't try to catch a falling knife."

In working on the rewrite of the segments in which I chronicle your departure, I would always end up crying incessantly. To paraphrase myself from the account of that period: "Just when you think you have nothing left to lose, you may find out otherwise."

• There really are mysteries without answers. Analysis in moderation is adviseable. If all mysteries were suddenly revealed to us with clarity, what would we choose to attain? Creativity and discovery, the spiciest dishes of life, would be reduced to just another recipe for ice cubes.

• Dreams will never be fulfilled without taking some action. My paralysis from trauma was like standing at the waters edge, as the waves lapped at my ankles. Slowly, the sand pulled my feet under the soft, flat surface. Hence, it required expending more effort to dislodge my footing, when I finally decided to move.

Effort does not always result in attaining success, but failure is nobler than torpor.

- Opportunity will never knock if there is no "Welcome Mat" at the door. Put out a sign to invite life to enter. Be a hospitable host to adventure and challenge. It's better to let them in through the front door than to have them enter surreptitiously through the bathroom window.
- Cherish the moment when a dog licks you on the nose. These creatures have good taste, and they also know what tastes good. Consider such a moment as an honor and a present. Keep empty spaces on your calendar schedule. Leave time to play fetch. And if it rains, grab a good book, listen to a new recording, write a poem or paint a picture.
- Accept praise, accept gifts, accept advice. Sincere gratitude really is a gift in return. It took me far too long to learn this valuable lesson. In turn, I remained unnecessarily frustrated, angry and uncomfortable for many years. Additionally, I was being unfair to others. Denying offers of assistance is actually more offensive than it is gracious. (I still find myself resisting this lesson much too often.)
- Do not equate a lost cause with "the blind leading the blind." Who is best qualified to understand our personal challenges than one who has been down the same road? But no two persons walk the exact same path. Find a comfortable pair of shoes, and bring along a snack.
- Life really *is* hard. Sometimes, everyone around us makes it look so easy. Don't be fooled. They might just be showing off, but check for masquerades, smoke and mirrors, or the man behind the black curtain, pulling the levers.

Sometimes you really *will* find yourself alone. People make other plans and do not include you. Others are always busy. Things just turn out that way. You are alone in being alone.

Don't expect all your calls to be returned. Many promises are scripted phrases. Try not to let yourself become equally as remiss in dealing with others.

Befriend yourself. And if you really do not like yourself, get a dog. And feed him. Then he will always pretend to like you.

• Take notes throughout life, there may be a test or at least a pop quiz. And, if in the end there isn't, your notes may be a good source of amusement later in life, or for others who follow.

KC, I want to avoid this book appearing as "Things My Dog Taught Me." There's a place for writing of that genre. And, your influence has been far more than just incidental. The stories are not about a blind man who faces adversity. Nor about a wise dog with awesome powers. (Although both those statements are true.)

Who am I to conclude this volume with such a professorial litany of profundities and unsolicited advice? When I come across as being pretentious, pompous, extraordinarily astute or arrogantly self-righteous, I ask others to excuse me. I'm far more humble than I appear. There are surely some noble truths in my assessments. But, I don't always take myself all too seriously, so why should any reader? Somewhere among my vast verbiage, I honestly hope that something I wrote will make a reader stop to ponder something they never previously considered.

In recent times, when peace and humor deserted me, I died. But, at night, I had vivid dreams. You were there, as was the whole cast of characters that have paraded through my days. I woke up, but never saw the sunshine that Annie promised. I got out of bed, with the images of dreams still swirling around my head. Something always kept me going. I cannot profess to know what it was, but I have become fond of stating, "I'm still here!" And, until I'm not, people will hear from me.

KC, my eternal best friend, today is July 16th, one full year from the day I kissed you goodbye. My eyes fill with tears each time your name is spoken, or memories of you resurface. They cling to me as close as your physical body once had. Not long ago, I thought it was just a cliché to say "you are always on my mind," but now I know it can be so. Your presence is always in the periphery of my attention. In your honor, I will not devote this day to mournful sorrow, but rather I will dedicate it to creative and productive endeavors. Proof of your enduring spirit is exemplified by a new milestone in my work.

They say that time heals everything. That is not true. Or, at least not time that can be quantified in human terms.

They also say that God never gives us more than we can handle. Why blame God for the things that happen to us?

Who is this "they" anyhow? It's certainly not a dog.

Why does Karma cry? Half the Earth's human population lives on less than two dollars-a-day. Yet, Karma lives a relative life of luxury. He just doesn't realize this fact. But I cannot blame him. I know that I compare well to so many others, yet, I am still too sad too often. Silly human!

Karma did not come with a manual. I cannot understand why he does not know how to keep busy while I work. He wants my attention all day long. Unable to keep himself amused, he looks around for mischief. He flips the rugs, pulls down towels, and sets up obstacles for me around the house. It's as if he is trying to kill me. I tell him that he is not named as beneficiary on any insurance policy. More likely, he just wants to incapacitate me enough, so that I cannot give more time to this keyboard than I give to him. His whining forces me to take him outside frequently. I use this time to open my mind to inspiration. I suppose that is why Karma cries.

Again, I distinguish myself in the neighborhood. What do the unfamiliar pedestrians think when they view a blind man being guided by a little five-pound pup, who has been described as "too cute to be real." When he behaves properly and walks directly in front of my swinging cane, I shout my mantra: "GOOD KARMA!"

KC, Have I told you lately that I love you?

Forever,
Dad

MORE DUST SETTLES

Sixty-three million years ago, a giant meteor was strongly attracted by the gravity of the verdant planet earth. Its violent impact, not far from Key West, caused a grave situation indeed. Things haven't been the same ever since. Residents of the planet were startled and devastated. This enormous impact thrust debris and dust skyward, and darkness reigned over the Earth. The atmosphere was strewn with clutter. Sunny days had come to an abrupt end for a very long time thereafter. Survivors found themselves wandering blindly through the prevailing darkness. Chaos seized the shattered remnants of previous environmental and social orders. Dinosaurs bumped into each other, uncertain whether they would eat or be eaten.

Blue skies were but a memory to this last generation. If it appeared to be a jungle out there *before* the calamity, those earlier times suddenly seemed like a walk in the park. Gone were the sweet days of large lounge lizards languishing in tropical paradise. The once-mighty fell into despair, and then fell into de swamps. Little did they know that they would become fossil fuel in eons to come, and, in turn, themselves would be the air pollutants. (Irony always has the last word.)

Time changes everything, but always seeks order. Nature rebalances the elements and reconstructs a new paradigm. The resulting universe cannot be judged as either good or bad, just different.

Eventually, humans emerged and tried to impose their own order on the planet where the ancient species once roamed. This impudent ape demanded a set of laws defining "good" and "bad." Trouble was, great divisions of opinion created even greater divisions among these domineering, Earth-dwelling latecomers. Hence, civilization was devised as a means to set the course for the human journey into the future. A "New World Order" would certainly provide all inhabitants with a sense of security. Leaders emerged. Order, at last, would again be restored.

History marched forward, and here we are. . .

The sane, rational and intelligent, of course, know right from wrong. Right?

The politically-correct know their right from their left. Correct?

The just and the righteous just know what cause is just right. Just because it's right!

The heart reveals the truth. The brain discerns the facts. Facts are truth. Right?

But for every heart, there is a mind. And sometimes these two disagree.

It's a good thing we all know deep down inside (wink) what's really right and wrong, good and bad, just and unjust, black and white, up and down. . .And, if we could only get others to see things as clearly as we do, harmony would prevail. Further, if we could all just agree on what is good, right, just and true, nothing bad would ever happen. Right? Sure!

Even with a common inherent interest – survival, more grandiose schemes take precedence, and each individual selects or designs a personal philosophy. Like art or obscenity, each heart and mind determines what is good or bad, right or wrong.

Self-preservation is an art, not a science. And, personal truths are not absolute. So who is best qualified to make the paramount judgments? The nearest we have come is to let our societies set standards. But separate societies are like separate individuals – cultures clash, populations have distinct perspectives and government/religious institutions vie for power. Even if a universal concept of an omnipotent God was accepted, humanity would still face the conundrum of whose will should prevail.

So, people have said things like, "Everyone ultimately gets what they deserve."

I wonder what the dinosaurs did that was so bad?

Cops, Lawyers, Insurance Agents

Earlier this summer, the City of Key West held a public forum to address issues regarding abundant allegations of excessively brutal police conduct.

Warren, the lawyer working on my behalf, took this as an opportunity to confront the Police Department spokesperson. Fiercely determined to hold them to their pledge to reconcile these mounting charges, he got the ball rolling once again.

Following this public meeting, Warren brought me up-to-date by telephone. He had suggested to the City Attorney that the city seriously reconsider our offer to settle out-of-court, inasmuch as I had recently engaged a lawyer who was ready to commence litigation. In light of the latest circumstances, the city's attorney suddenly concurred that the monetary amount, requested as a settlement, was really quite reasonable. He would recommend this course of action to the City Manager for final approval.

In the dim corridors of City Hall, our public servants huddled and conferred. Legal and social pressure brought my dormant, but still-breathing, issue back into the spotlight. When bright light is shone into the bureau drawers, one never knows what might become visible. The mounting litigation, the State Attorney's investigations, and the latest prospect of the formation of a Civilian Review Board, might just have enough candlepower to ignite a few small fires. Somebody was bound to get burned. The local authorities found themselves backed against the wall, fearful of getting screwed.

They were forced to dance. Yet, as was their habit, they still wanted to call the tune. Internal strategies needed to be reviewed. The faces of our public servants would not look good covered in fried egg.

My legal team played it cool. Sweltering, languorous summer days crawled by like feeble garden snails. Follow-ups and friendly reminders to city officials nudged things along. Even though the heat was on, the dance ritual would be two steps forward, and one step back. As I chronicle the continuing events here, it should be noted that time lapses between steps stretched the entire process out over a span of many months.

The City Attorney now viewed our previously-agreed-upon settlement as acceptable. He indicated that he would support this resolution before the City Manager. In the midst of this new political posturing and maneuvering, the City turned to its insurance provider. Insurance companies are always reluctant to pay claims, so it encouraged another round of bargaining. Warren received a new proposed offer that was roughly two-thirds of the originally-stated settlement amount. (The original sum was determined strictly by flat-out accounting, based wholly on verified, documented expenses directly resulting from the incident.) The monetary difference was an insignificant amount to the City or their insurance agencies, but was far more meaningful to me. Mainly because I wanted to hold them to their original agreement, and also, I had since incurred additional legal costs to reach this point.

We countered their counter-offer. They returned again with a new offer: they would increase the dollar amount by half the difference, providing that I submit a statement that I had. indeed, hit the vehicle with my cane. In return, they would issue a public apology.

I welcomed this proposal, not merely for the additional sum, but particularly for the confession of wrongdoing by the law enforcement officers. Never having denied that my cane had struck the vehicle, I would be glad to expose details that had been sorely omitted from public accounts. It had never been divulged that the vehicle, struck by the use of my cane, had initiated the confrontation by a reckless County detective, who nearly killed me.

I composed a concise statement, which subsequently was submitted. Eagerly, I awaited their own statement in return. But when it was clear to them that my "admission" was more damaging to them than vindicating, they rescinded their offer to make a public declaration of apology. Instead, they agreed to throw in a few extra bucks – hoping to avoid my open disclosure of the near-fatal traffic offense. Perhaps, in addition, the insurance agents consulted their own lawyers, and advised the City against a public acknowledgment of their role in this fiasco. Such an admission could make the City vulnerable to greater liabilities beyond my own case.

Unless further prompted by my lawyer, once more, things would have stagnated. There is no urgency to pay debts without external pressure. So as weeks passed, and another summer faded into autumn, it was time again to rattle the cage. In turn, a fax eventually arrived for our perusal. Three pages of legal mumbo-jumbo itemized the specific terms and conditions of our latest settlement agreement. A check would be cut in two weeks, contingent on my signing-off to all the designated provisions.

(Author's Note: These are open questions as of 10/ 16. I hope to have final answers next week.

– Did the offenders either get fired or reprimanded?

– Was my arrest record expunged?

– Could I now finally reveal the entire story without fear of retribution?)

I had been bullied, tyrannized and subjected to humiliation. The police conduct was demeaning, vicious and damaging. The subsequent handling of the case by the authorities displayed arrogance, impunity, insincerity and disrespect. . .proving once again that there really is no "just" in justice.

It seemingly comes out of nowhere and rocks our world. The darkness becomes so thick that solutions are indistinguishable from problems. But if the "problem" is a falling meteor, and the only "solution" is an umbrella, a plain, old rainy day starts looking pretty darn good.